POLITICS AND SOCIETY IN WALES,
1840–1922

Ieuan Gwynedd Jones.

POLITICS AND SOCIETY IN WALES, 1840–1922

ESSAYS IN HONOUR OF IEUAN GWYNEDD JONES

Edited by

Geraint H. Jenkins
J. Beverley Smith

CARDIFF
UNIVERSITY OF WALES PRESS
1988

©University of Wales, 1988

British Library Cataloguing in Publication Data

Politics and Society in Wales, 1840–1922:
   essays in honour of Ieuan Gwynedd Jones.
   1. Wales, 1840–1922
   I. Jones, Ieuan Gwynedd   II. Jenkins,
   Geraint H. (Geraint Huw), 1946–   III. Smith,
   J. Beverley (Jenkyn Beverley), 1931–
   942.9′07

ISBN 0-7083-1017-6

Printed in Great Britain at The Bath Press, Avon.

Contents

Illustrations

Foreword

In the autumn of 1985 Ieuan Gwynedd Jones retired from the Sir John Williams Chair of Welsh History at the University College of Wales, Aberystwyth, a position which he had held since his migration from the University College of Swansea, fifteen years earlier. Those who have been taught by Ieuan Gwynedd Jones or have worked closely with him will readily testify to his sharp intellect, boundless enthusiasm and gentle kindness. This volume is presented to him as a mark of the esteem in which he is held as a scholar of distinction and a friend of unfailing generosity. It was thought that it would be appropriate to present a volume of essays upon topics within the main field of his teaching and research activities. It was felt, too, that any tribute to Ieuan Gwynedd Jones should, along with the contributions of his colleagues, contain a representation of the work of a younger generation of historians which owes so much to his inspiration and example. Inevitably, a decision to publish a volume which concentrates upon his particular field of study meant that it was not possible to include the work of a number of writers who would otherwise have wished to contribute, nor was it possible to reflect the diversity of his intellectual commitments, not least his abiding interest in seventeenth-century studies. But the names of those who indicated their wish to subscribe to the volume reflect the respect and affection in which Ieuan Gwynedd Jones is held in the various academic and cultural circles which have been so enriched by his achievements and his presence.

We should like to express our thanks to the University of Wales Press for undertaking publication, and in particular to the Chairman, Professor J. Gwynn Williams, and Director, Mr John Rhys. We are indebted to Mrs Ceinwen Jones for her thoroughness in preparing the volume for the press and to Mrs Delyth Fletcher, who eased our work in innumerable ways. Dr Llinos Beverley Smith kindly undertook to prepare the index. Mr Philip Henry Jones generously supplied a list of Ieuan Gwynedd Jones's published writings and shares the joy felt by all those who have been associated with the volume that the list will continue to grow year by year for a long time to come.

GERAINT H. JENKINS
J. BEVERLEY SMITH

The Contributors

JOHN DAVIES, Senior Lecturer in Welsh History, University College of Wales, Aberystwyth.

RUSSELL DAVIES, Administrative Assistant, University College of Wales, Aberystwyth.

NEIL EVANS, Tutor in History, Coleg Harlech.

DEIAN HOPKIN, Senior Lecturer in History, University College of Wales, Aberystwyth.

PHILIP HENRY JONES, Senior Lecturer in Welsh Studies, College of Librarianship Wales, Aberystwyth.

KENNETH O. MORGAN, Fellow and Praelector in Modern History and Politics, The Queen's College, Oxford.

PAUL O'LEARY, Publicity Officer, Consumer Council for Wales, Cardiff.

PETER STEAD, Senior Lecturer in History, University College of Swansea.

CHRISTOPHER B. TURNER, Assistant Registrar, University of Wales College of Medicine, Cardiff.

GLANMOR WILLIAMS, Emeritus Professor of History, University College of Swansea.

SIAN RHIANNON WILLIAMS, Radio Producer, Education Department, BBC, Cardiff.

Abbreviations

AAC	Archives of the Archdiocese of Cardiff
BBCS	*Bulletin of the Board of Celtic Studies*
BL	British Library
BLPES	British Library of Political and Economic Science
CJC	*Cardiff Journal of Commerce*
CT	*Cardiff Times*
DNB	*Dictionary of National Biography*
DRO	Dyfed Record Office
DWB	*Dictionary of Welsh Biography*
EHR	*English Historical Review*
GRO	Glamorgan Record Office
LG	*Llanelly Guardian*
LL	*Labour Leader*
LM	*Llanelly Mercury*
LPArch	Labour Party Archives
MRC	Modern Records Centre, Warwick University
NLW	National Library of Wales
NLWJ	*National Library of Wales Journal*
PP	Parliamentary Papers
PRO	Public Record Office
RSG	*Railway Service Gazette*
SWDN	*South Wales Daily News*
SWP	*South Wales Press*
Trans. Cymmr.	*Transactions of the Honourable Society of Cymmrodorion*
UCNW	University College of North Wales, Bangor
WHR	*Welsh History Review*
WM	*Western Mail*

Ieuan Gwynedd Jones

GLANMOR WILLIAMS

PERHAPS the sharpest and most enduring image of Professor Ieuan Gwynedd Jones retained by many of his students, colleagues, and friends is one characteristic of him at his best. He sits at a desk or table, leaning forward, his head tilted back and cocked slightly to one side, his eyes flashing with eager enthusiasm, and his long, lean, sensitive, intelligent features—his whole being indeed—suffused with an urgent desire to communicate and convince. From time to time the flow of words is accentuated by the steady tapping of the right forefinger on the edge of the table, giving additional emphasis to what he has to say. Now and again he passes his hand over his hair as if to lend control and direction to those red-haired locks, still only faintly flecked with white, that seem to spring up as freely and spontaneously as the ideas that flow from him. In vain! Neither the curls nor ideas will readily submit to restraint or curb. Occasionally, the torrent of discussion is broken by the upsurge of deep chuckles of amusement or a shocked tut-tutting of simulated disapproval. Or he pauses to seek his listeners' views, and absorbs with typical care and thoughtfulness what they have to say, arching his tufted brows and wrinkling his forehead, deep in contemplation. That is the Ieuan beloved of all those who have come into contact with him: the warm, outgoing teacher and friend, enveloping and stimulating others with the currents of his own intellectual ferment. No one who has experienced him in that mood has ever wanted or been able to resist him.

It was not ever thus. Few such successful and apparently natural-born university teachers and intellectuals can ever have had a more unlikely early preparation for their later careers. Born in 1920 in the Rhondda Valley, on the eve of a long and painful economic depression, Ieuan was the son of a miner and a nurse. His father, a devout and sincere Christian believer, was a man who read his Bible with intense conviction and took his religion seriously enough literally to give a tithe of his scanty earnings to his church. His mother was another strong and independent character, whose family hailed originally from the Harlech area. But the 1920s and 1930s were an abnormally difficult era which put the mining communities of south Wales on the rack, and the family moved to Pyle. Ieuan attended the grammar school at Bridgend for a few years. With his father unemployed and himself one of the elder children of a large family, he left school at fourteen and joined the merchant navy. He went to sea for some time until he began to suffer from a stomach ailment which plagued him for years and from the effects of which he has never been entirely free. He later became a hospital nurse, but spent most of the war years as a railway signalman, riding to and from work on a bicycle. All the while he was trying to catch up on his reading and attending adult classes when he could. For a time he hoped to enter the ministry and exercise his talents as a preacher. Frustrating years these may have been, but they were not wasted. They taught him to be expert with his hands, and the serried rows of carefully-maintained tools in his workshop still bear witness to his practical skill and aptitude. Even more important, these years instilled in him the value of self-discipline and hard intellectual endeavour. They gave him an abiding interest in adult education and kindled in him a genuine sympathy for all students, but especially for those who had to learn the hard way without the advantages of a straightforward progression from school to university.

After the Second World War was over, he entered the University College of Swansea as a student. Those who knew him in those days remember an unusually lively and articulate undergraduate, who threw himself with delight and passion into the cut and thrust of debate and discussion. He already had an insatiable thirst for ideas and hypotheses, and a gift for expressing himself with that combination of clarity and subtlety that has always characterized his writings. Having graduated with First Class Honours, he went on to complete his MA. Then, armed with a University Fellowship, he proceeded to Peterhouse, Cambridge, where he studied for a Ph.D. in early Stuart history. This apprenticeship was a formative phase in his development, and he found the companionship of kindred spirits at Cambridge and the Institute of Historical Research particularly rewarding. In spite of the rigours of a debilitating complaint, which often left him convulsed with agony, he greatly enjoyed this period in his life. No physical discomfort, it seemed, could blunt his appetite for study or his natural cheerfulness.

In 1954 he came to a momentous decision. As things turned out, it was to change the whole course of his career and interests. He was invited by the University College of Swansea to take up a Research Fellowship for the study of the history of Wales in the second half of the nineteenth century—then a grossly neglected field. At first sight, it might have seemed a wholly disorienting switch of interest from early Stuart Parliaments to nineteenth-century Wales. In fact he accomplished it with uncanny ease and success. It proved to be a remarkable example of what educationists sometimes call a 'transfer of training'. To his new sphere he brought all kinds of fresh perspectives and subtle techniques of analysis never previously applied to it. He began to probe delicately for the hidden springs of political motivation and the interconnections between social conditions and political action—and inaction! Within a year or two, the fruits of this profound and novel interpretation of Welsh society in the two or three decades after 1850 began to be apparent. The late Charles Mowat, then resident in Swansea for a year as Fulbright Professor, was sufficiently impressed to urge Ieuan to publish some of the results of his research in the highly prestigious *Journal of Modern History*, which Mowat edited. It was an eloquent tribute by a master historian to the quality of the work of a hitherto-unknown Research Fellow.

Shortly afterwards, in 1957, Ieuan was appointed Lecturer in History at

Swansea. He himself was often worried that he had entered university teaching too late in life and that his published work was lagging a long way behind that of his younger colleagues. True though that may have been, he also possessed great advantages that more than compensated for it. He brought to his task the maturity and hard-won experience of a man whose path had been long and arduous. He had an unusually deep and intuitive sympathy with all students and a rare capacity for 'sparking them off'. I vividly recall one of the 'harder nuts' among mature students telling me, 'Oh! we all feel that he's so enthusiastic and so committed to every one of us that only a complete rotter could fail to respond to him'. The word he used was not 'rotter' but an old four-lettered Anglo-Saxon one; but I shall never forget how forcefully he made his point on behalf of himself and all the other students. Ieuan's teaching during these years had a profound impact in two fields: modern Welsh history and his special subject on early Stuart Parliaments. His influence on both undergraduate and postgraduate students right from the outset was far-reachingly memorable. He was always at his best in small groups, where it was possible to conduct genuine discussions or conversations with the class or an individual. He was not, at first, a great lecturer, being ill at ease with a large audience. Many may be surprised to hear that, knowing how in later years he developed into one of the *pregethwyr cyrddau mawr* (high festival preachers) of the historical profession in Wales, lecturing as he now does with compelling eloquence and virtuosity. In view of the quality of his research and teaching at this time, it was no more than a just reward that he should have been promoted to the rank of Senior Lecturer.

The news of his appointment in 1969 to the Sir John Williams Chair of Welsh History at Aberystwyth induced among his friends at Swansea a profound sense of loss and dismay, paralleled only by the general feeling of delight that he had been given the chance of extending his undoubted talents to a wider field of opportunity. During the preceding fifteen years he had given unmistakable proof of his own capacity for original, perceptive, and sensitive investigations into the field of nineteenth-century history and his unrivalled gift for bringing on young research students. He went to Aberystwyth convinced that the real justification for his appointment to the Chair would be the creation of a vibrant and dynamic research school. That, indeed, was to be his decisive contribution there. Though he was in many respects an excellent Head of Department and a gifted teacher at all levels, what he did supremely well was to foster and encourage vigorous and productive lines of research. His innovative flair and appealing style as a teacher attracted to him a large number of postgraduate students, most of whom he supervised himself. That is why it is singularly fitting that most of the contributions to this volume should have been written by his former research pupils. His ardour, concern, and willingness to put himself to endless trouble on their behalf have been proverbial down the years. All those who studied under him speak of him with unconcealed warmth, admiration, and affection.

Another gift of which he had provided clear evidence in Swansea was given fresh and enlarged scope at Aberystwyth. This was his ability to establish close

and fruitful contacts with other departments. At Aberystwyth he worked in
harmony with friends in sister departments such as History, Welsh, Economics,
Geography, Politics, International Politics, and Sociology. His enthusiasm for
the co-operative aims and integrated disciplines of the Centre for Advanced
Welsh and Celtic Studies was boundless. Outside the College he played a notable
role in the activities of the Ceredigion Antiquarian Society, becoming the General
Editor of its County History. He was Secretary of the History and Law Committee
of the Board of Celtic Studies and later its Chairman for many years. He also
had a decisive share in shaping the destinies of the Welsh Labour History Society
and its journal, *Llafur*, from their inception. He was an active member of the
Council of the National Library, which he regarded as the key nerve-centre
of all research into the life and literature of Wales. His long commitment to
the cause of adult education continued to be shown in his untiring efforts on
behalf of the Department of Extra-Mural Studies and of Coleg Harlech. It was
further revealed in his unsparing willingness to place his gifts at the disposal
of innumerable county and local societies all over Wales, with whom he was
in constant demand as a speaker.

These exacting activities inside and outside the College had not in any way
curtailed the spate of his own writings. Year in and year out, in Welsh and
in English, there came a stream of articles, intensively researched, penetratingly
argued, and beautifully written. Then, in 1976 and 1981, appeared two very
large and detailed volumes of documents relating to the Religious Census of
1851 in south Wales and north Wales. The immensely detailed and painstaking
work which went into the compilation of these volumes furnished unforgettable
evidence of the care, patience, and accuracy of their editor's scholarship. These
merits were even more apparent when his first volume of collected essays, entitled
Explorations and Explanations: Essays in the Social History of Victorian Wales, was
published in 1981. No one was in the least surprised that the degree of D.Litt.
of the University of Wales should unhesitatingly be awarded him for these works.
The *cognoscenti* had long recognized the worth of that succession of articles he
had earlier published. Those in Wales and elsewhere less familiar with the field
had almost certainly not realized until the books were published what a massive
contribution Ieuan Jones had made. A number of his articles had got
'lost'; tucked away in not very well-known journals. To refer to just one, but
possibly the most striking single example of an unjustly neglected article, out
of a number: the long, meticulously and ingeniously worked-out, and breath-
takingly seminal piece he wrote on Merioneth politics. It had first been published
in the transactions of the Merioneth Historical Society, an admirable county
journal, but hardly one that was seen or read widely enough for that revolutionary
analysis of nineteenth-century politics in general, not just of Merioneth or Wales,
to be appreciated at its true value. The exquisitely appropriate title of the book,
Explorations and Explanations, is itself an apt finger-post to the truly pioneering
paths he has blazed in opening up and explaining the nature of Welsh society
in the nineteenth century. The inwardness of its politics, religion, population
change, public health, and, above all, the essential secrets of its social beliefs,
aspirations, and institutions, have never been more tellingly revealed anywhere

than in his writings. His second volume of collected essays, *Communities: Essays in the Social History of Victorian Wales* (1987) confirms the view that no one has penetrated deeper into the very heart of Welsh working-class and Nonconformist culture than he. His own early life as well as his immensely receptive antennae as a historian had uniquely prepared him for the kind of empathy required of him. The techniques of his inquiry could profitably be extended to many areas outside Wales. It may well take generations before their implications are fully grasped and appreciated.

Un o'r rhesymau pennaf dros gyfrif Ieuan yn athro ac yn ysgolhaig mor atyniadol a chyffrous yw'r ffaith ei fod yn ddyn 'llawn', wedi ei gynysgaeddu â diddordebau eang a diwylliedig. Er iddo roi'r gorau ers llawer dydd i'r syniad o fynd i'r weinidogaeth, y mae'r grefydd Gristnogol a'r gwerthoedd moesol a meddyliol sydd ynghlwm wrthi yn dal eu gafael yn dynn ynddo o hyd. Bu'r elfen gyfriniol yn ei ddysgeidiaeth, a'i hemynau'n arbennig, yn rhan annatod o'i anian a'i gymeriad. Cydiodd prydferthwch Natur, unigeddau môr, maes, a mynydd, yn afaelgar yn ei ddychymyg erioed. Pan oedd yn iau, yr oedd yn ddringwr celfydd a beiddgar; a bu ef a'i gyfaill mynwesol, y diweddar John Collwyn Rees, cyn-Athro Gwleidyddiaeth yn Abertawe, yn dringo'n bell ac agos, yn y wlad hon a'r Cyfandir. Deil i gerdded yn egnïol, ac un o'i hoff adloniannau yw rhodio'r 'Prom' yn Aberystwyth gyda'r hwyr a myfyrio'n ddwys wrth syllu'n hir a meddylgar ar y môr mawr, beth bynnag fo hwyl hwnnw—ai mwynaidd, ai mileinig. Nid rhyfedd iddo ymhyfrydu ar hyd y blynyddoedd mewn llenyddiaeth Gymraeg a Saesneg. Llynca waith y pen awduron â chyfuniad neilltuol o angerdd a lledneisrwydd a adlewyrchir yn ei arddull ysgrifenedig ef ei hun. Gwelir hyn yn arbennig iawn yn y sensitifrwydd eithriadol hwnnw i ystyr, *nuance*, a thôn prioddull ysgrifenedig a llafar a'i nodwedda. Os gwir mai pennaf gyfrinach yr hanesydd yw ei fod wedi ymdrwytho i'r fath raddau yn llenyddiaeth ei gyfnod, mawr a mân, creadigol a rhyddieithol, nes iddo allu 'clywed pobl yr oes honno'n siarad â'i gilydd', yna'n sicr treiddiodd Ieuan i ddirgelion eithaf y ganrif ddiwethaf. Mae yn ogystal yn dipyn o gerddor; un a ymgolla'n llwyr wrth ganu mewn côr, chwarae'r piano, neu wrando ar gerddoriaeth mewn cyngherddau ac yn ei gartref. Er mai llais baritôn soniarus sydd ganddo, erfyniwyd arno i ganu tenor mewn un côr am flynyddoedd am ei fod yn un o'r gwŷr prin a dethol hynny sy'n meddu clust digon main a sicr i'w galluogi i wneud hynny! Cofiaf ofyn iddo unwaith pa un ymhlith cewri'r byd cerddorol oedd ei hoff gyfansoddwr. 'Anodd iawn dweud', oedd ei ateb, 'rwy'n ei chyfri'n fraint amhrisiadwy i mi allu cyfranogi o'r trysorau dihafal hyn o gwbl. Ond pan fyddaf yn gwrando ar un o bedwarawdau aeddfetaf Beethoven neu yn astudio un o'i *sonatas* mwyaf ar gyfer y piano teimlaf fy mod, a minnau'n greadur digon meidrol, yn y munudau hynny yn cael troedio ar flaenau fy nhraed yn wylaidd a gostyngedig i un o gysegrleoedd sancteiddiolaf holl enaid ac ysbryd y ddynoliaeth.' Yr un fyddai ei ymateb wrth ddarllen llenyddiaeth aruchel neu syllu ar gampweithiau celfyddyd neu bensaernïaeth. Ys dywedodd Robert Williams Parry, wrth gyfarch gwrthrych arall:

> Fe garodd bob rhyw geinder is y rhod
> Mewn natur, mewn celfyddyd, ac mewn dysg.

Rhywbeth yn debyg fu profiad ei gymar, Maisie. Gwraig rinweddol, medd awdur Llyfr y Diarhebion, sydd 'goron i'w gŵr'. Mae'n sicr fod hynny'n wir am Maisie, ac ni fyddai'r un deyrnged i Ieuan ond hanner cyflawn heb gyfeirio ati hi. Ym 1986 buont yn dathlu deugain mlynedd o fywyd priodasol hynod ddiddan a chariadus. Trwy gydol y blynyddoedd hynny bu hi'n gefn ac yn gynhaliaeth iddo ym mhob dim. Cydnabu yntau hynny wrth gyflwyno ei gyfrol, *Explorations and Explanations*, iddi. Er i'w hiechyd hithau fod yn fregus erioed ac er iddi ddioddef llawer iawn o boen a blinder, ni fennodd hynny ronyn ar ei serchusrwydd na'i rhadlonrwydd anghymarol. Helaethu a dyfnhau ei pherson-oliaeth a wnaeth, rhagor na'i chwerwi na'i diflasu. Chwedl yr hen ddihareb Gymraeg, 'A ddioddefws a orfu'. Cyfoethogwyd ei meddwl a'i chymeriad hithau gan lenyddiaeth a cherddoriaeth. Os Beethoven yw hoff gyfansoddwr ei gŵr, mae'n briodol iawn mai un o ffefrynnau mwyaf Maisie yw Schubert. Mae yn ei thymheredd ei hunan lawer o'r un cyseinedd melys, bywiogrwydd ysgafn, a llewyrch heulog a nodwedda fiwsig y cyfansoddwr ifanc hwnnw a ddioddefodd gymaint ond a adawodd inni beth o'r gerddoriaeth fwyaf serennaidd a hyfryd a gyfansoddwyd erioed. Mae caredigrwydd a lletygarwch Ieuan a Maisie yn ddiarhebol. Profodd llu o westeion y croeso twymgalon a haelfrydig a estynnir i bawb ar eu haelwyd. Mae rhyw athrylith naturiol ddigymell yn perthyn i'r ddau yn eu cynhesrwydd di-ben-draw at eraill. Hir oes iddynt ill dau ac i'w mab disglair a thalentog, Alun, sydd yn gannwyll eu llygaid.

As friends, Ieuan and Maisie are beyond praise. Those who know them would all wish to join in thanking them with the utmost warmth and sincerity for all they have given over the years. Though Ieuan has now formally retired from his Chair, it seems inconceivable that he will for a moment give up his 'explorations and explanations'. We can surely expect many more essays to continue flowing from his pen. His zest for seeking out historical truth remains undiminished, his passion for discussion and disquisition unabated, and his urge to convey his discoveries to others unquenched. For many years to come, as for many years gone by, he is likely to be one of the most regular and enthusi-astic clients of the National Library of Wales. We should all want to wish him and Maisie a long, happy and fruitful retirement. May they continue to give and receive as handsomely in the future as they have done in the past. To them belongs that art of friendship that masters Time itself and 'sits highest upon the forehead of humanity' (Keats).

Victoria and Victorian Wales

JOHN DAVIES

WRITING from Llandderfel in Merioneth on 27 August 1889, Queen Victoria requested Sir Henry Ponsonby, her private secretary, to inform the Prince of Wales 'of the excellent and enthusiastic reception we have all met with here, and ... to tell him how this naturally sensitive and warmhearted people feel the neglect shown them by the Prince of Wales and his family ... It is very wrong of him not to come here. It is only five hours from London and ... the Prince ... takes his title from this country, which is so beautiful.'[1] The neglect was not only that of the Prince of Wales. During her 64-year reign, the Queen spent a total of seven years in Scotland, seven weeks in Ireland, and seven nights in Wales—one at the Penrhyn Arms Hotel in Bangor in 1852; two at Penrhyn Castle in 1859 and four at Palé, Llandderfel in 1889. In addition, she cruised round the Welsh coast in 1847, a voyage which gave Prince Albert the opportunity to visit Pembroke and Penrhyn Castles and to walk along the bridge over the Menai Straits.[2] Before inheriting the throne, however, she had, in 1832, spent nearly eleven weeks in Wales, largely at hotels in Beaumaris and at 'dear Plas Newydd', the seat of the marquis of Anglesey.

From the accession of the Tudors until 1969, Victoria's sojourn in Anglesey in 1832 was by far the lengthiest visit to Wales by a member of the royal family. Medieval kings had had cause to have closer dealings with the country. With the exception of Stephen and Richard I, all the Norman and early Plantagenet monarchs had led expeditions in Wales, campaigns which culminated in the twenty-two months spent by Edward I in and around Gwynedd in 1282–4. Edward's eleventh child, Edward of Caernarfon, the first English Prince of Wales, won the loyalty of the Welsh official class, and in the crisis which terminated his reign it was to Wales that he withdrew (14 October to 16 December 1326). There is no evidence that Edward III (1327–77) ever visited Wales, although it was his son's thirty-three years as prince which firmly linked the principality with the heir to the English Crown. Like Edward II, Richard II found favour among the members of the Welsh official class, and the reign of Richard, like

---

[1] *The Letters of Queen Victoria*, 3, i, 528–9. The nine volumes of Victoria's correspondence, henceforth referred to as *Letters*, were published in three series of three volumes: first series (1837–61), ed. H. C. Benson and Viscount Esher (1907); second series (1862–85), ed. G. E. Buckle (1926); third series (1886–1901), ed. G. E. Buckle (1930).

[2] *North Wales Chronicle*, 23 September 1852; 15, 22 October 1859; E. Parry, *Royal Visits and Progresses to Wales* (Chester, 1850), 465.

that of Edward, came to an end following wanderings in Wales (28 July to 19 August 1399).

Henry IV, as heir to the Lancastrians and the Bohuns, was one of the chief lords of the March, while his successor, Henry of Monmouth, won his first experience of warfare during his campaigns against Owain Glyndŵr. Henry VI appears not to have visited Wales, but the dynastic wars which were the consequence of his feeble rule had extensive ramifications for the Welsh. The Yorkists, with their Mortimer inheritance, had their major power-base in the Welsh March, while their descent from Gwladus, daughter of Llywelyn the Great, allowed them to consider themselves the heirs of the senior Welsh dynasty. In comparison, Henry VII was only tangentially related to the royal houses of Wales, although his Welsh birth and residence and his use of Wales as the spring-board for his assault upon the English crown caused the Tudors to be considered a Welsh dynasty. Yet, following his seven-day march through Wales in August 1485, Henry VII made no further visits to the country; neither did any of his Tudor successors, thereby ensuring that the Tudors were the only dynasty of English sovereigns since the Norman Conquest not to set foot in Wales.[3]

The Stuarts proved a little more mobile. James I passed through the northern borderlands of Wales in 1617; Charles I made Raglan his headquarters for some weeks in the summer of 1645 and then travelled through Wales to Chester; James II went to 'heal and dine' at Holywell on 29 August 1687.[4] These, however, were the only royal visits to Wales in the seventeenth century. There were none at all in the following century; indeed, the first three Georges saw very little of any part of Britain outside the lower Thames Valley, with its Windsor–London axis.

With the sovereign so remote from the more peripheral parts of the kingdom, the common people of Wales may have had only the vaguest notion of the nature of kingship. Such at least is suggested by the recollections of John Evans (1723–1817), the revered pioneer of Methodism in east Merioneth. Reminiscing in 1811, he stated that many parents had refused to send their children to Madam Bridget Bevan's circulating schools because they thought that she 'was a Queen, and that after teaching the children, she would call them away to another kingdom'. Even more illuminating is Evans's childhood memory of a discussion about the King's death—it presumably occurred in 1727 and referred to George I.

'Where did he live?' John Evans's aunt asked the schoolmaster at Llanfor.

'In London,' was the reply.

'Well, the death of a man so far away can hardly matter to us.'

'Oh yes, it is a matter of great importance to us all.'

'Why, what was his work then?'

The schoolmaster sought to explain.

---

[3] Arthur, Prince of Wales, resided at Ludlow from November 1501 until his death in April 1502; Princess Mary was at Ludlow for eighteen months in the mid-1520s.

[4] Parry, *Royal Visits*, pp. 327, 407. During his travels in August 1687, James II also passed through Monmouthshire.

'Who will they have in his place?' asked John Evans's aunt. 'I hope they won't ask my husband Siôn; he was parish overseer last year and overseer of the roads the year before; this year he deserves to be left alone.'[5]

The first nineteenth-century monarch to visit Wales was George IV. Prince of Wales for fifty-seven years, he made a fleeting visit in 1806 to plant an oak tree at Llandrinio in Montgomeryshire. He gave a hundred guineas a year to the Welsh charity school in London, and its pupils regaled him at Carlton House on St David's Day before going on to the Freemason's Tavern to sing 'an ode to chastity'. A year after his accession, he set forth from Plymouth to Dublin, the first English monarch to visit Ireland since 1689. When he put in at Holyhead, news of the worsening health of his wife and mortal enemy caused him to disembark and spend the night at Plas Newydd. Returning to his yacht, he was informed of the Queen's death. 'Although it would be absurd to think that he was afflicted,' claimed John Wilson Croker, 'he was certainly affected.' Ordering the ships in the harbour to be dressed in mourning, he retired below deck and arrived in Dublin in a state of advanced intoxication. On the return journey heavy seas forced the yacht to dock at Milford Haven, from whence the King rapidly returned to London via Brecon, where he stopped briefly to give royal pardons to some of those convicted at the Assizes.[6]

Victoria's visit to Anglesey in 1832 was part of her mother's campaign to present the heir presumptive to the people—the 'Royal Progresses' which so delighted the Whigs and caused William IV to be 'indecent in his wrath'. The duchess provided her daughter with 'a book ... that I might write the journal of my journey to Wales in it'; this was the beginning of Victoria's diaries, which were eventually to fill 122 volumes.[7] Following the example of her uncle, the duke of Sussex, who had made a three-day visit to the Denbigh Eisteddfod of 1828, the princess and her mother became patrons of the Beaumaris Eisteddfod of 1832, an act which made a deep impression, judging by the number of references to it in the Welsh press over the next seven decades. Neither of the royal visitors actually attended the Eisteddfod, but the successful competitors—among them Samuel Roberts of Llanbryn-mair, who won second prize for an essay on agriculture—were summoned to Baron Hill where the duchess presented them with their awards.[8] The marquis of Anglesey, then Lord Lieutenant of Ireland, seems not to have visited Plas Newydd while the royal visitors were under its roof, but the weeks which she spent there linked Victoria closely with the Whig house of Paget. In the early years of her reign twelve of the marquis's close relations were members of the royal household, and that 'scurrilous ultra-Tory paper', *The Age*, referred to Windsor as the 'Paget Club House'. On her return

[5] *Y Drysorfa Ysbrydol*, 1809–13, p. 517; *Y Cymro*, 17 November 1981.

[6] Parry, *Royal Visits*, pp. 414–25; F. Jones, *The Princes and Principality of Wales* (Cardiff, 1969), p. 54; C. Hibbert, *George IV, Regent and King* (London, 1973), p. 207; *Seren Gomer*, October 1821; J. L. Jennings (ed.), *The Correspondence and Diaries of John Wilson Croker* (London, 1884), I, 201.

[7] *Letters* 1,1, 25; C. Woodham–Smith, *Queen Victoria, from her Birth to the Death of the Prince Consort* (London, 1972), pp. 88–9.

[8] *Y Dysgedydd*, October 1832; *North Wales Chronicle*, 7 August 1832; *Cambrian Quarterly Magazine*, 4 (1832); Parry, *Royal Visits*, pp. 435–62.

journey Victoria took refreshment at the home of Sir Stephen Glynne at Hawarden, a place to which she spurned all invitations when it was occupied by Sir Stephen's brother-in-law, W. E. Gladstone.[9]

The visit of 1852 was inspired by Albert's desire to see the newly completed Britannia bridge across the Menai Straits, while that of 1859 allowed the Prince Consort to view the *Great Eastern*, then in the harbour at Holyhead.[10] Albert was also the cause of the visit of 1889, for it stemmed from Victoria's wish to call at Bryntysilio, Sir Theodore Martin's home near Llangollen, and to see the desk at which Sir Theodore had written his five-volume biography of the Prince. Victoria visited the Penrhyn Quarry in 1852 and the Denbighshire coalfield in 1889—when her daughter, Princess Beatrice, went down a mine at Rhosllannerchrugog—but the burgeoning industrial communities of the south were wholly unknown to her.[11] Her knowledge of Wales was largely restricted to the banks of the Menai and the Dee, seen mainly through detours during journeys to or from Balmoral. These are localities with something of a Scottish feel about them, for the Menai, with its backcloth of mountains, has the appearance of a sea loch, while the valley of the Dee, from the lake at Bala to the romantic woodlands around Llangollen, has many counterparts in the Highlands.

The mention in the Queen's letter to Ponsonby of a journey of five hours from London suggests that it was to the north of Wales that Victoria was directing her son's attention. He had already been to those parts. When he returned from Ireland in April 1868, it had been noted that it was possible for him to be in Caernarfon on 25 April, the birthday of the first English Prince of Wales. He spent a few hours in the town, opening the new waterworks, before travelling on to stay with the duke of Sutherland in Staffordshire. He was pleased with his 'cordial reception'. 'It will', he said, 'encourage us to look forward to another visit on some future occasion.'[12]

Nineteen years later he paid an hour's visit to the Albert Hall, the setting of the National Eisteddfod of 1887. There he stated that he indulged 'in the hope that at no distant date it may be in my power to pay a visit to the ancient Principality whose name I am proud to bear'.[13] That hope was fulfilled in 1894 when, during a three-night stay at Penrhyn Castle, he attended the National Eisteddfod at Bangor. Entertained at the castle by the Penrhyn choir, he showed particular appreciation of its rendering of 'Gwŷr Philistia'. At the Eisteddfod itself, Lewis Morris, the Anglo-Welsh poet, explained that 'one cause or another had prevented his Royal Highness from coming before'. Morris offered an ode

[9] Parry, *Royal Visits*, p. 452; E. Pakenham, Countess of Longford, *Victoria, R. I.* (London, 1964), p. 38; Marquess of Anglesey, *One-Leg* (London, 1961), p. 309; A. Aspinall, *Politics and the Press, 1780–1850* (London, 1949), p. 342.

[10] *North Wales Chronicle*, 23 September 1852; 15, 22 October 1859.

[11] *Gwalia*, 28 August 1889; *The Times*, 27 August 1889.

[12] *Souvenir of the Visit of the Prince and Princess to North Wales* (Bangor, 1894), p. 19; *Byegones relating to Wales and the Border Counties*, 19 June 1901.

[13] H. T. Edwards, 'Victorian Wales seeks reinstatement', *Planet*, 52 (1985), p. 15.

which included the line: 'After six hundred years, the Prince of Wales comes home'. The Prince, his wife, and their hosts were made members of the Gorsedd of Bards, Edward as Iorwerth Dywysog, Alexandra as Hoffedd Prydain, Lord Penrhyn as Eryr Penrhyn and Lady Penrhyn as Blodeuyn Arvon. The following day, His Royal Highness went cruising off the coast of Anglesey. The chairman of the Llandudno Urban District, annoyed that his town was not to have a royal visit, hired a steamer to pursue him; catching up with the royal yacht near Ynys Seiriol, the chairman led the Llandudno Promenade Band in a rendering of 'God Bless the Prince of Wales'.[14]

Two years later the Prince came to Aberystwyth to be installed as chancellor of the University of Wales. No prospective king of England, noted the *Cambrian News*, had been to the town since 1485, although the resort had attracted a number of foreign royalties, a reigning king of Saxony amongst them. Edward was accommodated at Plas Machynlleth, the seat of the marquis of Londonderry, and fears were expressed that the occasion might be appropriated by the Tory aristocracy. These proved unfounded, for the Prince and his entourage were upstaged by the 87-year-old Gladstone, the recipient of an honorary degree and, for many leading figures in the university, the first choice as chancellor. The *Western Mail*, although piqued that the ceremony was not held in Cardiff, declared the installation to be 'the most brilliant pageant witnessed in Wales in modern times'.[15] The following day the Prince went by train from Machynlleth to Cardiff where, during a three-hour visit, he opened the town's Free Library. In 1897, while staying with the Grosvenors at Eaton Hall, he spent a day with Gladstone at Hawarden. In 1898, his son, the duke of York (later George V), was at Caernarfon, the last royal visit to Wales during the Victorian era.[16]

'Her Majesty', wrote Professor David Williams, 'was always disdainful where the principality was concerned,'[17] a view confirmed by the sparse references to Wales in Victoria's voluminous published papers. Although she urged Lord Lansdowne in 1849 to ensure that 'Welsh should be taught in Wales as well as English', she saw the issue in the context of 'her loyal and good Highlanders'; education in Gaelic, she argued, 'will tend more than anything to keep up their simplicity of character which [the Queen] considers a great merit these days.'[18] Seeking in 1868 to counter Disraeli's arguments in favour of a residence for the Prince of Wales in Ireland, she wrote: 'Every other place in the Queen's dominions—Wales and the colonies even—might get up pretensions for

[14] *Souvenir of the Visit*, pp. 24–44; *Transactions of the National Eisteddfod of Wales, Carnarvon, 1894* (Liverpool, 1896), pp. xxiv–xxxii.

[15] *Cambrian News*, 26 June 1895; E. L. Ellis, *The University College of Wales, Aberystwyth, 1872–1972* (Cardiff, 1972), pp. 118–21; *WM*, 31 December 1896.

[16] *SWDN*, 26, 27, 29 June 1896; *The Times*, 11 May 1897; *North Wales Chronicle*, 2 December 1899. The Queen embarked and disembarked at Holyhead while making her remarkable visit to Ireland in 1900; she refused all requests to break her journey in Wales (*North Wales Chronicle*, 17 March 1900).

[17] D. Williams, *The Rebecca Riots: a Study in Agrarian Discontent* (Cardiff, 1955), p. 265.

[18] *Letters*, 1, ii, 255.

residence, which are out of the question.'[19] She was surprised at the standard of the choirs which entertained her at Llangollen in 1889, composed as they were 'merely of shopkeepers and flannel weavers'.[20] As will be seen, the arrangements for the visit of 1889 suggest that Victoria's advisers either had no understanding of the situation in Wales or felt no compunction in offending Welsh susceptibilities.

Welsh issues impinged more closely upon the Queen in the last decade of her reign. In February 1893 she was appalled by the government's Suspensory Bill, introduced as a preliminary to Welsh disestablishment. 'I would never have agreed to [it]', she wrote in her diary, 'had I known [its] real bearing.' 'There is no "Church of Wales",' she informed Gladstone, 'and therefore this measure is in reality against the whole Church ... The Queen trusts Mr Gladstone may yet pause before taking so disastrous a step as to attempt to disestablish part of the English Church of which she is head; and of which she always thought Mr Gladstone a loyal member.' In his reply, Gladstone denied that he had used 'language which treated the Bill as being a first step towards the disestablishment or disendowment of the Church of England'. He reminded the Queen that Hartington, whom by 1893 she held in high favour, had stated that 'the question of Church establishment in Scotland was a local question, which ought to be decided according to the views of the people of Scotland ... It would be difficult to deny to Wales the application of the principle announced long ago in the case of Scotland.'[21]

The issue arose again when the earl of Rosebery replaced Gladstone. 'I was horrified', wrote the Queen in her diary in March 1894, '... by seeing in a draft of the Speech for the opening of Parliament the announcement of Bills going to [be] brought in for the discontinuance of the Ecclesiastical Establishments of Wales and Scotland ... I had promised at my accession to maintain the State Churches, and had always assured the Clergy their rights could never be interfered with.' 'She does not think', she wrote to Rosebery, 'that Lord Rosebery will destroy well-tried, valued and necessary institutions for the sole purpose of flattering useless Radicals.'[22] 'I don't want to be Prime Minister at all', wrote Rosebery to Ponsonby, 'but if I am to be, I must be a real one ... The Government came in ... on Welsh and Scottish disestablishment ... we could not exist for a moment without dealing with these questions ... The Welsh Party would simply vote the Government out on the Address ... If the Queen insists on her view, I have I am sorry to say no resource but to give up the Government.' The immediate crisis was resolved by changing the wording in the Queen's speech from 'Bills for disestablishment' to 'Measures dealing with the ecclesiastical establishment'.[23]

---

[19] Ibid., 2, i, 513.

[20] Ibid., 3, i, 528

[21] Ibid., 3, ii, 230, 232–3.

[22] Ibid., 375, 378.

[23] A. Ponsonby, *Henry Ponsonby, Queen Victoria's Private Secretary* (London, 1942), pp. 277–8; R. R. James, *Rosebery* (London, 1963), p. 336; *Letters*, 3, ii, 376, 379.

Rosebery was obliged to address himself to the question once more in January 1895 when Victoria sought to oppose the elevation of Dr Percival to the episcopal bench on the grounds that 'he is almost ... the *only* prominent clergyman in England who has declared himself in favour of Welsh Disestablishment'. 'Wales', Rosebery told the Queen, '... is different. There the Church of England has lost her hold on the mass of the people ... It is ... very much what Gibraltar is to Spain, a foreign fortress placed on the territory of a jealous, proud and susceptible nation.'[24] Rosebery's government fell in June 1895; thereafter Victoria was not troubled by Welsh issues nor by Welsh Members of Parliament, save in 1900 when Balfour told her of the 'extraordinary violence of the speeches of Lloyd George ... who actually went to the length of asserting that the Generals in the field had sacrificed the lives of troops to political considerations'.[25]

If disdain characterized Victoria's attitude to Wales, the general attitude of the Welsh to Victoria varied from warm approbation to rapturous adulation. Yet she was not without her Welsh critics for, as will be seen, anti-royalism and even outright republicanism were not absent from Victorian Wales. Disparagement of the Queen ebbed and flowed in unison with similar sentiments in England for, apart from attacks upon Victoria's neglect of Wales, there was little that was specifically Welsh about Welsh anti-royalism. Indeed, the adulation was more in accord with Welsh tradition, rooted as it was in an ancient sense of hierarchy and in pride in the Tudors. There was nothing in the Welsh press of the 1830s comparable with *The Times's* savage obituary of George IV or with the *Spectator's* derisive dismissal of William IV in 1837. Sidney Lee's comment that, before Victoria, the throne was occupied in succession by 'an imbecile, a profligate and a buffoon' is hardly reflected in the pages of *Seren Gomer*, the first Welsh-language weekly newspaper.[26] *Seren Gomer* found merit in George III, praising him for his farming skills and for his avoidance of carousing and libertinism. It found George IV less attractive, offering a mock heroic description of his visit to Anglesey and detailed reports of the Queen Caroline case; yet in its obituary, although it offered an unadorned catalogue of the King's life, it said nothing specifically derogatory about him. The paper published a number of *englynion* in praise of William IV and acclaimed him as 'the best representative of the Hanover family to have occupied the British throne'.[27]

Seren Gomer welcomed Victoria warmly, stating that she had always shown 'her love for freedom in Church and State'—a reference presumably to her parents' close association with the Whigs. She has saved us, it declared, from 'the enemy of the people's freedom', her vicious and obsessively reactionary uncle, the duke of Cumberland, and it urged unanimous support for the attempt to

[24] *Letters*, 3, ii, 468–71.

[25] *Letters*, 3, iii, 482, 568.

[26] F. Hardie, *The Political Influence of Queen Victoria, 1861–1901* (Oxford, 1935), p. 201; K. Martin, *The Crown and the Establishment* (Harmondsworth, 1962), pp. 29–30; H. Tingsten, *Victoria and the Victorians* (London, 1972), p. 73.

[27] *Seren Gomer*, 1 March 1820; 1 October 1821; 1 August 1830; 1 July 1837.

exclude Cumberland from the succession.[28] The entire Welsh press had been delighted by her stay in Anglesey—the cradle of the Tudors—where she received 'constant manifestations of the warm love of the race of Gomer'. Her visit, wrote the *Cambrian Quarterly Magazine*, would fortify the ancient traditions of the Welsh, for it would 'confirm inviolate our tiny Principality from that progression towards democracy ... which is lamentably stalking in some other parts of the Empire'.[29]

The Anglesey visit brought out two of the themes which would find constant expression in Victorian Wales—the Welsh lineage of the English royal house and the innate loyalty and passivity of the Welsh (particularly when contrasted with the alleged treachery and militancy of the Irish). These, together with the Protestantism of the Crown and the high moral tone of Victoria's court, were the chief components of the Welsh approbation of Victoria. The sovereign's Welsh descent, declared Alun at the Beaumaris Eisteddfod of 1832, more than compensated for the conquest of Wales: 'We have suffered a loss to our gain; we have no reason to clamour for repeal. A descendant of our native princes now fills the British throne ... and so long as blood flows through the veins of an Ancient Briton, loyalty and attachment to the House of Brunswick will flow likewise.'[30] John Williams ab Ithel, in the Abergavenny Eisteddfod of 1853, made even more extravagant claims. 'It is grievous to recollect', he stated, 'that any persons should withhold their support for such meetings ... A weak plea was once made on the ground ... that if we were too national, we might loosen the ties which bind us to the English government and try to acquire the independence of Wales. Never was there a more ridiculous idea! Wales is strictly and emphatically independent ... Victoria is peculiarly our own Queen—Boadicea rediviva—our Buddug the Second ... We can address our English friends: "We have ... more right in Victoria than thee", a larger quantity of Celtic than of Saxon blood flowing through her royal veins.' Ab Ithel went on to trace her ancestry through Henry Tudor back to Madog ap Locrine ap Brutus, to Ieuan ap Japheth ap Noah, to Adam and to God.[31]

The uniquely loyal character of the Welsh was extensively proclaimed throughout the nineteenth century. 'There has been riot and commotion in England, Scotland and Ireland', wrote Robert Jones, Rhos-lan, in 1820, because those peoples 'neither feared God nor honoured the King ... but our nation remained wonderfully faithful to the government in all troubles.' 'In these days of sedition and threatened anarchy', said Alun in 1832, 'the principality has always been tranquil and happy as a Goshen.' 'We, the Welsh', wrote *Y Gwladgarwr* in 1866, 'have been loyalists for centuries ... more so than the English themselves.' 'In no part of the Empire', stated *Y Genedl Gymreig* on the death of the Queen in 1901, 'is distress and grief deeper and more heartfelt than in Wales'—

---

[28] Ibid., 1 August 1837. 'Noting the attitude of the Whigs to your nearest successor', King Leopold of the Belgians told Victoria: 'It is enough to frighten them into the most violent attachment to you.' (*Letters*, 1, ii, 93).

[29] *Yr Eurgrawn Wesleyaidd*, September 1832; *Cambrian Quarterly Magazine*, 4 (1832).

[30] *North Wales Chronicle*, 7 August; 4 September 1832.

[31] *Report of the Abergavenny Eisteddfod of 1853* (Abergavenny, 1853), p. 10; H. T. Edwards, *Gŵyl Gwalia* (Llandysul, 1980), pp. 303–4.

sentiments echoed in *Young Wales* in its references to 'the absolute love and loyalty of the Welsh' and to the 'hush of our national sorrow and bereavement'.[32]

Like the Queen herself, the Welsh press was fully aware that Victoria owed her throne to the Protestantism of her line, a fact which was linked, in the minds of Nonconformists, with growing religious toleration. To *Seren Gomer*, the reign of George III had seen a significant advance in the rights of Dissenters; this was even more true of the reign of Victoria, a point seized upon in 1901 by most of her Welsh obituarists.[33] David Rees, editor of *Y Diwygiwr*, was delighted by her marriage to Albert; the Prince's ancestors, he noted, 'were the foster-fathers of the Protestant Reformation and one of them safeguarded ... the life of Luther'. Enthusing over the royal family in 1863, *Y Traethodydd* declared that 'it is only in Ireland that one finds a few—and they are all Papists— who dare show their poisonous infidelity'. Recalling Howell Harris's eagerness to defend the House of Hanover, the Calvinistic Methodist *Goleuad* wrote in 1889: 'Our denomination from its beginnings has always shown loyal allegiance to the Crown.'[34]

Even more emphatic were the Welsh tributes to Victoria's high sense of morality. 'No sovereign, from the days of Sennacherib to our own', declared Talhaiarn in 1853, 'has wielded so bright and unsullied a sceptre.' 'The family virtues of the court', wrote Roger Edwards in 1863, 'call for the utmost praise and imitation.' The Queen, stated *Y Genedl Gymreig* in 1901, had 'purified the court' and 'her beneficent influence had elevated the life of the entire Kingdom.' Even the irrepressible radical, Dr E. Pan Jones, felt obliged to agree that her personal life was beyond reproach. 'One has to praise her moral character', he wrote, 'especially bearing in mind the corruption in high places.' The fact caused him some surprise when he considered her ancestry. 'When one remembers she was related to the Georges, it is astonishing that she had any merits at all.'[35] Victoria would have agreed with at least some of Pan Jones's comments. It was in reaction to her licentious relations, and those of the Prince Consort, that the royal couple had adopted a rigid code, particularly in sexual matters. She was fully aware of 'the corruption of aristocratic circles'. One of her motives in publishing her *Leaves from the Journal of our Life in the Highlands* was to reform 'Highborn Beings by showing them an example of a good simple life at the summit'. A moral court, she argued, would retard 'democratic feeling [which] was caused by the fact that the sins of the upper classes were forgiven while the lower classes were punished'. Like the bulk of her subjects, particularly those of the middle class, she believed in moral progress. In the time of her predecessors, she remarked, 'even the best people were excessively coarse'; in her reign, 'modern

[32] R. Jones, *Drych yr Amseroedd* (Llanrwst, 1820), p. 204; *North Wales Chronicle*, 7 August 1832; *Y Gwladgarwr*, 22 September 1866; *Y Genedl Gymreig*, 29 January 1901; *Young Wales*, February 1901.

[33] *Letters*, 2, i, 377; *Seren Gomer*, 1 March 1820.

[34] *Y Diwygiwr*, 1840, pp. 31, 96–7; I. Jones, *David Rees, Y Cynhyrfwr* (Swansea, 1971), pp. 239–40; *Y Traethodydd*, 18 (1863), 257; *Y Goleuad*, 22 August 1889.

[35] *Y Traethodydd*, 18 (1863), p. 257; *Report of the Abergavenny Eisteddfod of 1853*, p. 5; *Y Genedl Gymreig*, 29 January 1901; *Cwrs y Byd*, March 1901.

women had more accomplishments, men drank less and dogs behaved better towards the furniture'.[36]

While Victorian Wales produced a large body of prose in praise of the Queen, it produced an even larger body of verse. At the London Eisteddfod of 1887, where the chair was offered for an *awdl* on Queen Victoria, there were seventeen competitors, a fact which suggested, wrote the adjudicator, 'that the poets of Wales, as a class, are highly loyal'. Indeed they were. As Dr R. Tudur Jones has pointed out, a compilation which included all the *englynion*, *pryddestau* and *awdlau* sung to Victoria would form a very substantial volume. In 1887 the chair was won by R. A. Williams (Berw), whose 750 lines on 'un ohonom ni sy'n hanu' (one who issues from us) were warmly praised, although the adjudicator considered the genealogical details somewhat tedious.[37] Berw had many predecessors. Robert ap Gwilym Ddu had sung to George IV in 1821 and Robert Davies, Nantglyn, had greeted Victoria at Beaumaris in 1832. Eben Fardd hailed her accession and included felicitous references to the royal house in his 'Battle of Bosworth Field' (1858). Emrys and Islwyn wrote elegies to Albert the Good. At the Caernarfon Eisteddfod of 1861, the coming-of-age of the heir to the throne inspired Ceiriog's 'Prince of Wales Cantata', which contains some of the best-known Welsh lyrics of the century. With its references to Buddug and to 'Eich Dyn' (Your Man—an adaptation of the Prince of Wales's motto much favoured by nineteenth-century Welsh royalists), and with its choruses of Welsh noblemen singing of their inability to rule themselves, Ceiriog's cantata is the finest example of the readiness to consider that the conquest mattered little compared with the connection with the royal house.[38] The marriage of the Prince in 1863 moved William Roberts (Bardd Berw) to compose a lengthy ode, and the Prince's recovery from typhoid in 1871 led to a rash of versifying. There was, in addition, a vast outpouring of more ephemeral compositions; indeed, hardly an issue of *Y Geninen* appeared without at least one *englyn* to some member of the royal family. Several Welsh versions of 'God Save the Queen' were published, and James Elroy Flecker added an extra verse to the anthem praising 'The Golden Dales/Of thine old Christian Wales'. Anglo-Welsh poets were also enthusiastic royalists. Lewis Morris, hoping perhaps to succeed Tennyson as Poet Laureate, was always on hand with panegyric. 'Our Cymric eyes grow bright to see our sovereign come,' he sang in 1889, and continued, with a curiously Wildean touch:

[36] Longford, *Victoria*, pp. 375, 381, 597. 'Compared with the Prince Consort's family', wrote Giles St. Aubyn, 'the Hanoverians might have come out of a monastery.' (G. St. Aubyn, *Edward VII, Prince and King* (London, 1979), p. 19).

[37] *Cofnodion a Chyfansoddiadau Eisteddfod Genedlaethol 1887, Caerludd* (Cardiff, 1890), pp. 1, 21, 28–42; *Y Cymro*, 26 May 1981.

[38] W. Williams (ed.), *Gardd Eifion* (Dolgellau, 1841), pp. 135–8; *Gweithiau Barddonol Eben Fardd* (Bangor, n.d.), pp. 299–327; *Y Dysgedydd*, October 1832; *Y Beirniad*, 16 (1875), 24–33; Bardd Berw (William Roberts), *Cân newydd ar yr achlysur o Briodas Tywysog Cymru a'r Dywysoges Alexandra o Denmark* (Caernarfon, 1863); J. Ceiriog Hughes, *The Prince of Wales Cantata* (Wrexham, 1862); Edwards, *Gŵyl Gwalia*, pp. 343–51; Anthropos (Robert David Rowland), *Y Frenhines Victoria, ei hanes, ei nodweddion a'i dylanwad* (Caernarfon, 1901), pp. 19,27,35; J. B. Smith, *Llywelyn ap Gruffudd, Tywysog Cymru* (Cardiff, 1986), pp. 198–9; Ll. B. Smith, 'Llywelyn ap Gruffudd and the Welsh Historical Consciousness', *WHR*, 12 (1984–5), 7–8.

> Dear Lady, we are feeble folk and weak,
> But our old tongue and loyal hearts we keep:
> We cherish still the love we may not speak—
> The old affection deep.[39]

Praise of Victoria came to its peak in 1901, when even the radical *Baner ac Amserau Cymru* published black-edged editions in her memory. This was partly the result of the sheer length of her reign. 'Our gracious Queen', wrote Anthropos, 'had been with us so long that her name and her history are interwoven with our memories of youth.' She had become an awe-inspiring symbol of maternity. To *Y Genedl Gymreig*, Victoria was 'Y Fam Wen Fawr' (The Great White Mother). During her tenure of the throne there had been unprecedented prosperity, progress and peace. *Y Geninen*, rhapsodizing at the time of the Diamond Jubilee, concluded that 'Victoria must have had a hand in these improvements'.[40] Her life was combed for its Welsh connections. Her descent from the Tudors and Llywelyn Fawr, her grant of a Civil List pension to Idrisyn (the translator of her *Leaves*), the sympathetic remarks on the Welsh language which she had made to Bishop Connop Thirlwall, her presentation of prizes following the Eisteddfod at Beaumaris, all were pressed into service, giving the impression that throughout her reign the Queen had cherished an intimate relationship with Wales. Stories of her devotion to Protestantism, her gift to an African chief of a Bible ('the foundation of my kingdom') and her insistence upon reinstating a servant dismissed for preferring chapel to church, might cause the reader to suppose that she could pass as a Welsh Nonconformist—that she was, as W. J. Gruffydd put it, 'of so sterling a quality that she would qualify for full membership of Bethel Chapel'.[41]

There was also a widespread belief that Victoria was the ideal constitutional monarch. An observer as acute as Walter Bagehot declared that she was, after 1861, a 'retired widow' and that her role consisted merely of the right 'to be consulted, to encourage and to warn'.[42] 'She keeps out of the way in matters relating to government and administration,' wrote Lewis Edwards in *Y Traethodydd* in 1845. In initiating a debate in 1879 on the abuse of the prerogative of the Crown, Lewis Llewelyn Dillwyn, MP for Swansea, went to great lengths to exclude the Queen from his strictures. She 'thoroughly understands her duties as a constitutional monarch,' he informed the House of Commons, 'and never interferes improperly in public affairs',[43] an assumption shared by most of her obituarists in 1901. Yet, as Edmund Gosse put it in a frank and lengthy article in the *Quarterly Review* shortly after her death, they also 'accepted her view of

---

[39] P. A. Scholes, *God Save the Queen* (London, 1954), p. 152; *The Works of Lewis Morris* (London, 1890), pp. 498–9.

[40] *Baner ac Amserau Cymru*, 26 and 30 January 1901; Anthropos, *Y Frenhines Victoria*, p. 10; *Y Genedl Gymreig*, 29 January 1901; *Y Geninen*, July 1897; *Young Wales*, Celebration Number, August 1897.

[41] W. J. Gruffydd, *Hen Atgofion* (Aberystwyth, 1936), p. 42 (D. M. Lloyd (trans.), *The Years of the Locust* (Llandysul, 1976), p. 37).

[42] W. Bagehot, *The English Constitution* (London, 1964 ed.), pp. 82, 111; Hardie, *Queen Victoria*, p. 239.

[43] *Y Traethodydd*, 1 (1845), 72; *Parl. Debates*, Third Series, 246, p. 242.

her own functions and tacitly concluded with her that she ruled, a consecrated monarch, by Right Divine'.[44]

'Her view of her own functions' became apparent with the publication of her later letters in 1926 and 1930. They proved that she had no real understanding of the meaning of constitutional monarchy. 'It is a defect of our much-famed constitution', she wrote in 1892, 'to have to part with an admirable Government like Lord Salisbury's ... merely on account of the number of votes.'[45] Her letters and diaries laid bare her systematic harassing of Gladstone during his last three ministries, her encouragement of the Liberal split of 1886, and her eager collusion with the Tories from 1874 onwards. They also showed that the Queen was a determined opponent of almost all the causes embraced by the radicalism which flourished so mightily in Wales in the last three decades of her reign. As has been seen, she abhorred disestablishment. Egalitarianism and democracy were anathema to her; attacks upon landed estates she abominated; suggestions for the reform of the House of Lords she denounced; home rule in any guise she execrated; education which would expand the horizons of working-class children she considered a danger; Nonconformity, Sabbatarianism and teetotalism she viewed with disfavour. Gladstone, venerated by the Welsh almost to the point of idolatry, she declared to be 'a half crazy and really in many ways ridiculous old man'.[46]

Very little of this was known to the public during Victoria's reign. The two volumes of her *Leaves* do not suggest that she played an active political role, and her lengthy stays at Balmoral and Osborne give the impression of a monarch far removed from the centre of decision-making. 'There can seldom have been a bigger political secret', wrote Frank Hardie, 'than ... the extent of [Queen Victoria's] political influence ... The *éminence grise* of the Victorian constitution was Victoria herself.'[47] 'Gladstone', claimed Kingsley Martin, 'could have revived republicanism by telling a tithe of what he suffered from the Queen.' Intense royalist that he was, he chose to remain silent, although he did privately record his view that the partisanship of the sovereign could cause the downfall of the throne.[48]

Some of Victoria's actions, of course, could not be concealed. Peel's resignation in 1839 on the issue of the Ladies of the Bedchamber, which resulted in the removal of a Conservative ministry, was welcomed by the Welsh radical press; David Rees urged readers of *Y Diwygiwr* to write to the Queen to congratulate her.[49] Her role in the dismissal of Palmerston in 1851 for recognizing Louis

---

[44] *Quarterly Review*, 193 (July 1901), 337. Gosse's article, in which Victoria was described as 'a rather ordinary mortal ... with a certain vital persistence', was widely attacked.

[45] L. Strachey, *Queen Victoria* (London, 1921), p. 300; Longford, *Victoria*, p. 518.

[46] Longford, *Victoria*, pp. 32, 214, 217; Ponsonby, *Henry Ponsonby*, p. 206; *Letters* 2, iii, 131; 3, i, 168; 3, ii, 384.

[47] F. Hardie, *The Political Influence of the English Monarchy, 1868–1952* (London, 1970), p. 1.

[48] Martin, *The Crown*, p. 53; *Personal Papers of Lord Rendel* (London, 1931), pp. 66, 78, 93; Philip Guedalla, *The Queen and Mr. Gladstone, 1880–1898* (London, 1933), *passim;* M. Balfour, *Britain and Joseph Chamberlain* (London, 1985), p. 90; Ponsonby, *Henry Ponsonby*, p. 256.

[49] Jones, *David Rees*, p. 239.

Napoleon's *coup d'état* also found support, Anthropos gloating over the matter as late as 1901.[50] The role of the Queen and Prince Albert in the Crimean War, as revealed in 1878 in the third volume of Theodore Martin's *Life of the Prince Consort*, caused considerable unease. Aroused by the comments of Dunckley, editor of the *Manchester Examiner and Times*, Thomas Gee published a series of articles in the spring of 1878 in *Baner ac Amserau Cymru* criticizing the political influence of the court. 'How mistaken we have been throughout the years,' he wrote. 'We used to think that the ministry was responsible for the policies of the kingdom. But no! [In 1854] Prince Albert was the Alpha and Omega of everything.' With Russia and Turkey again at war in 1878, Gee suggested that Martin's volume had been published specifically in order to inflame anti-Russian feeling and to involve Britain in a 'futile and unnecessary conflict'.[51] Had he been aware of the degree to which the Queen was then bombarding her ministers with demands for forceful action, Gee's strictures would undoubtedly have been more hostile.[52]

Welsh comments on Victoria's treatment of Gladstone were subdued, presumably because the extent of the Queen's enmity was not fully realized. While most Welsh Liberal activists probably agreed with Dilke's dictum 'that the Liberal Party exists for the purpose of doing the things she does not like', their comments were very restrained.[53] The Queen, wrote *Y Diwygiwr* in 1901, 'naturally tended towards the Conservative way of thinking, and it is likely that that inclination showed itself occasionally, especially in her dealings with Mr Gladstone.' Dr Pan Jones, always the most thoroughgoing of Welsh radicals, noted that Victoria had been 'well disposed to the Liberals in her youth, but at that time the Liberals were closer to the Conservatives'. It was her imperialism which angered Jones, a defect he also detected in many of his fellow Liberals. 'She died of a broken heart', he wrote in 1901, 'caused by the stubborn refusal of the Boers passively to submit to be killed by her butchers.' He stoutly denied that she had made any contribution to the progress which characterized the Victorian era. Great improvements, he agreed, had occurred during the lifetime of the Queen, but they had also occurred during the lifetime of his neighbour, 'Ann Jones, Verulam Street, who died at the age of 84 and who was buried on the same day as the Queen'.[54]

To the extent that there was anti-royalism in Victorian Wales, it was not the political role of the Queen which was its main component. Its main component was money. On her accession Parliament voted Victoria a Civil List of £375,000; with the revenues of the duchies of Cornwall and Lancaster and the payments to other members of the House of Hanover, the total receipts of the royal family during the early years of her reign were in the region of half a

---

[50] Anthropos, *Y Frenhines Victoria*, pp. 103–4; *Y Genedl Gymreig*, 29 January 1901.

[51] *Baner ac Amserau Cymru*, 20, 27 March; 10, 24 April 1878; T. Gwynn Jones, *Cofiant Thomas Gee* (Denbigh, 1913), pp. 520–1; Theodore Martin, *The Life of ... the Prince Consort*, 3 (London, 1877), esp. pp. 83ff.

[52] See the Queen's correspondence for 1877 and 1878 in *Letters*, 2, ii.

[53] S. Gwyn and G. M. Tuckwell, *The Life of the Rt. Hon. Charles W. Dilke* (London, 1917), 1, 286; Hardie, *Queen Victoria*, p. 243.

[54] *Y Diwygiwr*, February 1901; *Cwrs y Byd*, March 1901.

million pounds a year. By the later years of her reign, the increase in the revenues of the duchies and the grants to her children and to some of her grandchildren brought the annual receipts of the family close to a million pounds. In present-day values this would be about £30,000,000, broadly similar to the current costs of maintaining the House of Windsor, although it should be borne in mind that Victoria's income represented a far higher proportion of the revenue of the state than does that of Elizabeth II.[55]

The misappropriation of funds in the interests of the upper classes was a regular theme among early nineteenth-century English radicals, with Cobbett and others thundering against 'The Thing'. Their Welsh disciples followed suit. While the thrust of the attack was upon jobbery among the clergy and the aristocracy, the royal family did not escape censure. Within a year of Victoria's accession, David Rees in *Y Diwygiwr* contrasted the 'less than six thousand a year' received by the President of the United States with the half a million pounds received by Victoria. By 1844 he was expressing dismay at the financial implications of the Queen's fecundity—she had given birth in 1840, 1841, 1843 and 1844. 'If Her Majesty continues like this for another twenty years,' he wrote, 'Britain will have the largest royal family in Europe.'[56]

There were few such comments in the Welsh press in the next two decades, but the Queen's virtual seclusion following the death of Prince Albert in 1861 encouraged attacks on the expense of the monarchy. 'The experience of the last nine ... years', wrote Bradlaugh in 1870, 'proves that the country can do quite well without a monarch and may therefore save the extra expense of monarchy.'[57] In 1871 *Baner ac Amserau Cymru* reported with glee the claim of the anonymous pamphlet *What does she do with it?* that Victoria hoarded money on a vast scale. Commenting sarcastically on the debate over Princess Louise's £30,000 dowry, Thomas Gee wrote, 'of the few fanatics who were opposing so reasonable a grant ... they are straining at a gnat and swallowing a camel.' He offered his readers a translation of a letter in *Reynolds News*, which exulted at the death of a newly-born child of the Prince and Princess of Wales on the grounds that 'the working classes were thus relieved from maintaining another addition to the long list of royal mendicants'. Although Gee expressed astonishment that any newspaper should publish such a letter, he reproduced it in full.[58]

The question flared up again in 1888 over the issue of gifts to the Prince and Princess of Wales on the occasion of their silver wedding. John Price,

[55] *The Times*, 9 January 1987. In the 1880s the annual receipts of Queen Victoria and her family represented about 1.5 per cent of the total sum raised in taxation; if the House of Windsor were to receive a similar proportion today, it would amount to over £1,600 million.

[56] *Y Diwygiwr*, 1844, p. 68; Jones, *David Rees*, p. 238.

[57] R. J. Grossman, 'Republicanism in Nineteenth-century England', *International Review of Social History*, 7 (1962), 51. Commenting on the Queen's unwillingness to undertake her duties, General Grey informed Gladstone in 1869 'that neither health nor strength are wanting were inclination what it should be. It is simply the long unchecked habit of self-indulgence which now makes it impossible for her, without some degree of nervous agitation, to give up, even for ten minutes, the gratification of a single inclination, nor even *whim*' (P. Magnus, *Gladstone, a Biography* (London, 1954), p. 200).

[58] *Baner ac Amserau Cymru*, 22 February; 19 April; 20, 27 September 1871. The author of the pamphlet was the Liberal MP, Sir George Otto Trevelyan.

vice-principal of Bangor Normal College, demanded to know what the Prince had done that Bangor Corporation 'should spend even one, two or more shillings on him'. What form should a testimonial take—'a statue of Mr Sullivan the pugilist or that of a burlesque actress?' His fellow councillor, William Jones, argued that fathers quite as good as the Prince of Wales had raised large families on 15s. a week. 'What of the character of the Prince?' he continued. 'Has he made himself known as a Sunday School teacher or anything of that sort? ... I don't know of a more poor lot on the face of history than the English Kings and Monarchs ... their histories are stinking in the nostrils of the Welsh nation', a comment which put paid to any suggestion that the Prince of Wales should visit the Bangor Eisteddfod of 1890.[59]

A far bigger controversy broke out in 1889 over financial provision for the Queen's grandchildren. She had told Salisbury in 1888 that 'the grandchildren (children of the younger sons) of the Sovereign have always been provided for ... the Queen thinks it most unjust that *she*, in her old age and with endless expenses, should be asked to contribute so largely'. In July 1889 a committee was established to consider the matter and the Queen was appalled to find that it included among its twenty-three members 'that horrible lying Labouchere and ... that rebel Parnell'.[60] The issue gave Gladstone an opportunity to give expression to his ardent royalism and it was he who was mainly responsible for the decision to add £36,000 to the annual income of the Prince of Wales to enable him to make provision for his family.[61]

The grant was discussed by some of the newly established county councils of Wales, causing the Tory newspaper, *Gwalia*, to castigate the Jacobinism of Welsh radicals. Thomas Gee was saddened by Gladstone's role in the matter, but delighted by that of Labouchere. He gave full coverage to Labouchere's minority report which claimed that the Queen, since her accession, had received a global sum of £20,020,000. The Prince of Wales had had annual grants totalling £1,040,000, together with £601,760 from the investments of the duchy of Cornwall and £1,450,000 from the duchy's income; £44,650 of state money had been spent on Marlborough House, £32,400 on the Prince's military offices, £23,450 on his marriage, and £60,000 on his visit to India, while the allowances to his wife amounted to £240,000. With the grants to the rest of Victoria's children, her family had received, between 1837 and 1889, the sum of £26,188,023.[62]

When the additional allowance to the Prince of Wales was debated in the House of Commons, William Abraham (Mabon), MP for the Rhondda, declared that the Queen had 'accumulated sums sufficient to endow a 100 grandchildren'

[59] *Caernarvon and Denbigh Herald*, 9 March 1888; Edwards, 'Victorian Wales', p. 15.

[60] *Letters*, 3, i, 435, 509–10; Salisbury informed the Queen: 'It is comparatively immaterial [which opposition members are chosen] so long as they are a minority ... There are *no* Moderate Liberals in the present day' (ibid., 510).

[61] Ibid., 462; H. W. Hutton and H. J. Cohen (eds.), *The Speeches of the Rt. Hon. W. E. Gladstone* (London, 1902), pp. 103–16.

[62] *Gwalia*, 21 August 1889; *Baner ac Amserau Cymru*, 24, 31 July 1889. Labouchere's motion was supported by 116 MPs, among them L. Ll. Dillwyn, D. A. Thomas, J. B. Roberts, A. J. Thomas and W. Bowen Rowlands.

and that she had 'for over twenty years almost entirely neglected the public duties of her royal position'. He claimed that he was speaking in the name of the overwhelming majority of the workers of Wales, an assertion that George Osborne Morgan, MP for East Denbighshire, sought to deny. A wrangle then ensued over whether Mabon or Morgan represented the true voice of Wales. The South Wales Liberal Federation supported Mabon, as did a mass meeting of miners at Mountain Ash, although Morgan won himself some complimentary remarks in the Welsh Conservative press.[63] Even *Y Goleuad* felt constrained to declare the hope that Parliament would not accede to unreasonable demands from the Queen, while Michael D. Jones in *Y Celt* drew on the analogy of the American President. 'The President', he wrote, 'receives £10,000 a year; Victoria and her family get more than that in five days.' 'If the Queen', he continued, 'is worth the money that is paid to her, then I must believe that Solomon in all his glory is unworthy of being compared with her.'[64] He was delighted to hear that during Victoria's visit to Wales in 1889, the Bala baker, Mari Williams, had refused to sell bread to her on the grounds that the Queen was a 'wasteful old woman'; Labouchere, argued Jones, should visit Bala in order to get a supply of such uncontaminated bread.[65] In 1889 even the mild-mannered Tom Ellis was provoked to talk of the 'expensive ornaments and figureheads [of] the court of Victoria'. A year later, David Lloyd George, in his second speech to the House of Commons, attacked the 'positively monstrous grants' to associates of the Queen; 'royal vagabonds', he wrote, 'are spending the nation's money on idle frippery.'[66]

To many Nonconformists, even more offensive than the cost of the monarchy was the relationship between Throne and Altar. Several of Victoria's ministers sought to disabuse her of her notion of her role in the Established Church, but she stubbornly adhered to the belief that she was Head of the Church of England, a belief shared by most of her subjects, Anglican and Nonconformist.[67] To David Rees, the concept was highly repugnant. 'The essence of Nonconformity', he wrote in *Y Diwygiwr* in 1838, 'is the recognition that Christ alone is King.'[68] The Church issue was the cause of the only spasm of Welsh anti-royalism during Victoria's reign to receive widespread publicity in both Wales and England. That was on the occasion of Victoria's visit to Wales in 1889, when the intention of the clergy of the diocese of St Asaph to offer her a memorial led to the suggestion that it would be fitting if the Nonconformist ministers did likewise. A group of Wrexham ministers drew up a highly laudatory memorial

---

[63] *Baner ac Amserau Cymru*, 24, 31 July 1889; *Y Genedl Gymreig*, 21 August 1889; *Parl. Debates*, Third Series, 338, pp. 1336–7, 1470–4. Mabon was a favourite with Victoria. (T. I. Ellis, *Thomas Edward Ellis, Cofiant* (Liverpool, 1948), 2, 279).

[64] *Y Goleuad*, 8 August 1889; *Y Celt*, 23 August 1889.

[65] E. Pan Jones, *Oes a gwaith ... Michael D. Jones* (Bala, 1903), pp. 100–4; R. T. Jenkins, *Edrych yn ôl* (London, 1968), p. 69.

[66] T. E. Ellis, *Speeches and Addresses* (Wrexham, 1912), p. 103; *Parl. Debates*, Third Series, 348, pp. 904–5; K. O. Morgan (ed.), *Lloyd George Family Letters* (Cardiff and London, 1973), p. 32.

[67] E.g. *Letters*, 2, ii, 352 and Gladstone to Asquith, 26 February 1893, cited in K. O. Morgan, *Wales in British Politics, 1868–1922* (Cardiff, 1980 ed.), p. 135.

[68] Jones, *David Rees*, p. 136.

stressing the growth of religious liberty during the Queen's reign; this was sent on 8 August 1889 to their fellow-ministers in the counties of Denbigh, Flint and Merioneth with a note that 'we shall assume your concurrence if we do not hear to the contrary by [13 August]'.[69]

In order to appreciate the strength of feeling this letter aroused, it should be borne in mind that the Queen, after virtually ignoring Wales during the previous fifty-two years of her reign, was proposing to visit precisely those parts of the country most affected by the Tithe War of 1887–8. At the beginning of August 1889 Lord Salisbury's government introduced a bill for the recovery of tithe which many Welsh radicals considered of a nature similar to the Irish Coercion Acts. The Queen's escort was to be drawn from the Ninth Lancers, who a few months earlier had been involved in the suppression of the tithe rioters. She was to be accompanied, as Minister-in-Waiting, by the Postmaster-General, R. C. Raikes, a man whose bitter attacks upon Nonconformity had made him the *bête noire* of Welsh Liberals. Sir Theodore Martin, a leading local Tory activist, was to be singled out for special attention by the Queen. An invitation to stay with the Gladstones at Hawarden had been ignored and Tom Ellis, MP for Merioneth and the darling of the Welsh radicals, was denied any role in the visit.[70]

'Considering the circumstances under which the Queen is coming amongst us', wrote a correspondent of *Baner ac Amserau Cymru*, 'why should the Nonconformists of Wales thank her; she intends her visit to be a check upon the rising tide of Radicalism.' 'It is proper', declared Thomas Gee, 'for parsons to recognize their "Head", for it is by virtue of the relationship between the Church and the Crown that they receive their tithes ... To the extent that religious freedom has been won over the past fifty years, it has been won despite the Church of the Queen. [Praising her] would make us contemptible lapdogs, ready to kiss every scourge—and the scourger too ... If Her Majesty is allowed to travel through these counties without being hooted, she should feel grateful.' 'The ministers [organizing the memorial]', wrote *Y Genedl Gymreig*, 'are the object of the contempt of the clerical party ... Buddug and her progeny have always been cold and indifferent towards Wales, and that has begotten among the people an equivalent coldness and indifference, to say the least.' *Y Celt*, believing that the request for the memorial from the ministers originated with R. C. Raikes, argued that 'royalist sentiment in Wales must be at a low ebb if a minister of the Crown has to go around begging for a vain and empty address to Victoria'.[71]

Not all the Welsh press was as forthright. *Gwalia*, while also complaining of the neglect of Wales by the royal family, declared that Thomas Gee had made a fool of himself; 'a few generations ago', it wrote, 'he would have faced

---

[69] *Baner ac Amserau Cymru*, 14 August 1889. Thomas Gee pointed out that the letter would probably be received on Saturday 10 August, when many ministers would have already left home for their Sunday preaching engagements.

[70] Ibid., 7, 17 and 21 August 1889; Ellis, *Cofiant*, 2, 83; *The Times*, 23 August 1889.

[71] *Baner ac Amserau Cymru*, 7, 17, 21 August 1889; *Y Genedl Gymreig*, 21 August 1889; *Y Celt*, 23 August 1889.

24

The Roberts family of harpists playing before the Queen at Palé in 1889. (*By permission of the National Library of Wales.*)

execution or exile.' His attitude was condemned by *Y Goleuad*, much to the gratification of 'A Welsh Unionist', who reported the condemnation to *The Times*. *Seren Gomer* doubted the wisdom of Gee's attacks, arguing that 'an honest believer in democracy [*gweriniaeth*] can respect the sovereign while the monarchy still stands'.[72] Gee was unrepentant. A justice of the peace and the chairman of the Denbighshire County Council, his uncompromising comments won widespread attention. He was delighted when *The Times* published a translation of his most critical article. 'Let us hope', he wrote, 'that the Queen has read [it]. We have sure proof that it is approved of by the bulk of the Welsh nation.' Dr Pan Jones agreed: 'Eight out of ten', he declared, 'are tired of fawning flattery.'[73] *Punch* attempted some mulish wit at Gee's expense and the *Spectator* suggested that his 'simple Celtic mind' rendered him incapable of understanding the British constitution.[74] The memorial was presented, but was not publicly read, much to the disappointment of its organizers; it contained, said Gee, 'the names of hundreds who did not want to be associated with it'.[75]

Criticism of Victoria, whether on the grounds of her political influence, her income, her role in the Church or her neglect of Wales, was not in itself proof of republican sentiments. Indeed, some of her critics hastened to state their support for the principle of monarchy. 'No sensible man', wrote David Rees in 1838, 'can be a republican.'[76] Yet there developed in Wales a tentative tradition of republicanism. The rejection of hereditary monarchy is implicit, and sometimes explicit, in the writings of the Welsh radicals of the 1790s. It is also implicit in much of the rhetoric of the Chartists: in 1839 John Frost, two years after he had proclaimed Victoria's accession at Newport, was declared President of the Provisional Government.[77] Thackeray announced in 1840 that he was in favour of a republic, and his popular lectures on the Four Georges, parts of which were paraphrased by Thomas Gee, did much to remind the public of the awfulness of the Hanoverians.[78] By the mid-nineteenth century, the belief that democracy necessarily implied republicanism had many upholders—the Queen among them.[79] As the frequently repeated comparisons with the American President suggest, nineteenth-century republicanism was not socialist in origin. It drew its inspiration from the United States, where the absence of a monarch, a territorial aristocracy and an Established Church seemed to ensure progress, liberty and personal enrichment. In the early 1870s, when republicanism won a considerable following in Britain, the movement was led by that advocate of Anglo-Saxon hegemony, Sir Charles Dilke, a baronet whose father

---

[72] *Gwalia*, 28 August 1889; *Y Goleuad*, 22 August 1889; *Seren Gomer*, September 1889; *The Times*, 23 August 1889.

[73] *The Times*, 23 August 1889; *Baner ac Amserau Cymru*, 14, 21 August 1889.

[74] *Punch*, 24, 30 August 1889; *Spectator*, 17, 24 August 1889.

[75] *Baner ac Amserau Cymru*, 14 August; 4 September 1889.

[76] *Y Diwygiwr*, 1835–6, p. 409.

[77] G. A. Williams, *When was Wales?* (London, 1985), pp. 169–70; J. Jones, *Seren Tan Gwmmwl* (London, 1795); D. Williams, *John Frost* (Cardiff, 1939), p. 212.

[78] Compare *Baner ac Amserau Cymru*, 1 July 1891 with W. M. Thackeray, *The Four Georges* (London, 1873), p. 176.

[79] *Letters*, 2, iii, 131; Martin, *The Crown*, pp. 27–57.

had been a friend of the royal family. (When he was eight years old, Victoria stroked Dilke's head; 'I must', she is reputed to have stated in 1871, 'have rubbed the brains the wrong way.') The victory of the North in the American Civil War was seen as a triumph for republican virtues and the fall of the French throne in 1871 augured well for the enemies of monarchy. In 1871 Dilke's republican lecture tour attracted large and enthusiastic audiences and in most substantial towns republican clubs were formed.[80]

Baner ac Amserau Cymru gave detailed and sympathetic accounts of Dilke's campaign, although it did suggest that, as part of his attack upon hereditary titles, Sir Charles should renounce his baronetcy. Gee described with enthusiasm the republican demonstration in Hyde Park in April 1871, a demonstration considered by the Home Secretary, H. A. Bruce (later Lord Aberdare), to be 'insignificant both with regard to the number and the character of those who took part in it'. 'The banners of America were carried,' wrote Gee; 'the crowd was very large, including some toughs, but others were of the middle class.' Later in the year he wrote of the 'thousands welcoming Dilke at Middlesborough and the vast throng at Leeds'. There were unruly scenes at a meeting in Dilke's constituency of Chelsea, he admitted, 'but attempts to sing the National Anthem failed because of the hootings of the majority'. Votes of thanks to Dilke, he reported, 'were pouring in from radical societies'.[81]

The republican campaign proved short-lived. The severe illness of the Prince of Wales in December 1871 caused 'a great epidemic of typhoid loyalty' from which organized anti-royalism failed to recover. Dilke's motion on the Civil List in March 1872 was defeated by 174 votes to 2; in 1880, in order to ensure that Victoria would accept him as a member of Gladstone's third ministry, Dilke apologized for the views he had held when he was 'very young and foolish'.[82] From 1874 onwards, the Queen, inspired by Disraeli's flattery, became less of a recluse and consented to participate, from time to time, in grand state occasions. The later years of her reign saw the invention of much royal tradition, the pomp of her two jubilees, in particular, causing her subjects to believe, erroneously, that Britain had always possessed a particular genius for royal ceremonial.[83]

Yet although organized republicanism faded, republican sentiments did not. In 1889 the letter columns of the Welsh radical press suggest that there was in Wales considerable grass-roots republicanism. 'As long as men are lunatic enough to maintain oppressive and wasteful monarchies,' wrote a correspondent of *Baner ac Amserau Cymru*, '... so long will the poor be downtrodden and the wealthy exalted.' The Prince of Wales's involvement in the card-swindling case of 1891 led to a revival of anti-monarchist sentiment. In the wake of the scandal,

---

[80] Martin, *The Crown*, pp. 27–57; Grossman, 'Republicanism', pp. 55–60; Gwyn and Tuckwell, *Charles W. Dilke*, 1, 10.

[81] *Baner ac Amserau Cymru*, 22 April, 25 November, 9 December 1871; H. A. Bruce to Victoria, 17 April 1871 (*Letters*, 2, ii, 130).

[82] Martin, *The Crown*, p. 50; *Letters* 2, iii, 87.

[83] D. Cannadine, 'The British Monarchy and the "Invention of Tradition"' in Eric Hobsbawm and T. Ranger (eds.), *The Invention of Tradition* (Cambridge, 1983), pp. 101–64.

Thomas Gee published a series of articles entitled 'Monarchy or Republic', in which he quoted extensively from the English newspapers, all of them uniformly hostile to the Prince. While such papers as *The Times* indulged in lofty condemnation, the *Star* declared that 'monarchy would expire through its own weakness and madness'. A new motto was suggested for the Prince: 'Ich Deal'. 'What will happen after the death of our Queen,' wrote Gee, '... when this man will be the Head of the State Church and Defender of the Faith ... All the shameful and empty pleasures which have been associated with [the Prince] will have substantial and open encouragement.'[84] Victoria shared his fears. In 1871, her daughter, Princess Alice, stated that the Queen 'thinks the Monarchy will last her time and it is no use thinking what will come after if the principal person himself does not'.[85] This point of view gathered strength in the last years of her reign. Even Michael D. Jones declared that he was prepared 'to recognise Victoria as long as she occupies the throne'. 'How much longer will it last, we wonder?' asked the *Pall Mall Gazette* on the occasion of the Golden Jubilee. 'As long as the Queen lasts, yes, but after the Queen? Who knows?'[86] The tables had been turned. In the 1860s there were those who saw merit in monarchy, but little in Victoria; by the late 1880s and 1890s there were those who saw little merit in monarchy but much in Victoria.

Yet some of the younger Liberals warmed to the Prince of Wales, who moved in less exclusively Conservative circles than did his mother, and who made no secret of his admiration for Gladstone.[87] In 1892, Samuel Thomas Evans, MP for Mid Glamorgan, refused to rise to toast the Queen at the Lord Mayor of London's banquet, although he rose to toast the Prince. His action, although warmly endorsed by the Neath Fabian Society, led to a flurry of comment in the *Western Mail*. The paper's editor, also present at the banquet, attempted to throw a glass of wine at Evans. Lloyd George thought that his friend Sam has been unwise. 'The proper thing ... is to merely get up and not pledge the old lady by raising a glass. I adopt the latter course.'[88]

Two years later the royal family was the subject of a far more heartfelt protest. In June 1894 the birth to the duke and duchess of York of a son (later the duke of Windsor) coincided with the death of 251 miners in an explosion at Cilfynydd. Keir Hardie, then MP for West Ham South, was incensed by the decision of the House of Commons to move an address of congratulation on the former event and its refusal to move an address of sympathy on the latter.

---

[84] *Baner ac Amserau Cymru*, 17 August 1889; 10, 13, 17, 24 June; 1 July 1891; Longford, *Victoria*, p. 512.

[85] Longford, *Victoria*, pp. 391–2.

[86] *Y Celt*, 23 August 1889; *Pall Mall Gazette*, 22 June 1887.

[87] In addition to visiting Hawarden, the Prince served as pallbearer in Gladstone's funeral and as chairman of the memorial appeal fund. The degree to which the decline of the Whigs and the split over home rule had led to the weakening of the Liberal presence at the court was a matter of grave concern to Gladstone. 'At the present juncture', he wrote to the Queen in 1892, 'the views of Your Majesty's actual advisers ... are hardly at all represented ... in the powerful circles with which Your Majesty has ordinary personal intercourse' (*Letters*, 3, iii, 172).

[88] *WM*, 6, 7, 8 June 1892; *SWDN*, 15 June 1892; Morgan, *Lloyd George Family Letters*, p. 53. In 1886 over a hundred of those present at a Liberal parliamentary dinner failed to stand for the loyal toast (Longford, *Victoria*, p. 514).

'The government', he told the House on 28 June, 'will not find an opportunity for a vote of condolence with the relatives of those lying stiff and stark in a Welsh valley ... Time and occasion can be found in this House only for rank and title.' He mocked the rule that a Minister of the Crown had to be present at the birth. 'It is a matter of small concern to me whether the future ruler of the nation be the genuine article or a spurious imitation.' With remarkable clairvoyance, he outlined the future of the newborn child: 'He will be surrounded by sycophants and flatterers by the score ... He will be sent on a tour around the world and probably rumours of a morganatic alliance will follow ... and the country will be called upon to pay the bill.'[89]

He continued his attack in the *Labour Leader*: 'For the lick-spittles of the press who have no care for the cry of the poor widow and infant and who attempt to see in the birth of a child to the Duke and Duchess of York an event of Divine significance ... there can be nothing but contempt. The life of one Welsh miner is of greater commercial and moral value ... than the whole Royal crowd put together, from the Royal Great Grandmama down to the puling Royal Great Grandchild.' Hardie won no support in the House of Commons; when the 'Ayes' and 'Noes' were called, his was the only 'No'. His protest, it has been argued, made him appear an 'irresponsible fanatic', an indication of the degree to which republicanism was a spent force.[90] The Labour movement drew its own conclusions and thereafter was reluctant to attack the royal family openly.

The Welsh of the Victorian era found cause to prize and censure the monarchy. Today, the approbation might be considered excessive; the disapprobation certainly would. Republicanism receded in the wake of the decline in the power of the Crown, for, despite Victoria's determined interference in politics during the last decades of her reign, the widening of the franchise and the increasing coherence of party organization were rapidly undermining the authority of the sovereign. 'The more democratic we become', wrote Bagehot, 'the more we shall get to like state and show.' Equally apposite, perhaps, is Kingsley Martin's comment in 1936: 'If we drop the trappings of monarchy in the gutter, Germany has taught us that some guttersnipe will pick them up.'[91] At the beginning of Victoria's reign, the Welsh were willing to acclaim the monarch without expecting anything in return. With the erosion of deference, that willingness diminished. 'Loyal enthusiasm', wrote *Y Genedl Gymreig* in 1889, 'is not a thing which is on official call. It must be nurtured.'[92] For good or ill, that is a lesson which Victoria's successors have learned.

[89] *Parl. Debates*, Fourth Series, 26, pp. 460–4.
[90] *L(abour) L(eader)*, 30 June 1894; K. O. Morgan, *Keir Hardie, Radical and Socialist* (London, 1975), p. 71.
[91] Cannadine, 'The British Monarchy', pp. 122, 149.
[92] *Y Genedl Gymreig*, 21 August 1889.

Irish Immigration and the Catholic 'Welsh District', 1840–1850

PAUL O'LEARY

DURING the 1820s a curious Welshman at Cardiff was prepared to pay the substantial sum of a half-crown to one of the handful of Irish labourers at the port for the privilege of seeing for himself a Catholic priest. As there were so few Catholics in the town, the labourers depended upon the ministrations of the parish priest of Merthyr Tydfil who visited Cardiff to celebrate mass every Sunday. Witnessing the arrival of the Sunday coach from Merthyr, the credulous Welshman was astonished to discover that the priest resembled a 'gentleman' and that he did not conform to the alarming stereotypes of anti-Catholic demonology which he had expected. His half-crown had been a poor investment.

This incident, known to history as 'the Welshman and the Half-Crown', has achieved almost mythical status in Catholic historiography in Wales. Yet the story is reliably documented. It was first recorded in print some sixty years after the event occurred, at a time when oral recall of the incident was failing and when the great debate concerning immigrant 'leakage' from the church was gaining momentum.[1] In this context, the main features of the anecdote are of more than a passing or superficial interest. Through retelling the story, the equation of the categories Irish and Catholic on the one hand and Welsh and Protestant on the other became fixed, an almost unquestioned axiom intended to reinforce the reflex identification of ethnicity and religion at a time when these identities were in a state of flux. Significantly, the priest was the central figure in the story and clerics were mainly responsible for perpetuating the story in print. In this respect, the story has come to resemble the genesis myths identified by social anthropologists as the means by which cultural groups seek to legitimize their present behaviour by reference to their origins in the past. The ill-conceived and ineptly executed reports of the Parliamentary Commissioners on Education in 1847 can be seen to have played a similar role in the Welsh Nonconformist community.[2]

---

[1] Fr. F. Signini, 'The Welshman and the Half-Crown', *St. Peter's Chair*, February 1889, pp. i–iii; reprinted in *St. Peter's Magazine* (September 1924), 269–70; B. Doran, 'The Welshman and the Half-Crown', *Menevia Record* (February 1959), 23–4.

[2] Royal Anthropological Institution of Great Britain and Ireland, *Notes and Queries on Anthropology* (6th ed., London, 1951), pp. 204–6; J. Vansina, *Oral Tradition as History* (London, 1985).

It is only in recent decades that the relationship between orthodox Catholicism and Irish culture in the nineteenth century has come to be considered as in any way problematic, and it would appear that this relationship is far more complex than has been allowed hitherto. In Wales the precise impact of ecclesiastical reorganization upon the religious culture of the immigrant Irish has yet to be examined in detail. This essay is an attempt to evaluate the degree to which a realignment of Catholic activity on more specifically Welsh lines in the 1840s by the creation of the Welsh District facilitated or frustrated the acceptance of immigrant Catholicism, and to establish the extent to which everyday piety differed from the ideals of religious behaviour promoted by the clergy.

In 1840 Pope Gregory XVI announced a reorganization of the Catholic church in England and Wales, a move that was greeted by the clergy in particular as a much-needed and long-awaited departure from the unsatisfactory arrangement which existed. Since 1688 the two countries had been divided into the London, Midland, Northern and Western Districts. The Western District comprised the thirteen counties of Wales, together with the six counties of south-west England. Considering the parlous conditions of roads in this period and the fact that the Western District was effectively bisected by the Bristol Channel (its fickle winds and tides made navigation under sail unreliable), it seems remarkable that this nightmarish administrative unit remained in place for as long as it did. The reorganization of 1840 multiplied the number of districts from four to eight and a new diocese, called the Welsh District, was carved out of the unwieldy Western District. The new area comprised the thirteen Welsh counties, with the English county of Herefordshire tacked untidily onto the south-eastern flank. Transport within this new unit was no easier than previously, but the new arrangement did have the virtue of reducing the overall geographical dimensions of the bishop's responsibilities and consequently held out the possibility of his acquiring a more intimate knowledge of the scattered congregations in his care.

Critics of the new scheme were swift to point out that too much of the old order remained embedded in the new. They believed that the church had responded sluggishly to the changed social conditions it now had to confront, and many sections of the clergy felt that timid remedial action of this kind would be hopelessly inadequate. Their criticisms crystallized in the single issue of the status of the bishops, which remained unchanged after 1840. Since the seventeenth century, Catholic bishops in England and Wales had held the subordinate title of 'Vicar Apostolic' of a district in Britain. Without claiming episcopal authority over an area in England or Wales, the vicars apostolic were also accorded the nominal title of a diocese outside Europe, enabling them to use the title 'bishop'. By this means a conflict with the Protestant Establishment over alleged attempts by Rome to encroach upon Protestant territory was avoided. Thus the new Vicar Apostolic of the Welsh District was Thomas Joseph Brown, bishop of Appollonia *in partibus infidelium*. Apart from reinforcing the foreign image of Catholicism, such practices were constant reminders that the church in England and Wales remained directly subordinate to Rome, together with those countries accorded the status of missionary field. Reluctance on the part of Rome to take the final step of creating full diocesan bishops by restoring the hierarchy tended to undermine clerical morale. Indeed, problems arising from the changing status of the clergy within the Catholic community were to become a significant element in exacerbating relationships between the clergy and laity at parish level. However, the remaking of the Catholic church in nineteenth-century Wales was a development that was far from being confined to the ranks of the clergy and needs to be placed against the background of population growth associated with the Industrial Revolution.

Population growth in society at large and immigration from Ireland served to place the demographic basis of Catholicism on a new footing. It has been estimated that the increase in the number professing the Catholic faith in England and Wales as a whole was in the region of 212 per cent, from 80,000 in 1770 to approximately 250,000 in 1850.[3] In Wales the pattern of growth was even more pronounced. In 1773 Mgr Charles Walmesley, Vicar Apostolic of the Western District, reported to Rome that there were only 750 Catholics in the whole of Wales. By 1839, on the eve of the establishment of the Welsh District, the number of Catholics had reached 6,269, an increase of 735 per cent. This increase had occurred before the great influx of Irish famine refugees in the late 1840s.[4]

During this period of growth, the character and geography of Welsh Catholicism changed appreciably. The depletion in the number of Welsh Catholics by the late eighteenth century left them concentrated geographically in the border counties, particularly north-east Monmouthshire and Flintshire. The congregations in these areas consisted of small clusters of tenants and servants focused on a landed family which had provided protection against the intrusion of the penal legislation. The Herberts of Llanofer in Monmouthshire and the Mostyns of Talacre in Flintshire are examples of landed families who maintained their staunch Catholic allegiance and who supported socially integrated congregations on and around their estates.

These congregations were small 'closed' communities which kept a low profile in society and avoided ostentation in worship, clerical dress and ecclesiastical architecture. Nevertheless, there is some evidence that, at the end of the eighteenth century, these inward-looking and isolated congregations were regaining some of their former confidence while remaining dominated by their upper-class patrons. Relaxation in the penal legislation was an important factor in creating a more optimistic climate of opinion. By the time small groups of Irish immigrants began to establish themselves in the iron- and coal-producing villages of industrial south Wales in the 1820s, Welsh Catholicism was slightly more receptive to outside influences, if woefully ill-prepared in terms of the geographical distribution of resources. New, or renewed, congregations sprang up in coastal towns

[3] J. Bossy, *The English Catholic Community, 1570–1850* (London, 1975), p. 298.

[4] J. H. Whyte, 'The Vicars Apostolic Returns of 1773', *Recusant History*, 9 (1967–8), 212; W. M. Brady, *The Episcopal Succession in England, Scotland and Ireland, AD 1400–1875* (3 vols., 1876–7), 3, 315–16.

such as Swansea, Cardiff and Newport, in the upland iron-town of Merthyr Tydfil and in a sprinkling of lesser industrial villages. The numerical superiority of the 'old Catholics' disappeared at some point during the late 1820s or early 1830s.[5]

Initial reactions to this new Catholic presence were not all critical. At Maesteg in Glamorgan in 1824, a Welsh Franciscan priest, Fr Edward Richards, found that the Irish were 'eminent propagandists of the Faith',[6] but priests in the same situation invariably wrote of their frustration, the absence of co-operation on the part of the Irish, and their 'insolent' response to requests for financial help. In part, this picture is the result of the disappointment of a clergy fired by missionary zeal upon discovering that the objects of their enthusiasm had not lived up to their expectations. Yet in some measure the overall picture is accurate. Ireland before the Great Famine fits the description of a 'Catholic country' in a very loose way. As far as everyday religious practice is concerned, the Catholic Counter-Reformation had been singularly ineffective in its attempts to enforce a code of religious observance with the emphasis on regular mass attendance and sacramental participation. Religious observance on this model was certainly not in place before the Famine of the 1840s and a spirituality expressed through festal and communal rites was the norm. The failure to reform popular practice, combined with the restrictions of the penal legislation, resulted in a situation where the ratio of priests to laity before the Famine was approximately 1 to 2,100; church attendance was possibly as low as 33 per cent of the Catholic population, although there were considerable regional variations. In addition, either there were not enough churches or insufficient seating in the churches to accommodate all.[7]

It cannot be taken for granted, therefore, that the labouring Irish who found employment within the industrial concerns of Wales in the early nineteenth century would seek out a priest on their arrival or make arrangements for one to visit their often temporary accommodation. Moreover, it would be dangerous to assume that, even where a church and priest were at hand, the Irish would be instantly punctilious in the discharge of their duties. This basic fact confounded the receiving clergy and frequently evoked vehement denunciations of Irish habits.

As has been seen, the number of Catholics in Wales increased noticeably during the opening decades of the nineteenth century. Of the 6,269 recorded Catholics in Wales in 1839, more than half lived in Monmouthshire, while three-quarters of the remainder were to be found in Glamorgan. The man appointed to shepherd these congregations was Dr Thomas Joseph Brown, OSB. In 1838 an acquaintance summed up his suitability for the post in glowing terms: 'his

---

[5] See, e.g., 'The Catholic Registers of Abergavenny, Mon., 1740–1838' in *Publications of the Catholic Record Society*, 27 (London, 1927), 98–235.

[6] D. Attwater, *The Catholic Church in Modern Wales* (London, 1935), p. 70.

[7] J. Bossy, 'The Counter-Reformation and the People of Catholic Ireland, 1596–1641', in T. D. Williams (ed.), *Historical Studies*, 8 (Dublin, 1971), 155–69; E. Larkin, 'The Devotional Revolution in Ireland, 1850–75', *American Historical Review*, 78 (1972), 626, 636; S. J. Connolly, *Priests and People in Pre-Famine Ireland, 1780–1845* (Dublin, 1983).

learning, talents and every estimable quality are beyond all praise.'[8] In many respects his education and upbringing were that of a typical English cleric of the 'old Catholic' variety. Born at Bath in 1798, he was educated by the Benedictine order near Shrewsbury and at Downside. Becoming a Benedictine himself, he was ordained to the priesthood and appointed Professor of Theology at Downside shortly afterwards. His position within the order was strengthened in 1829 by his successful accomplishment of delicate business with the Roman *Curia*, and his public reputation as a skilful master of theological debate was enhanced during the 1830s by the publication of a number of pamphlets setting out the terms of theological disputes in which he had taken part. In 1834 Brown became Prior of Downside and received his doctorate in divinity. In October 1840, at the age of forty-two, he was consecrated bishop at Bath. Yet his appointment as Vicar Apostolic of the Welsh District marked him off in no uncertain terms from the more aristocratic and distant 'old Catholics'. Evangelical notions of service to the 'holy poor' were gaining ground and inspired the clergy to many sacrifices on behalf of the Irish in particular; writing soon after Brown's death some forty years later, an acquaintance described him as having been 'in a very literal and primitive sense a bishop in poverty'.[9] By comparison with the thousands of desperate Irish who thronged the ports of Wales in the late 1840s, Brown occupied a rare position of privilege, but at the same time the Welsh District was anything but a choice perquisite to be milked for personal gain.

The enthusiastic bishop did not see his brief solely in terms of providing the means of worship for those who could be identified as being in some way Catholic already; he understood that his duties also encompassed a mission to convert the Protestant Welsh. Initially, Brown intended to release Frs Joseph Jones and Peter Lewis, both of whom where Welsh-speakers, as itinerant missioners to evangelize the people and prepare the ground for new missions. However, a shortage of clergy in the established missions rendered this ambitious plan a dead letter and the two missioners were deployed elsewhere. This was not to be the last occasion in the Welsh District when spiritual aspirations were curbed by material restrictions.

Detailed reports of the condition of the Welsh District appeared in the *Catholic Directory and Annual Register*, and from 1843 this publication was used as a vehicle to solicit financial aid from Catholics in the rest of Britain and beyond. The Society of St David, established in June 1842, was the formal means of channelling funds to Wales and it could boast patrons among the old English landed families and contacts for contributions in Scotland and Ireland. Appealing to the pocket by way of the heart, the *Register* reminded its readers that in the seven Welsh counties of Anglesey, Merioneth, Montgomery, Cardigan, Radnor, Pembroke and Carmarthen:

---

[8] Archives of the Archdiocese of Cardiff (hereafter AAC), no number, J. Rathbone to George Oliver, 23 June 1838.

[9] *DNB*, VIII (London, 1886), 33–5; B. Hemphill, 'Bishop Joseph Brown, OSB, the Modern Apostle of Wales', *Studies*, 29 (1950), 31–9.

forming a territory a hundred and thirty miles from north to south and a hundred miles from east to west; even the meanest covering cannot be found under which a priest of God may break the bread of life to famishing multitudes.[10]

In truth these 'famishing multitudes' were a numerically dominant, articulate and increasingly politically-aware Nonconformist Protestant people. Even so, by November 1843 this emotional appeal had realized £1,423 15*s*. and substantial additions were made to this total in the following years. The application of these funds presented no problems for the bishop. 'We are advised by venerable authority', he wrote, 'to look first to the head, and afterwards we shall be able to throw new life and energy into the body.'[11]

Here Brown was moving in a direction consistent with wider intellectual trends in the church. The early nineteenth century saw the decline of Gallicanism, which had been associated with the cherishing of local customs and the limitation of papal influence. By the mid-nineteenth century there were more concerted efforts to impose more 'Roman' devotions and forms of piety, accompanied by the growth of papal power and the rise of the Ultramontane movement. The propriety of concentrating financial resources at a central depository was perfectly intelligible in the context of a clerical hierarchy, and Brown's prudence was rewarded during the trade depression of 1843 in south Wales. Catholic congregations at Cardiff, Rhymni, Pontypool and Nant-y-glo were seriously depleted when iron production stagnated and Irish workers sought work elsewhere. Individual missions were normally financed by the voluntary contributions of those attending mass on a Sunday and it was believed that, had it not been for assistance from the funds of the Society of St David, a number of these missions would have closed.[12] Given the working-class composition of these congregations, monetary contributions towards the upkeep of the priest and chapel could never be large or regular without causing considerable hardship. The age of religious voluntarism based on self-help brought its own peculiar problems for congregations of this kind.

Accommodation and the priest's upkeep were perennial problems. At Merthyr in 1841, Fr J. M. Carroll eked out his living by selling salt fish. His parish covered twenty-six miles of iron and coal-mining country of difficult terrain:

> There is no chance of forming additional congregations in a district which cannot be made to pay the rent even of the poor places in which I celebrate Mass. If they contribute anything for the intended new Chapel it is deducted from what a few were in the habit of contributing monthly for the support of the priest, the newcomers mostly declaring that they do not care whether Mass is said here or not, whilst others refuse to subscribe. . . .[13]

Carroll's case was representative of a more general problem. Where funds existed small chapels could be erected but, more frequently, mass was celebrated in

---

[10] *Catholic Directory and Annual Register for the year 1843* (hereafter *Directory* plus date), p. 102.
[11] *Directory*, 1844, pp. 130–1.
[12] Ibid., p. 71.
[13] AAC, no number, Carroll to Bishop T. J. Brown, 7 September 1841.

the room of a private house, as at Cardiff, or at an inn, as at Abersychan, Tredegar and Rhymni. However, this solution to the problem of accommodation was itself precarious, and in 1844 the mission at Nant-y-glo in north-west Monmouthshire, served from Pontypool, was jeopardized when the Catholic owner of the house where mass was celebrated moved away.

Faced with this situation, which was greatly exacerbated by the refugees from the Irish Famine in the late 1840s, Bishop Brown tackled the problem of church accommodation in a pragmatic way. Where it was possible to erect a simple chapel, it was put to use as a schoolroom also; in Brown's view, its educational use was almost as important as its religious *raison d'être*. His correspondence with the clergy reveals the minute attention to detail and costing that resulted from his abhorrence of debt, and he enjoined his priests to follow the same example. This was not merely a case of parsimony masquerading as policy; Brown's flexible approach to the use of buildings and a rigid position on fiscal matters were well suited to a situation where he possessed limited capital resources for building and where the majority of the Irish congregation refused— or were unable—to contribute to projects requiring investment. Undoubtedly, many Irish men and women regarded themselves as sojourners in a foreign land and would not invest, either financially or emotionally, in a future that was not their own. As a result, Brown occasionally found it necessary to veto extravagant projects, such as the projected church tower in Usk, in favour of more basic needs. His policy was to suggest projects and help initiate them if possible, but to insist on the self-sufficiency of the particular mission concerned thereafter, restricting his contribution to advice on investment and improvements. He responded most readily to those heartfelt pleas grounded in a genuine evangelical concern, but his fiscal policies were formed in accordance with economic orthodoxy which stressed the overriding importance of 'sound money'.

Despite the magnitude of these problems connected with the Irish influx, Brown had still not abandoned the mission to the Welsh. Since his initial plan of commissioning roving missionaries to evangelize the Welsh and to establish new congregations had lapsed, he looked increasingly to Brittany as a potential source of Welsh-speaking clergy. The culture shock experienced by English-speakers when confronted by Welsh-speaking communities on the one hand, and the widely held belief in the close affinity between the Welsh and Breton languages on the other, led Brown to this conclusion. The shaky, if not false, impression absorbed by many contemporaries that a structural linguistic affinity between the Welsh and Breton languages would facilitate the trouble-free learning of one language by a speaker of the other was to be exposed cruelly by the experience of two Breton priests in mid-Wales during the years 1845–9.

In 1844 Brown secured the services of Fr Joseph Mahé of the diocese of Quimper in Brittany and contributed funds for the education of two students in the seminary there. Mahé arrived in mid-Wales in January 1845 and soon found that the prospects of establishing a self-sufficient congregation at either Welshpool or Newtown were not encouraging and so he removed to Aberystwyth. Personality clashes between the priests and their failure to acquire any fluency in Welsh were buried under the irrepressible evangelical zeal of Fr Mahé, who succeeded in dragging out the ill-starred Breton presence until 1849, thereby placing a considerable strain on diocesan funds.[14]

This experience finally convinced Brown that it was futile at that time to attempt to keep a constructive balance between the mission to the immigrant Irish on the one hand, and make systematic endeavours to convert the native Welsh on the other. As has been seen, the general picture of low levels of church attendance and sacramental participation in pre-Famine Ireland was reproduced in industrial Wales and provides evidence that the Irish as a group would not revitalize the Welsh mission overnight. The presence of a baptized, but largely unchurched constituency was a novel problem for the Catholic church in Wales.

The case of Fr Kavanagh and the Irish congregation at Cwmafan near Swansea helps to elucidate the complex nature of the relationship between the Catholic priest and laity in mid-nineteenth-century Wales. By all accounts, Kavanagh was a tireless pastor at Swansea, tending to the sick and needy, and dispensing both material help and spiritual succour during the cholera epidemic of 1847. Kavanagh's heroic actions were formally recognized by the local community when, in the winter of 1849–50, a public subscription realized fifty sovereigns for one:

> whose long unwearied exertions during the late visitation of cholera in the town and neighbourhood, regardless of personal risk or inconvenience, and impartially exercised towards all in need, independent of creed or opinion, justly entitle him to be considered as a public benefactor whose valuable services cannot be too highly appreciated.[15]

Notwithstanding this glowing newspaper testimonial, Kavanagh's devotion to the people was not reciprocated by his parishioners at Cwmafan. There the congregation preferred the ministrations of a suspended Irish priest to those of Kavanagh because of the latter's alleged Protestant sympathies and his unwanted interference in the affairs of that community. According to Timothy Murphy, who lived at Cwmafan, 'Kavanagh is liked better by all the Protestants than by the Catholics so that they are glad never to see him'.[16] This comment suggests that it was not the priest's nationality, but his sacerdotal function, that was of paramount importance in the relationship with his congregation. In a study of Catholicism in Manchester, G. P. Connolly has summed up that sacerdotal function as being the bearer of 'spiritual peace'. By creating dissension in his relationship with the Irish at Cwmafan, Kavanagh can be seen to have broken that spiritual peace and decisively undermined respect for his special position within the community.[17]

Kavanagh's reception is more easily understood when it is remembered that the Catholic clergy in mid-nineteenth-century Wales were not simply concerned to enjoin the Irish to regular attendance at mass. Of greater significance was

---

[14] AAC box 21, Correspondence of Fr. Mahé with Bishop T. J. Brown, 1844–9.

[15] *The Cambrian*, 21 December 1849.

[16] Archives of St David's Priory, University College, Swansea, (37), b, f–h.

[17] G. P. Connolly, 'Little Brother be at Peace: the priest as holy man in the nineteenth-century ghetto', *Studies in Church History*, 19 (1982), 191–206.

their campaign to restructure popular practices and incorporate them within the ambit of orthodox piety. A rediscovered evangelical approach to the poor enabled the church to make the vital connection between spiritual values and everyday life in urban slums, thereby delaying the emerging dichotomy between spirituality and a secular world.

Churches, parish sodalities and the all-important Catholic schools underlined the ability of organized religion to adapt, however tardily, to the problems of industrialization and urbanization. However, a stumbling-block which prevented the clergy from achieving complete success was the way in which the Irish perceived the priest himself. In pre-Tridentine Catholic culture, the priest occupied a special position which stressed his magical qualities, and this perception persisted into industrial society. An anecdote recalled by William Flynn, who was born in Merthyr Tydfil in the 1840s, illustrates how tales emphasizing the magical qualities of the priest served to strengthen the mystique surrounding a celibate man at once part of, and set apart from, society. Flynn recalled the tradition that Fr Carroll would walk down to Merthyr from Dowlais to say mass and that he was regularly insulted on his return:

> One Monday when coming home to Glebeland Place, he [Fr Carroll] was passing though Old Arch in Castle Street when a Welshman spat upon him. He spoke to a passer-by in Irish:
> 'Are you an Irishman?'
> 'Yes, Father,' was the reply, 'don't you see that man spitting upon you?'
> 'Yes,' replied Fr. Carroll, 'but by this time tomorrow he won't do so.'
> This man then walked home with Fr. Carroll for protection from the jeering man who followed him.
>   The following day at about the same hour in the afternoon, a procession up Castle Street brought the dead body of the man who had spat upon Fr. Carroll the day before. He had been killed in the works. Fr. Carroll's remark to the Irishman was town's talk for some time afterwards.[18]

In this context, belief that the curse of a priest was especially harmful was not so much an irrational delusion as the embodiment of a means of adjustment to the strains and frustrations of an unpredictable life in a frequently hostile environment. When viewed in conjunction with a compatible peasant 'folk culture', beliefs of this kind can be seen as supplying an explanation for misfortune and a means of dealing with it. The perception of the priest as a thaumaturge enhanced his status in one direction, but did not accord him the centrality in the Irish community that he desired. That centrality could only be acquired by the cultivation of a host of social relationships which often appeared to be wholly secular. The priest's attempt to establish himself at the heart of the immigrant community was legitimized by the rapidly developing 'cult of martyrdom' associated with the priests who had lost their lives in serving the Irish during the typhus epidemic of 1847 in particular. In Wales the memory of Frs Mulcahy (Bangor), Metcalfe (Newport), and Carroll (Merthyr), who all died in their attempts to serve the 'holy poor', was actively kept alive. As with the

---

[18]   Glamorgan Record Office, D/Dxha, 4/1, Papers of Fr. J. M. Cronin.

story of 'the Welshman and the Half-Crown', the stature of these figures attained mythical proportions as time passed.

Attempts to reform popular Irish practices were broadly related to 'Romanizing' tendencies within the church. Priests who arrived in Wales in the 1840s and 1850s rejected the circumspection in dress and behaviour which had characterized the old Catholicism. The Institute of Charity, or Rosminians, were foremost in this movement. Italian priests of the Institute were active in Newport, Cardiff and Merthyr Tydfil and were credited with introducing the Roman collar as a permanent feature of clerical dress. By 1864 there were more Italian than Irish priests in Wales, while Dutch and Breton clergy supplemented the Welsh, Irish and English clergy in the parishes.

Reformers of popular piety occasionally let their evangelical enthusiasm develop into excessive criticism of the Irish, thereby accelerating their alienation from formal religion. Bishop Brown was increasingly critical of the 'unreformed' practices of Irish Catholics whose experience was derived from pre-Famine Ireland. He complained to the third marquis of Bute, a Catholic convert, of the 'imperfect early religious training of many Catholics from Ireland' which, he believed, resulted in their neglect of Sunday mass at Cardiff.[19]

Brown was deeply aware of the fact that the perpetuation of a religion such as Catholicism, in which tradition and authority played a major part, depended primarily upon the transmission of a teaching and moral code. In nineteenth-century Wales, where there existed a plurality of religions, the maintenance of religious continuity between generations of Catholics was established through Catholic schools. Yet when, in 1866, Bishop Brown looked back upon the first year of his episcopate, he recalled that in south Wales 'there was not a single school-room fit for its purpose, nor indeed do we recollect that there existed one poor-school'.[20] Educational provision was organized on confessional lines, with keen competition between different denominations for the allegiance of parents and the attendance of their children. This situation was the result of the voluntarist and uncompromisingly competitive ethic of the age, and attendance at state-funded day schools did not become general until the passing of Forster's Education Act in 1870.

As early as 1842 Fr Carroll alternated between Merthyr Tydfil and Tredegar, teaching a total of sixty children. 'Education makes but little advances', he wrote:

> I keep up two day schools, assisted in the expenses by two charitable friends; 60 children of both sexes attend the schools ... hours from nine to twelve and two till five ... The children of both sexes are employed so early picking or piling minerals or coals. They are removed about seven years of age, which early removal generally deprives them of all taste for instruction.[21]

He went on to suggest that schools with a more technical and scientific curriculum

---

[19] AAC box 123, Bishop T. J. Brown to the third marquis of Bute, undated.

[20] Attwater, *Catholic Church*, p. 95.

[21] Parliamentary Papers (hereafter PP), 1842, XV, First Report from the Commissioners for Inquiring into the Employment and Condition of Children in Mines and Manufactories, 506.

would 'tend greatly to elevate the social condition and character of the working classes'. Carroll was mindful of the presence of the Chartist movement in the area and the increasing importance of Irish issues for British radicals. Denominational schooling was underpinned by the unshakeable belief that the inculcation of literacy could be positively harmful unless it was placed firmly within a religious framework.

By 1843 there were four Catholic poor-schools in Wales, three being maintained 'with great difficulty' by the priests at Merthyr, Wrexham and Cardiff. The fourth was probably in Newport where, in 1846, the school boasted an annual income of £46 16s., besides £18 in school pence.[22] In 1845 the *Catholic Directory* published a résumé of the District finances, which included an Education Fund (in existence since 1840) which provided some £19 annually.[23] The impact that these fledgling schools had on their mainly Irish pupils can be evaluated even less precisely than the sketchy evidence on their funding. An impression of the type of education offered and the proportion of Irish children reached by it can be gained from the evidence for Cardiff reproduced by the Education Commissioners in their report of 1847. Although the Commissioners did not examine the town's Catholic school personally, Fr Millea, the parish priest, contributed a written report on the state of Catholic education there and his document was reproduced in the published report.

According to Millea, his congregation was composed, with few exceptions, of the poorest of the labouring classes and only 80 or 90 of the 220 children in need of instruction actually attended school. The highest charge was 4d. per week, but many parents felt that even this sum was beyond their means and Millea referred to the common belief among the congregation that the most basic ability to read was adequate education in itself. Consequently, few would strive for any additional educational provision. The curriculum included arithmetic, geography and English grammar, as well as some elementary practical skills; class books of the National Schools of Ireland were also in use. A Sunday school catered for general religious education. Up until that time the school had been held in 'some back place only fit for cattle', whereas during 1847 a new and larger school was in the process of construction.[24]

Cardiff's school was unexceptional in so far as it experienced only partial success in attracting Irish children to its classes. This unpalatable fact was the most important factor militating against the schools becoming the bulwark of orthodox Catholicism at this time. The Irish community was characterized by high geographical mobility, a factor hardly conducive to a settled education, and the Catholic schools could hope only to develop basic literacy and numeracy and inculcate the elementary tenets of the Faith. This state of affairs strengthened clerical commitment to the expansion of educational facilities. Towards the end of the decade funds were channelled to Wales to construct and support schools

---

[22] *Directory*, 1842, p. 43.

[23] *Directory*, 1845, p. 68.

[24] PP, 1847, XXVII, Report of the Commissioners of Inquiry into the State of Education in Wales (Part 1), 371–2.

through the Catholic Poor-School Committee of England and Wales, with Dowlais receiving £20, Merthyr £17, Newport £20, Cardiff £20, Wrexham £15, Bangor
£15, Abermarlais £10 and Chepstow £20. Capital allowances of £100 and £90
had been made to Pontypool and Swansea respectively. However, as Fr Millea
emphasized in 1847, an effective system of education would need to be free,
compulsory and devoid of religious prejudice.[25] It was only under these conditions that the Catholic schools could perform their stated function adequately
and those conditions would not obtain until after the Act of 1870 was passed.

Despite these attempts to broaden the base of Catholic education, Brown's
reference to the 'imperfect early religious training' of the Irish leading directly
to their non-attendance at church remained the crux of the problem facing the
church. Attendance at church was taken by the the clergy as a measure of
the success of organized Catholicism in imposing orthodoxy. Where serial statistics exist, they suggest strongly that those Irish who participated fully in the
rituals of the church were themselves a minority. Attention to Easter duties—the
minimum participation required of a practising Catholic—fluctuated considerably from 1841 to 1861 at Cardiff. In the mid-1840s the energetic Fr Millea
was responsible for an increase in practice, reaching 50 per cent in 1847, but
his unaided resourcefulness was insufficient in the face of the Famine upheaval.
By 1853 the percentage of the total Catholic population at Cardiff fulfilling their
Easter duties had dropped to 15.8 per cent. In 1854 the Fathers of the Institute
of Charity took care of the mission and they managed to stabilize the practice
of Easter duties in the town at 23.5 per cent, rising to 25.5 per cent in 1861.[26]

Comparable statistics for other parishes in Wales appear not to have survived.
However, it is possible to achieve a synchronic view of Catholic attendance
at mass on a particular Sunday in 1851 by using the returns of the Religious
Census compiled in that year. In his study of religion and the Industrial Revolution in south Wales, Canon E. T. Davies used these returns to draw attention
to the discrepancy between the number of Irish-born residing in a number of
the Enumeration Districts used in the Census of Population for 1851 when compared with the attendances at mass recorded in the Religious Census of the
same year. Davies found that this discrepancy was greater in those areas where
the Irish were more dispersed, whereas in a town such as Newport the gap
was much narrower. Accordingly, Davies maintained, the frequency of Catholic
attendance at mass was a product of the density of Irish settlement.[27]

In so far as the close proximity of Irish settlers in a locality acted as a spur
to the establishment of a mission to them and the erection of a place of worship
for their use, the density of Irish settlement undoubtedly facilitated the more
regular attendance of baptized Catholics at services. However, this explanation
is predicated on the belief that, in order to fill the pews, the church had
the comparatively simple task of bringing the facilities of worship closer to the

---

[25] Ibid.
[26] Based on figures in J. Hickey, *Urban Catholics* (London, 1967), pp. 90–4. Here the percentages are
of the total Catholic community, including children.
[27] E. T. Davies, *Religion in the Industrial Revolution in South Wales* (Cardiff, 1965), pp. 187–91.

immigrants. As has been shown above, the religious culture which the Census statistics sought to express was considerably more variegated than this interpretation allows.

The raw data provided by the Census need to be treated with caution, especially when attempts are made to abstract information concerning non-Protestant bodies and in specific localities. Horace Mann, the civil servant responsible for conducting the Religious Census, was duly sensible of the limitations of the enumeration in this respect.[28] As he pointed out, the pattern of Roman Catholic attendance differed from that of Protestants; the latter organized morning, afternoon and evening services, while the former tended to hold a number of masses during the morning. Protestants would be expected to attend more than one service on the Sabbath, while one attendance at Sunday mass was deemed sufficient. The importance of regular attendance for the maintenance of the identity of a particular denomination could also vary. Protestant Nonconformity was sustained partly by its relationship with the Established Church and the failure to attend a place of worship other than that of the Established Church meant that the non-attender was claimed as a *de jure* member of the state Church. As regards Irish immigrants, particularly in Wales, non-attenders were regarded as *ipso facto* supporters of Catholicism and so it did not appear vitally important to attend a religious service regularly in order to preserve an ascribed religious identity. This was the case despite the exhortations of parish priests to attend at least once a week on a Sunday. It was possible to be Catholic by identification in nineteenth-century Britain as well as by practice, an identification which was nourished from within the group but which was also sustained by the attitudes of outsiders.

When the Religious Census of 1851 was published, it revealed that in Wales and England, taken together, the attendances at Nonconformist chapels and at the places of worship of the Established Church were roughly equal. By comparison, the figures for Wales alone revealed a startling picture of religious activity. Decades of vigorous Nonconformist activity among the Welsh-speaking working class and mass alienation from the Established Church had produced a situation where the chapels accounted for an overwhelming preponderance among worshippers in Wales on Census Sunday.[29] In England Catholicism was recognized as a religion with a special mission to the urban poor; in Wales the Nonconformist denominations towered over the religious landscape in both town and country.

The statistics collected on Census Sunday do not record the number of individuals attending a place of worship but rather record the total number of attendances at each service. Adopting a method utilized by Professor Ieuan Gwynedd Jones in his study of denominational growth in Swansea, it is possible to arrive at an index of attendance for the Irish-born in specific localities which is in

[28] H. Mann, 'On the Statistical Position of Religious Bodies in England and Wales', *Journal of the Statistical Society of London*, 18 (1855), 144n.

[29] I. G. Jones, 'Religion and Society', in *Explorations and Explanations: Essays in the Social History of Victorian Wales* (Llandysul, 1981), p. 227.

some measure comparable to that for the native Welsh.[30] This index is arrived
at by expressing the total number of attendances at all services on Census Sunday
as a proportion of the total population of the district. Although failing to take
account of different habits of worship among the various churches and chapels
and tending to favour the Nonconformist bodies, calculations of this kind are
an accurate means of ascertaining differential rates of attendance.[31] By expressing the total number of attendances at all services in Catholic chapels (in areas
where it is known from other sources that native Catholicism is numerically
insignificant) as a proportion of the Irish-born population, it is possible to arrive
at a rudimentary index of attendance for Irish Catholics in Wales. Although
the Census of Population recorded the Irish-born only and did not distinguish
their British-born children from the native inhabitants, an index based on these
statistics can provide a comparative picture of differential rates of attendance
(Table 1). This method is particularly applicable in Wales where the growth
areas of Catholicism were associated almost exclusively with Irish immigration.

Table 1: Index of Religious Attendance, 1851

District	Total no. of Irish-born	Total Catholic Attendances	Irish Index of Attendance	District Index of Attendance
Newport	2,737	2,200	80.4	64.4
Cardiff	3,317	1,450	43.7	70.3
Merthyr	3,706	750	20.2	80.1
Swansea	1,369	500	36.5	71.1
Wrexham	711	360	50.6	74.4

These figures seem to suggest that the typical index of attendance for Irish
Catholic communities was approximately 35–50 and that church attendance
was more frequent among the other denominations. It should be remembered,
of course, that these figures are crude pointers to the extent of religious practice
and that they must be used with caution. Nevertheless, it can be seen that
the experience of Catholicism at Merthyr Tydfil on the one hand, and at Newport
on the other, was exceptional. Certainly, the Irish population of the Merthyr
district was dispersed over a wide area, but the density of Irish settlement cannot
explain the difference in rates of attendance between Newport and towns such
as Cardiff, Swansea and Wrexham. An important element which accounts for
the difference between Newport and other towns in Wales was the fact that
its mission was far more securely established. An impressive Gothic church
was under construction at the time of the Chartist Rising in Newport in 1839
and a poor-school was established early in the 1840s on the initiative of Dr
Baldacconi, the parish priest; it was reported in 1849 that there were 'flourishing

---

[30] 'Denominationalism in Swansea and District', ibid., pp. 53–80.
[31] I. G. Jones and D. Williams (eds.), *The Religious Census of 1851: A Calendar of the Returns relating to
Wales*, 1, South Wales (Cardiff, 1976), xi–xxxv.

schools' under the supervision of the Brothers of the Order of Charity and the
Sisters of the Order of Providence. The combination of a Catholic education
and a succession of priests acutely aware of the evangelical nature of their aposto-
late made a decisive impact. The mission also received a visit from Fr Luigi
Gentili of the newly formed Institute of Charity in 1846. Gentili was reputedly
the first priest to convert a man on a train, but he failed to build up his usual
head of steam in south Wales because of ill health. His uninspiring sermons
before two mixed Catholic and Protestant congregations served to reinforce the
favourable standing of the local parish priest, Fr Furlong.[32]

The exceptional circumstances of Catholicism in Newport merely underline
the overwhelming impression left by the census statistics that a large proportion,
in many places a majority, of Irish men and women—nominal Catholics who
had been baptized in the church—were habitual non-attenders at mass. This
state of affairs has often been obscured in writings by Catholic commentators
intent on fusing the frequently divergent categories of 'Catholic' and 'Irish'.
Here we are not dealing with a backsliding people dominated by unbelief, but
rather with a variant of popular religion at odds with theological and ritual
orthodoxy.

It should not be forgotten that the Religious Census was compiled at a time
when the Famine immigration was in full flood; it was not until the civil Census
of 1861 that the highest number of Irish-born was recorded in Wales. Consequently, the church felt that, by the beginning of the 1850s, its resources were
strained to the utmost. Many Irish settlements were provided with a permanent
chapel and a resident priest in later decades, and church-building became a
desperate remedial action. While thirteen Catholic chapels were built during
the decade of the Welsh District, a further fourteen were constructed in the
period 1851 to 1860, and another sixteen in the decade 1861 to 1870. Thereafter,
building activity slackened until the first decade of the twentieth century.[33]

The crude vital statistics for the Catholic church in Wales as a whole in
1851 nevertheless reveal a remarkable improvement on the position reported
to Rome in 1839 when the total number of Catholics was enumerated as 6,269.
Eleven years later there was a total Irish-born population of 19,747 distributed
among the eight Welsh counties that were served by at least one priest; the
vast majority of these would have been baptized Catholics. Even if the British-
born children of these immigrants are ignored, we are left with an increase
in the bedrock Catholic constituency of some 200 per cent, and in the following
decade numbers continued to grow. This population was served by twenty-five
priests from nineteen churches and chapels, but the total number of Catholic
attendances on Census Sunday was only 5,585.

By the time the Census was conducted, the Welsh District had been divided.
In the previous year Pope Pius IX had put an end to mounting speculation

[32] C. Leetham, *Luigi Gentili: A Sower of the Second Spring* (London, 1965), pp. 3, 244–5.

[33] *Directory*, 1840, and following years; cf. I. G. Jones, 'Ecclesiastical Economy: Aspects of Church Building
in Victorian Wales', in R. R. Davies *et al.* (eds.), *Welsh Society and Nationhood: Historical Essays presented to
Glanmor Williams* (Cardiff, 1984), pp. 216–31.

by announcing the restoration of the Hierarchy in England and Wales, an act which revived the traditional vitriolic anger of Protestant 'No Popery'. In this reorganization provocative plans to rename the Welsh District as the diocese of St David's—technically an illegal act because it usurped the title of a diocese of the Established Church—were put aside in favour of creating two new dioceses, both containing English counties. The six northern counties of Wales were annexed to the diocese of Shrewsbury, while the southern counties of Wales and the English county of Hereford were regrouped to form the diocese of Newport and Menevia.[34] It was not until 1916 that Catholics in Wales were brought into a single Metropolitan District with their own archbishop.

Unquestionably, in the precise form of its existence between 1840 and 1850 the Welsh District was a flawed arrangement. On the eve of industrialization, Catholicism in Wales remained rural-based and marginal to the new areas of urban growth. In contrast to a county like Lancashire, which retained a Catholic presence in its towns, the church in Wales had to cope with two vexing developments: that of Irish immigration to urban areas with a small or non-existent receiving community, and the difficulty of addressing that problem from a rural base. By annexing the counties of north Wales to the diocese of Shrewsbury in 1850, this problem remained unresolved. While it is true that the Welsh District had a short life expectancy, given the well-known intention of restoring the Hierarchy at some point in the future, it was not inevitable that Wales would be divided in precisely the way it was in 1850.[35]

In terms of diocesan organization, the decade under consideration was uniquely important in Wales, for it saw not only the continuation of Benedictine influence but its consolidation and extension. Bishop Brown was himself a member of that order and soon after his appointment to the see of Newport and Menevia under the new Hierarchy of 1850 a pre-Reformation system of diocesan organization was resurrected, albeit in a radically different social context. This system was based on the Benedictine community at Hereford, which subsequently supplied all members of the diocesan Chapter of Canons. Under this arrangement diocesan affairs became a reflection of the internal politics of the Benedictine Order, a fact which can be fully appreciated when it is remembered that it was Benedictine influence which perpetuated the inclusion of the English county of Herefordshire in the Metropolitan District of Wales in 1916.

These developments in the mid-nineteenth century need to be viewed against the longer-term picture of the decline of the influence of the Catholic gentry and the rise of the clergy as the undisputed leaders within the church. During the period of penal legislation, the Catholic community was beset by problems concerning where authority within the church resided. The increase in the number of Districts in 1840 and the restoration of the Hierarchy in 1850 can be seen as the completion of this change in the ecclesiastical balance of power

---

[34] G. Albion, 'The Restoration of the Hierarchy, 1850', in G. A. Beck (ed.), *The English Catholics, 1850–1950* (London, 1950), pp. 86–115; A. H. Williams, *Efengyliaeth yng Nghymru, c. 1840–1875* (National Museum of Wales, 1982), pp. 21–3.

[35] Cf. R. Tudur Jones, *Ffydd ac Argyfwng Genedl, 1890–1914*, I (Swansea, 1981), 34.

in favour of the clergy. In the Welsh District more than in any other, the transference of power to the Benedictines under Bishop Brown's firm control exemplified this process. Also, the change in Wales was in favour of the English clergy. Unlike Australia, New Zealand and Canada, where Irish bishops dominated the church, and in contrast to Scotland, where native bishops retained their control over affairs, the Catholic church in Wales remained firmly in the grasp of English prelates.[36]

Under these circumstances, resources were not channelled towards the centres of Irish settlement in the industrial areas of Wales as effectively as they might have been. In 1851 there were five places of worship served by the same number of priests in Herefordshire, although there were only 119 attendances at mass on Census Sunday and an Irish-born population of only 363. In the same year in the rapidly industrializing county of Glamorgan, there were only three Catholic priests and the same number of chapels despite a higher number of attendances (2,000) on Census Sunday and an Irish-born population of 9,737. Far too many Catholic places of worship were to be found in the rural areas of Monmouthshire and Herefordshire, where congregations were small and where the Irish were generally absent.

The scale of these problems was dimly perceived in the 1840s and the Welsh District had only begun to provide the context within which they could be addressed. The unfortunate and arbitrary assignment of the six counties of north Wales to an English diocese meant that the Catholic church abandoned its recognition of Wales as a territorial unit at the same time as Protestant Nonconformity was beginning to articulate its religious identity in terms of Welsh nationality. Paradoxically, by the end of the Welsh District's life, Catholicism was regarded as more, not less, alien than before. Neither was the clergy's desire to see the errant Irish brought within the realm of orthodox practice achieved more swiftly by dividing Wales. When the Welsh District came to an end in 1850, it had become patently obvious to the isolated parish priests who alternately denounced and cajoled the Irish immigrants to whom they ministered, that the reluctant foot-soldiers of the Faith would not meekly march in the direction pointed out to them by their aspiring clerical officers.

[36] S. Gilley, 'The Roman Catholic Church and the Nineteenth Century Irish Diaspora', *Journal of Ecclesiastical History*, 35 (1984), 188–207.

Iaith y Nefoedd mewn Cymdeithas Ddiwydiannol: y Gymraeg a Chrefydd yng Ngorllewin Sir Fynwy yn y Bedwaredd Ganrif ar Bymtheg

SIAN RHIANNON WILLIAMS

Er gwahaniaethu mewn credo, yr ydym oll yn unol yn ein crediniaeth mai yr iaith fwyaf gweddus i annerch yr Hollalluog Dduw ydyw ... iaith gwlad ein genedigaeth. Yr oedd y syniad yma ym meddwl fy annwyl dadcu a'm hannwyl famgu pan adeiladasant a gwaddolasant yr Eglwys hon ...[1]

GEIRIAU'R CYRNOL HERBERT, Llan-arth (Aelod Seneddol) yw'r rhain wrth iddo ddadorchuddio cofeb i goffáu Benjamin ac Augusta Hall (Arglwydd ac Arglwyddes Llanofer) yn eglwys Aber-carn ym 1907. Er 1862 bu'r eglwys hon yn enghraifft unigryw yn hanes crefydd yng Nghymru. Yn y flwyddyn honno, cytunodd cynulleidfa o eglwyswyr i drosglwyddo'u heglwys i ofal y Methodistiaid Calfinaidd, a hynny er mwyn gallu parhau i addoli yn eu mamiaith. Er mor neilltuol yr oedd yr uno o safbwynt diwinyddol,[2] ac er mor ddiddorol y gwrthdaro rhwng yr Eglwys yn esgobaeth Llandaf a Benjamin Hall, y diwydiannwr a'r gwleidydd a oedd yn un o'i phrif noddwyr, i'r hanesydd cymdeithasol nid dyma wir arwyddocâd y trosglwyddo. Ei bwysigrwydd, yn hytrach, yw'r cipolwg a rydd ar y berthynas gymhleth a fodolai rhwng crefydd a'r iaith Gymraeg yn y gymdeithas ddiwydiannol.

Yn ystod y bedwaredd ganrif ar bymtheg cafwyd cyfnewidiadau cymdeithasol aruthrol yng nghymoedd gorllewinol sir Fynwy a achosodd yn y pen draw ddirywiad yn hanes yr iaith Gymraeg mewn rhannau helaeth o'r ardal. Erbyn 1907, a'r Adroddiad Brenhinol ar Sefyllfa'r Sefydliadau Crefyddol[3] ar fin cael ei gyhoeddi, yr oedd dylanwad crefydd yn gwanhau. Nid enciliad yr iaith oedd yr unig achos, ond yr oedd y ffaith fod erbyn hynny gysylltiad mor glòs rhwng

---

[1] NLW, C[alvinistic] M[ethodist] A[rchives], 14702–3. Abraham Morris, 'The History of Calvinistic Methodism in Monmouthshire', t. 63.

[2] D. Parry Jones, 'The Use of Aber-carn', *Province*, 18 (1968–9), 58–64, 97–105, 131–8.

[3] *Royal Commission on the Church of England and Other Religious Bodies in Wales and Monmouthshire*, PP, 1908–10 (Cd. 5432–9), xiv–xix.

crefydd a'r Gymraeg nes eu bod i raddau helaeth yn gyd-ddibynnol yn ffactor allweddol yn nirywiad y naill a'r llall. Yr oedd 'yr hen Gymraeg yn marw a'r Beibl yn ei llaw'.[4] Serch hynny, parhâi'r Ymneilltuwyr, ynghyd â rhai Eglwyswyr hefyd, i bwysleisio cryfder y berthynas rhwng y ddwy elfen a fu mor bwysig yn eu gorffennol, a hynny hyd yn oed wrth iddynt wylio eu capeli yn troi i addoli yn Saesneg. Cafodd yr agwedd ddeuol hon ddylanwad nid yn unig ar sefydliadau crefyddol y sir ond ar hanes yr iaith yn ogystal.

Yn sgîl y Chwyldro Diwydiannol daeth poblogaeth fawr, amrywiol a symudol i ardal a fu cyn hynny yn wasgaredig ei phoblogaeth. Yn Gymry, Saeson a Gwyddelod, daethant â'u hieithoedd, eu traddodiadau, eu moes a'u hanfodes gyda hwy. Mae disgrifiadau sylwebyddion hanner cyntaf y bedwaredd ganrif ar bymtheg o gymoedd Mynwy—y 'black domain' o 'deyrnasoedd haearn' a'u poblogaeth anystywallt—yn hen gyfarwydd i fyfyrwyr hanes Cymru erbyn hyn.[5] Felly hefyd yr ymgyrch fawr o'r 1830au ymlaen i grefyddoli a moesoli'r boblogaeth ddiwydiannol newydd hon a ymddangosai yn fygythiad mor frawychus i ddosbarth canol y cyfnod. I arweinwyr crefyddol, yr oedd hyn yn sialens, ac aethant ati gyda sêl y croesgadwr i geisio dofi, gwareiddio a sobri'r 'lliaws gweithfaol'. Yn hyn o beth yr oedd yr Eglwyswyr a'r Ymneilltuwyr yn gytûn. Ond os oedd y ddwy ochr yn fodlon cydweithio â pherchenogion y gweithfeydd, yr oeddynt hefyd yn arch-elynion, a'r gystadleuaeth rhwng y naill a'r llall i ennill teyrngarwch y gweithwyr yn hir a chwerw. Rhan annatod o'r frwydr hon oedd yr iaith Gymraeg; hyhi oedd iaith mwyafrif mawr poblogaeth cymoedd Gwent am gyfran helaeth o'r ganrif.

Oherwydd natur hyblyg eu trefnyddiaeth gallai'r enwadau Ymneilltuol ymateb i ofynion crefyddol y boblogaeth yn ôl y galw. Gwyddai'r addolwyr beth oedd eu hanghenion, ac i raddau helaeth cawsant lwyddiant wrth ddarparu adeiladau a chyflogi gweinidogion, gan dynnu ar eu hadnoddau hwy eu hunain yn unig. Er bod nawdd diwydianwyr yn bwysicach iddynt erbyn ail hanner y ganrif, ym mlynyddoedd cynnar y gweithfeydd yr oedd y mwyafrif o'r cynulleidfaoedd yn hunan-gynhaliol ac, er gwaethaf dyledion trwm, yn rhydd i geisio helaethu darpariaeth grefyddol eu henwad fel y cynyddai'r boblogaeth.

Nid felly'r Eglwys. Esgobaeth dlawd oedd Llandaf, ac yr oedd ceisio darparu addoldai yn y canolfannau poblog newydd yn broblem aruthrol o dan y drefn anhyblyg a oedd ohoni. Hen eglwysi a adeiladwyd yn wreiddiol i wasanaethu poblogaeth amaethyddol, wasgaredig oedd eglwysi plwyfi Bedwellte, Mynyddislwyn ac Aberystruth, ac fe'u lleolid yn uchel ar y llethrau ymhell o fwrlwm y gweithfeydd newydd. Yr oedd yn anos felly i'r Eglwys ymateb i'r sefyllfa nag ydoedd i Ymneilltuaeth ac, wrth i'w phroblemau gael eu dwysáu gan y ffaith fod gan y boblogaeth ddiwydiannol ddwy iaith, ni fu'r trigolion newydd yn hir cyn sylweddoli pa un a gâi'r flaenoriaeth ganddi.

Mewn traethawd a anfonwyd i gystadleuaeth yn Eisteddfod Cymreigyddion

---

[4] Yr oedd y testun, 'Mae'r hen Gymraeg yn marw a'i Beibl yn ei llaw', yn deitl i ddarlith Miss E. Evans, Coleg y Barri, a draddodwyd gerbron sawl Cymdeithas Gymraeg yn sir Fynwy rhwng 1918 a 1922.

[5] *Report of the Commissioners of Inquiry into the State of Education in Wales*, PP, 1847 (870), xxvii.

y Fenni ym 1838, gresynai'r awdur (a'i galwai ei hun yn Einion ab Haiarn) at y modd yr oedd offeiriad yn esgeuluso anghenion y trigolion Cymraeg:

> Peth cyffredin oedd eu gweled yn dyfod yn fintai mawrion i fynwentydd y llannau cyn amser y gwasanaeth, ond mor fuan a gwybyddent nad oedd y cyflwyniad efengylaidd yn cael ei weinyddu yn eu hiaith, ymwasgarent yma a thraw ... arferiad a ddygodd anfri ar yr Eglwys oedd hyn, a roddodd ddrws agored a lle addas i osod cyflawn sylfaen Ymneilltuaeth.[6]

Cyhuddwyd yr Eglwys o anwybyddu'r mwyafrif Cymraeg eu hiaith er mwyn plesio nifer bychan o gymunwyr o safle cymdeithasol uwch. Yn ôl yr eglwyswr, Dyfnwal Gwent, ym 1844, '... a thrwy mai Saeson ydynt y meistri haiarn a'u teuluoedd ... gadawyd idd y gwasanaeth Cymreig gael ei esgeulusaw ... mal y dechreuasant y gwrandawyr Cymreig ymadael'.[7] Nid oedd ond un lle iddynt fynd—i'r capel.

Sais o'r enw Edward Copleston oedd Esgob Llandaf ar y pryd. Yn ystod ei gyfnod ef yn yr esgobaeth (1828–49) cynyddodd y boblogaeth yn aruthrol. Yn sicr, yr oedd Copleston yn ymwybodol o'r angen i geisio darparu adeiladau a chynnal gwasanaethau ar gyfer y ddwy garfan ieithyddol. Mynnai fod pethau'n gwella, ond bod ceisio cyflawni'r 'ddyletswydd ddwbl' hon yn gwasgu'n annioddefol o drwm ar adnoddau prin yr esgobaeth.[8] Yn wahanol i'r portread a geir yn nhraddodiad hanesyddol Ymneilltuaeth, nid oedd holl aelodau'r 'hen Estrones' yn elyniaethus i'r Gymraeg. Yn wir, daeth mwyafrif yr ymosodiadau ar fethiant, neu ddiffyg, polisi ieithyddol esgobaeth Llandaf (o leiaf hyd at y 1870au) o blith yr eglwyswyr eu hunain. Yn sir Fynwy yr oedd carfan gref o eglwyswyr Cymreig yn gysylltiedig â chylch teulu Llanofer. Benjamin Hall, Arglwydd Llanofer, oedd y mwyaf llafar efallai, ond yr oedd nifer ohonynt, megis y Parch. David Howell (Llawdden) a'r Parch. David James (Pant-teg) yn wŷr amlwg yn y byd diwylliannol Cymraeg. Trwy gyfrwng y wasg Gymraeg a mudiad y Cymreigyddion yn arbennig, cafwyd ymgyrch i Gymreigio'r Eglwys drwy ddarparu esgobion ac offeiriad Cymraeg eu hiaith a thrwy godi eglwysi Cymraeg yn y trefi diwydiannol newydd. Hawliai'r garfan hon mai'r Eglwys oedd gwir gartref ysbrydol cenedl y Cymry, a'u bwriad oedd adfer ei safle fel Mam Eglwys.

Er gwaethaf y feirniadaeth a'r problemau, gellid dadlau bod y cyfnod ar ôl 1837, pan basiwyd deddf i geisio diwygio'r Eglwys, yn gyfnod pan welwyd ysbryd newydd yn yr Eglwys, ysbryd efengylaidd a oedd i raddau yn ymateb i dwf Ymneilltuaeth. Dywedwyd am gyfnod Copleston: 'This may be called a period of transition from an almost utter inefficiency to a state of importance and influence ... destined to produce visible and permanent results'.[9] O safbwynt

---

[6] NLW, MS. 13961E, f. 59a.

[7] *Seren Gomer*, Mehefin 1844.

[8] E. Copleston (Bishop of Llandaff), *A Charge Delivered to the Clergy of the Diocese of Llandaff in September 1836* (London, 1836); idem, *A Charge Delivered to the Clergy of the Diocese of Llandaff at the Triennial Visitation in October 1842* (London, 1842); W. J. Copleston, *A Memoir of Edward Copleston DD, Bishop of Llandaff* (London, 1851).

[9] Copleston, *Edward Copleston*, t. 225.

y ddarpariaeth Gymraeg, gormodiaith yw hyn, er y cafwyd rhai adeiladau newydd a mwy o barodrwydd nag o'r blaen i benodi curadon Cymraeg eu hiaith
i gynorthwyo offeiriaid di-Gymraeg y plwyfi dwyieithog. Yn yr ychydig fannau
hynny lle y llwyddodd yr esgobaeth (fel arfer drwy gymorth y cwmni haearn
neu lo yn yr ardal) i sefydlu eglwysi cwbl Gymraeg a phenodi offeiriaid a oedd
yn Gymry Cymraeg, fe wobrwywyd ei hymdrech gan iddynt dyfu'n sefydliadau
poblogaidd, ffyniannus. Yr enghraifft orau yn sir Fynwy yn ddi-os yw Eglwys
Dewi Sant, Rhymni, a fu, o dan ofalaeth y Parch. Lodwick Edwards a'r Canon
William Evans, yn ganolfan fywiog i'r diwylliant Cymraeg yn y dref am bron
i ganrif.[10] Yr oedd eglwys Aber-carn hefyd yn cymharu'n ffafriol â'r capeli
Ymneilltuol lleol o ran aelodaeth, disgyblion Ysgol Sul a gweithgarwch diwylliannol.

Ond eithriadau oedd eglwysi fel Rhymni ac Aber-carn, ac erbyn cyhoeddi
Cyfrifiad Crefydd 1851 yr oedd hi'n amlwg fod yr Eglwys yn colli'r dydd yn
ei hymdrech i adennill teyrngarwch y Cymry Cymraeg.[11] Bu'r blynyddoedd
rhwng 1848 a 1851 yn gyfnod o bolareiddio barn ar grefydd. Ar ôl cyhoeddi
Adroddiad Addysg 1847 ystyrid yr offeiriaid lleol yn fradwyr oherwydd iddynt,
yn eu tystiolaeth i'r Comisiwn, ddatgan y farn fod y Gymraeg yn faen tramgwydd
i ddatblygiad y Cymry fel cenedl.[12] Ond o gofio agweddau llawer o'r gweinidogion Ymneilltuol ynglŷn ag addysg Saesneg, mae'n amheus a fuasai eu hatebion
hwythau i'r cwestiwn penodol ar sefyllfa'r iaith yn wahanol iawn pe buasent
wedi cael cyfle i'w ateb. Er na fuasent mor ddilornus o'r Gymraeg (oherwydd
gwelent ei gwerth moesol ym myd crefydd), mae'n debyg y buasent wedi croes-
awu'r ffaith fod y Cymry cyffredin yn dechrau dysgu'r iaith Saesneg, gan ystyried
hynny'n gam ymlaen yn y broses o addysgu'r genedl. Ond ni chawsai eu tystiolaeth weld golau ddydd, ac yr oeddynt felly'n rhydd i gondemnio agwedd
yr eglwyswyr. Rhoddodd 'Brad y Llyfrau Gleision' sail i'r Ymneilltuwyr hawlio
mai hwy oedd ceidwaid yr iaith a'r genedl, ac ar ôl cyhoeddi Adroddiad 1847
daeth Cymreictod ac Ymneilltuaeth yn anwahanadwy.

Yn sgîl sefydlu 'Y Gymdeithas er Ehangu Darpariaeth Eglwysig' yn esgobaeth
Llandaf ym 1850, cafwyd nifer o ddatblygiadau adeiladol o safbwynt y ddarpariaeth Gymraeg. Serch hynny, methiant fu ymdrech yr Eglwys i fagu delwedd
wir Gymreig yn ail hanner y ganrif oherwydd na fedrai gystadlu â'r ddelwedd
rymus o Gymreictod a feddai'r Ymneilltuwyr. Yr oedd yr Esgob Ollivant yn
fwy Cymreig ei gefndir ac yn fwy ymwybodol o'r problemau ieithyddol na'i
ragflaenydd, neu o leiaf fe roddai'r argraff ei fod. Ond er gwaethaf nifer o ddatgan-
iadau o blaid y Gymraeg, dengys ei areithiau mai'r hyn a ddymunai oedd unffurf-
iaeth ieithyddol. Ystyriai mai problem dros dro oedd y Gymraeg, anghyfleustra
i'w goddef hyd nes i bawb ddysgu Saesneg. Drwy gydol y 1850au a'r 1860au,
beirniadwyd Ollivant am ei agwedd anghyson at yr ymdrech i Gymreigio'r esgobaeth. Daeth i wrthdrawiad â'r eglwyswyr Cymreig yn sir Fynwy wrth i gwestiwn

---

[10] I. Jenkins, 'The Church in Industrial Rhymney, 1800–50', *Journal of the Historical Society of the Church in Wales*, 16 (1966), 77–87.

[11] I. G. Jones and D. Williams (eds.), *The Religious Census of 1851, Vol. 1: South Wales* (Cardiff, 1976).

[12] *Report of the Commissioners of Inquiry*, 1847, 2, 297–302.

Yr Eglwys Gymraeg, Aber-carn. (*Drwy ganiatâd Cyhoeddiadau Yr Eglwys yng Nghymru.*)

The Welsh Church, Aber-carn. (*By permission of Church in Wales Publications.*)

yr iaith godi yng nghyswllt amryw o eglwysi yn y blynyddoedd hyn, er enghraifft, yn Llan-ffwyst, Rhisga a Thredegar. Credai ei wrthwynebwyr na wnaethai ddigon o ymdrech i wneud iawn am y driniaeth a gawsai'r Cymry gan yr Eglwys yn y blynyddoedd blaenorol. Mewn llythyr maith at y *Star of Gwent*, meddai 'Glanhirllyn' (Benjamin Hall, mae'n debyg):

> ... the only compensation at all which has been made to the Welsh people for this ... aggression upon their ancient religious rights has emanated from ... the Llandaff Church Extension Society ... by which means sums ... have been granted towards making provision ... for the performance of Welsh services in schoolrooms ... ill-adapted for such a purpose ... Can it be a source of surprise that they should have left the Establishment in disgust and taken shelter under the ever advancing banner of Dissent?[13]

Hyd yn oed mor ddiweddar â'r 1880au yr oedd y ddarpariaeth ar gyfer addolwyr Cymraeg ymhell o fod yn gyflawn. Yn sir Fynwy cafwyd gwrthdaro yn sgîl penodi offeiriad Cymraeg ei iaith ym mhlwyf y Goetre ym 1886, a bu'n rhaid sefydlu Comisiwn Eglwysig i gymodi rhwng Ollivant a'r plwyfolion lleol. Ond at ei gilydd nid oedd yr iaith yn bwnc mor llosg yn yr Eglwys yn y sir erbyn hynny. I raddau helaeth cawsai Ollivant ei ddymuniad o weld y problemau ymarferol yn lleihau wrth i'r iaith encilio. Eto i gyd, er bod agwedd yr Eglwys at yr iaith yn fwy cadarnhaol a'r ddarpariaeth ar gyfer plwyfolion Cymraeg yn well erbyn ail hanner y ganrif, nid oedd wedi llwyddo i ddiwallu'r anghenion. Hwyrach fod argyfwng 1862–3, pan drosglwyddwyd eglwys Aber-carn i ofal y Methodistiaid Calfinaidd, yn symbol amserol o fethiant yr Eglwys i adennill y boblogaeth Gymraeg. Yn sicr, yr oedd y rheini a gredai mai'r Gymraeg oedd yr unig wir gyfrwng i annerch yr Hollalluog yn colli'r dydd o fewn yr Eglwys yn sir Fynwy. Ond nid oedd yr Ymneilltuwyr heb eu problemau ychwaith.

Yr oedd 1862, blwyddyn datrys problem iaith eglwyswyr Aber-carn, yn ddechrau degad o newid sylweddol i'r ardal gyfan. Pe bai rhaid dewis un cyfnod a welsai grisialu llawer o'r dylanwadau mwyaf arwyddocaol o safbwynt y Gymraeg a'r gymdeithas, mae'n debyg mai'r ysbaid rhwng Cyfrifiadau 1861 a 1871 fyddai hwnnw. Dyma'r cyfnod pan wasgai dylanwad masnach gydwladol ar weithfeydd haearn blaenau'r cymoedd. Rhaid oedd iddynt ymateb i ofynion technoleg newydd, a phroses boenus oedd honno. Dioddefodd sawl ardal ddirwasgiad enbyd, a chollodd rhai mannau (fel y Blaenau, lle bu'r gweithfeydd yn segur rhwng 1862 a 1872) gyfran helaeth o'u poblogaeth. Ond wrth i'r diwydiant haearn wynebu argyfwng, yr oedd y diwydiant glo ager ar gynnydd. Yn is i lawr y cymoedd, suddwyd pyllau dyfnach, codwyd pentrefi o'u cwmpas, a rheilffyrdd i'w cysylltu, ac yn y rhannau hynny yr oedd y mewnfudo'n parhau. Y mae effaith y newidiadau hyn ar batrwm symudiadau'r boblogaeth yn allweddol wrth ymdrin â hanes yr iaith. Yn wahanol i hanner cyntaf y ganrif, pan ddeuai mwyafrif y mewnfudwyr i sir Fynwy o rannau eraill o Gymru, am y tro cyntaf yn awr deuai cyfran uwch o'r newydd-ddyfodiaid o Loegr. Yr oedd y ffaith fod twf diwydiannol enfawr yn digwydd yn sir Forgannwg yn yr un

---

[13] *Star of Gwent*, 18 February 1854.

cyfnod yn dylanwadu ar gyfansoddiad y mewnfudo i sir Fynwy. Erbyn hyn, tuedd y mewnfudwyr o orllewin Cymru oedd ymsefydlu yng nghymoedd Morgannwg yn hytrach nag yng nghymoedd Mynwy, ac ar yr un pryd câi llawer o Gymry sir Fynwy eu denu i Gwm Rhondda ac i fannau eraill yn sir Forgannwg yn ogystal ag i'r Amerig, Awstralia a mannau pellennig eraill.

Felly, yr oedd dwy elfen yn tanseilio'r gymdeithas a oedd wedi dechrau ymsefydlu yng nghymoedd Gwent yn ystod y blynyddoedd blaenorol—cyfnod o ddeng mlynedd ar hugain neu ragor—sef, ar y naill law, mewnfudo gwŷr a gwragedd di-Gymraeg, ac ar y llall, allfudo Cymry Cymraeg. Hyd yn hyn, ni chafwyd astudiaeth ystadegol i gadarnhau'r dystiolaeth a gesglais wrth ymdrin â'r pwnc hwn mewn man arall[14] ond, yn sicr, teimlai trigolion sir Fynwy eu bod yn byw yn ystod cyfnod o drawsnewid mawr. Gellir synhwyro ymdeimlad o argyfwng wrth ddarllen eu sylwadau. Sonnir am 'ugeiniau o filoedd' o fewnfudwyr yn dod â'r iaith Saesneg i'r sir fel 'trên ruthrol, tanllyd yn prysuro ymlaen'; am y Saesneg 'yn dyfod yn genllif arnom' a 'Mynwy yn agos cael ei lanw â Saesneg ac â Saeson'. Ar yr un pryd ceir adroddiadau am 'ymfudo a sôn am ymfudo' a gresynu at '. . . y cyfnewidiad difrifol i'r eithaf. Cymry yn ymadael wrth yr ugeiniau, a'r Scotch, Irish, Cornish a phob "trash" yn dyfod yn eu lle'.[15] Adlewyrcha'r sylwadau hyn yr ofn a deimlid wrth i'r Saesneg ennill tir yn yr ardal, ond nid yr effaith ar yr iaith Gymraeg oedd yr unig bryder. I grefyddwyr yn arbennig, yr oedd rhywbeth amgenach yn peri gofid wrth i golledion eraill ddod yn sgîl colli'r iaith. Fel y dywedodd y Parch. Thomas Rees, Cendl, yn ei araith gerbron cyfarfod o'r Undeb Gynulleidfaol ym Mryste ym 1865:

> Englishmen, English capital and enterprise, English customs and unhappily, English vices, are rushing in upon us like mighty, irresistible torrents carrying away before them our ancient language, social habits, and even our religious customs and influence over the masses.[16]

Nid yr iaith yn unig a oedd dan fygythiad, ond crefydd a moesoldeb yn ogystal. Ystyrid y mewnfudwyr yn hebryngwyr anfoes a llygredd, yn rhegwyr digrefydd a fyddai'n dinistrio traddodiad crefyddol y Cymry. Yng ngeiriau William Williams (Myfyr Wyn), y dychanwr craff o Sirhywi:

> Mae cymoedd glofaol a gweithfaol Mynwy wedi syrthio llawer o ddigris yn ish nag o'n nhw . . . yn achos fod cymaint o fforinars wedi emigrato o Wlad yr Ha, Dyfnaint a pharthau eraill. Hwynt hwy sydd yn cyflawni mwyaf o droseddau yno, a hwynt hwy sydd yn difwyno cymeriad moesol a chyntefig y tir . . .[17]

---

[14] Sian Rhiannon Williams, 'Rhai Agweddau Cymdeithasol ar Hanes yr Iaith Gymraeg yn Ardal Ddiwydiannol Sir Fynwy yn y Bedwaredd Ganrif ar Bymtheg' (traethawd Ph. D. Prifysgol Cymru, 1985). Gweler yn arbennig Rhan I, penodau 2 a 3.

[15] Daw cyfeiriadau'r paragraff hwn o adroddiadau amrywiol gan ohebwyr i'r cylchgronau enwadol: *Y Tyst Cymreig*, 29 Mehefin 1867, 30 Ebrill 1863; *Seren Cymru*, 18 Medi 1863; *Y Diwygiwr*, Tachwedd 1865.

[16] T. Rees, 'Congregational Churches and the English Population in Wales', yn T. Rees, *Miscellaneous Papers* (London, 1867), t. 86.

[17] W. Williams (Myfyr Wyn), 'Llythyra Newydd gan Fachan Ifanc', Llith V yn David Williams (Myfyr Ddu) (gol.), *Cân, Llên a Gwerin* (Aberdâr, 1908).

Yn nhyb y sylwebyddion hyn, âi nodweddion cenedlaethol law-yn-llaw â'r iaith.
Iaith sanctaidd oedd y Gymraeg, iaith aruchel a weddai i bwrpas dwyfol megis
gweddïo a chanu mawl i Dduw. Wrth i'r iaith honno gael ei gwthio o'r neilltu,
byddai'r Cymry'n sicr o gael eu llygru gan y dylanwadau drwg a ddeuai yn
sgîl goruchafiaeth y Saesneg:

> Look for a moment at those districts where the Welsh language has been supplanted
> by the English tongue. The inhabitants have degenerated in body and mind ...
> and religion is like the shadow of a shadow,[18]

meddai Dr E. Pan Jones o flaen cynulliad o delynorion a gwladgarwyr yn Llanofer ym 1869. Atseiniwyd ei sylw sawl gwaith yn ystod y ganrif wrth i grefyddwyr
resynu at y ffordd yr oedd nodweddion y Saeson, 'anturiaeth fasnachol ac anfoes-
oldeb cyffredinol', yn dod yn sgîl y newid ieithyddol i ddiorseddu nodweddion
cenedlaethol y Cymry Cymraeg, sef 'gwres teimlad, crefyddoldeb, moesoldeb
a chareidd-dra'.[19]

Nid ffenomen unigryw i'r bedwaredd ganrif ar bymtheg oedd yr ymdeimlad
fod cysylltiad organig rhwng y Gymraeg a chrefydd, ond cred a wreiddiwyd
yn ddwfn yng nghof hanesyddol y Cymry.[20] Erbyn y 1860au, fodd bynnag,
yr oedd y gred hon wedi magu arwyddocâd cymdeithasol a gwleidyddol yn
y gymdeithas ddiwydiannol. Dwysáwyd yr argyfwng ieithyddol gan y cysylltiad
a wnaethpwyd rhwng yr iaith a chrefydd, a daeth yn nodwedd a fyddai'n effeithio
ar y berthynas rhwng y boblogaeth ddi-Gymraeg a'r Cymry Cymraeg am sawl
cenhedlaeth. Argyfwng i'r Ymneilltuwyr, yn anad neb, oedd hwnnw, ac fe'i
achoswyd gan drawsnewid ieithyddol y 1860au. Erbyn hyn yr oeddynt mor
agos gysylltiedig ag achos y Gymraeg fel na fedrent osgoi wynebu dilema gwirion-
eddol wrth i'r iaith a amddiffynnai eu crefydd ddod dan fygythiad.

Gwraidd yr anhawster oedd y ddeuoliaeth a fodolai yn agwedd crefyddwyr
yr oes at yr iaith Saesneg. Ar y naill law, Saesneg oedd iaith addysg oleuedig,
masnach a llwyddiant gwladwriaethol. Yn ddigon naturiol credent ei bod yn
angenrheidiol i'w plant gael y cyfle gorau mewn bywyd, ac os oedd y Cymry
am fod yn gyfartal â'r Saeson rhaid oedd iddynt gystadlu ar eu hamodau hwy.
Ar y llaw arall, ystyrid y Saesneg yn iaith llygredd ac anfoes, ac ofnid ei dylanwad
ar foesau'r genhedlaeth ifanc wrth iddi ledaenu yn eu plith. Ceisiwyd datrys
y sefyllfa ddryslyd hon drwy neilltuo'r Gymraeg i fyd crefydd: rhwydd hynt
i'r Saesneg arglwyddiaethu mewn meysydd eraill, ond y Gymraeg fyddai iaith
popeth crefyddol.

Credid am gyfnod hir y byddai'r rhesymeg hwn nid yn unig yn diogelu eneid-
iau'r Cymry ifainc ond dyfodol y Gymraeg yn ogystal. 'Tra mai'r Gymraeg
yw iaith yr efengyl', meddid, 'ni fydd i Dduw adael iddi ddiffodd.'[21] Parhaodd
y syniad hwn ymysg crefyddwyr sir Fynwy hyd yn oed pan oedd realiti'r sefyllfa
ieithyddol yn wahanol iawn, ac er bod yr ewyllys yno mewn gair, nid felly
mewn gweithred. Profodd yn amhosibl cynnal y Gymraeg ym myd crefydd ar

---

[18] *Star of Gwent*, 30 October 1869.
[19] *Y Diwygiwr*, Gorffennaf 1868.
[20] Gweler, er enghraifft, G. Williams, *Religion, Language, and Nationality in Wales* (Cardiff, 1979), tt. 1–33.
[21] *Seren Cymru*, 4 Mawrth 1864.

ôl ei halltudio o bob maes arall, a hyd yn oed cyn y 1860au yr oedd y Saesneg wedi treiddio'n bell i fyd y cysegr sancteiddiolaf.

Gellir olrhain gwreiddiau'r duedd hon yn ôl i ddyddiau cynnar Ymneilltuaeth sir Fynwy. Gosodai Coleg y Bedyddwyr yn y Fenni (1807–36, a symudwyd wedyn i Bont-y-pŵl), megis y gwnaeth yr athrofa gyntaf ym Mhen-y-garn (1734– 60), bwyslais mawr ar hyfforddi gweinidogion yn yr iaith Saesneg. Mae'r rhestr o feibion y capeli Cymraeg a aeth i'r weinidogaeth Saesneg yn faith, ac yn eu plith ceir gwŷr hyddysg yn y diwylliant Cymraeg fel y Parch. D. Rhys Stephen (Gwyddonwyson).[22] Yn fuan iawn sefydlwyd yr arfer o gynnal gwasanaethau Saesneg mewn capeli Cymraeg (yn aml er mwyn codi arian), a cheir amryw o enghreifftiau o weinidogion yn pregethu yn Saesneg er mwyn plesio'r lleiafrif na ddeallai Gymraeg.[23] Yr oedd Ysgolion Sul yr Ymneilltuwyr yn sir Fynwy yn dysgu Saesneg yn y 1840au, fel y dengys tystiolaeth Comisiwn Addysg 1847.[24] Felly, hyd yn oed cyn iddynt deimlo effaith y mewnlifiad mawr o Saeson, nid oedd yr Ymneilltuwyr a gollfarnai eu gwrthwynebwyr Eglwysig mor hallt am eu Seisnigrwydd yn hollol ddi-fai yn hyn o beth ychwaith.

Wrth gwrs bu peth galw am bregethu Saesneg mor gynnar â'r 1820au a'r 1830au, a sefydlwyd eglwysi i gyflenwi'r fath angen yn y prif drefi, megis Casnew-ydd, Pont-y-pŵl a Thredegar. Ceir, yn wir, nifer o enghreifftiau o eglwysi Saesneg yn methu ac yn gorfod troi yn ôl at y Gymraeg, a hyd yn oed ar ôl eu sefydlu mewn pentrefi diwydiannol (fel Abersychan, er enghraifft) buont am flynyddoedd yn llawer llai niferus eu haelodaeth na'r capeli Cymraeg. Ond erbyn 1853 yr oedd Ymneilltuwyr sir Fynwy ar flaen y gad ·yn y mudiad i sefydlu achosion Saesneg. Yn y flwyddyn honno cynhaliwyd cynhadledd ar y pwnc yng Nghendl, o dan arweiniad y Parch. Thomas Rees, prif ysgogydd yr ymgyrch yn ystod y blynyddoedd nesaf.[25] Ei ddadl ef a'i debyg oedd bod y Saesneg yn sicr o oroesi yn y pen draw ac y dylai'r eglwysi, felly, ragweld hynny a pharatoi mewn pryd er mwyn amddiffyn eu treftadaeth grefyddol. Ni ellir amau dilysrwydd yr ymdeimlad cryf o ddyletswydd at y Saeson a'r awydd i rannu gweledigaeth â'r rheini na chawsai (yn nhyb y Cymry) yr un breintiau crefyddol yn rhan gynhenid o'u magwraeth. Ni ellir dadlau ychwaith nad oedd angen darparu gwasanaethau Saesneg ar gyfer mewnfudwyr mewn llawer man. Yn wir, lle bynnag y cyflenwid angen penodol cynulleidfa o Saeson a Chymry di-Gymraeg yr oedd gwaith y mudiad yn llwyddiannus ac yn tystio i gryfder ac afiaith Ymneill-tuaeth Gymraeg. Ond ei gwendid, o ran sicrhau dyfodol y Gymraeg, oedd y ffaith iddi fynd yn genhadaeth ffanatig bron, a'r enwadau yn cystadlu am y gorau â'i gilydd i sefydlu achosion Saesneg ym mhob tref a phentref, heb fod angen yn aml, a hynny ar draul y gynulleidfa Gymraeg leol.

Cymry Cymraeg neu fewnfudwyr Saesneg a oedd wedi dysgu Cymraeg oedd sefydlwyr yr achosion Saesneg yn sir Fynwy. Cyfaddefodd Thomas Rees:

> It requires not a small amount of the grace of self-denial to persuade a dozen

[22] *Y Bywgraffiadur Cymreig hyd 1940* (Llundain, 1953), t. 866.
[23] T. Rees a J. Thomas, *Hanes Eglwysi Annibynol Cymru* (4 cyf., Lerpwl, 1871–5), 1, 147.
[24] *Report of the Commissioners of Inquiry . . . 1847*, 2, 289.
[25] J. Thomas, *Cofiant y Parch Thomas Rees DD* (Dolgellau, 1888); *Y Diwygiwr*, Ebrill 1854.

or twenty of the most intelligent, respectable and wealthy members to separate and form the nucleus of an English cause.[26]

Erbyn 1867 yr oedd tystiolaeth fod dulliau'r Gymdeithas Genhadol Gartrefol o weithredu yn cael effaith andwyol ar yr eglwysi Cymraeg. Mewn papur a gyflwynwyd gerbron Cyfarfod Chwarter yr Annibynwyr yn y Farteg y flwyddyn honno, galwodd y Parch. D. Hughes am drefn newydd a fyddai'n sicrhau na fyddai'r capeli Cymraeg yn dioddef oherwydd y baich a osodwyd arnynt o orfod ffurfio a chynnal 'moeth-eglwysi' Saesneg. Beirniadodd y gorawydd i sefydlu eglwysi Saesneg newydd ac i droi capeli Cymraeg yn achosion Saesneg heb fod angen. Siaradodd yn ddiflewyn-ar-dafod:

> ... yr ydym ni fel Cymry yn ymylu ... ar gashau ... ein cenedl ein hunain, ac yn magu a meithrin yn hytrach yr hyn a berthyn i genedl arall ... Oni ellid meddwl, os oes eisiau achosion Saesonig ... mai Saeson ac nid Cymry ... ddylai fod yn eu gwneud i fynu. Nis gellir mewn un modd edrych ar yr ysbryd hwn o broselytio aelodau allan o eglwysi Cymreig at Eglwysi Saesonig yn fawr amgen na chloddio bedd i'r Gymraeg a'r eglwysi Cymreig yn ein plith, a hyny cyn bod y naill na'r llall ohonynt yn hollol barod i'w CLADDU.[27]

Nid polisïau'r Gymdeithas Genhadol Gartrefol yn unig oedd yn gwanhau'r Gymraeg yn y capeli. Yn aml, byddai mewnfudo yn cael effaith uniongyrchol ar iaith gwasanaethau, a cheir sawl enghraifft o gapeli Cymraeg yn sir Fynwy yn newid iaith dros nos pan ddeuai nifer sylweddol o Saeson i fyw i'r ardal. Fel arfer, fodd bynnag, yr oedd yn broses arafach ac yn achosi anghytundeb ymysg yr aelodau ac ambell rwyg difrifol. Unwaith eto yr oedd yr ymdeimlad o ddyletswydd i droi i'r Saesneg er mwyn 'gwareiddio a chrefyddoli' Saeson yn amlwg yn y dadleuon. Wrth feirniadu'r mewnfudwyr a oedd 'yn difwyno cymeriad moesol a chynhefig y tir', yr oedd Myfyr Wyn yr un mor hallt wrth gystwyo'r Cymry a oedd yn 'aberthu eu capeli a'u hiaith i draethu'r efengyl iddynt ...' Gwell ganddynt hynny, meddai, na gadael i'r mewnfudwyr 'fyned ar ddisberod bythol yn eu rhyfyg pandemonaidd.' 'Pam', gofynnodd, 'na fuasai'r Cymro, ac yntau'n gwpod y petha hyn ... yn cauad ceg y Sais am ddylanwad gwareiddiol y Saeson yng Nghymru?'[28]

Dengys y cwestiwn eto beth oedd wrth wraidd dilema ieithyddol crefydd y cyfnod. Y gair 'gwareiddiol' yw'r allwedd i'r cwestiwn a'n hymgais ninnau i'w ateb. Yn wir, yr awydd i 'wareiddio' cymdeithas oedd sail ymdrechion yr Eglwys ac Ymneilltuaeth i ddal gafael ar eu dylanwad dros boblogaeth yr ardaloedd diwydiannol. Yr oedd y gweithiwr o Gymro, megis y masnachwr o Sais, a'r gweinidog o Gymro, megis y diwydiannwr o Sais, yn credu os oedd un cyfrwng yn debyg o wareiddio'r genedl (ac eithrio crefydd) yr iaith Saesneg oedd hwnnw. Ar y naill law, fel y dangoswyd, fe'i gelwid yn iaith isel a barbaraidd, ond ar yr un pryd fe'i hystyrid yn iaith aruchel a goleuedig a oedd yn prysur ennill dylanwad ym mhob cwr o'r byd. Gwyddai pawb fod y Cymry dan anfantais

---

[26] Rees, *Miscellaneous Papers* (1867), t. 87.

[27] D. Hughes, *Yr Achosion Saesneg yng Nghymru: Papur a gyfansoddwyd yn unol â phenderfyniad Cyfarfod Chwarterol Undeb Cymraeg Sir Fynwy, ac a ddarllenwyd yn Sardis, Farteg, Rhagfyr 31, 1867* (Tredegar, 1868), tt. 11–12.

[28] Williams, *Cân, Llên a Gwerin, passim.*

ddirfawr wrth fethu â siarad Saesneg. Yr oedd swyddi breision, menter fasnachol a chyfle cyfartal mewn addysg oll yn dibynnu i raddau helaeth ar wybodaeth dda o'r Saesneg. Wrth ddysgu Saesneg hefyd, gallai'r Cymro brofi i'r Sais ei fod cystal os nad gwell nag ef. Nid rhyfedd felly fod yr Ymneilltuwyr (fel yr Eglwyswyr hwythau), er cymaint eu gwawd o Saesneg 'barbaraidd' y 'trash' o Wlad-yr-Haf neu swydd Henffordd, yn ddigon parod i geisio efelychu'r Sais addysgedig. Yr oedd y frwydr dros addysg, a honno'n addysg uniaith Saesneg i bob pwrpas, yn rhan ganolog o waith y capeli Ymneilltuol Cymraeg o'r 1850au ymlaen. Cefnogwyd nid yn unig y Gymdeithas Frutanaidd a Thramor wrth iddi sefydlu ysgolion yn y mwyafrif o bentrefi diwydiannol y cymoedd, ond daethpwyd â gwersi Saesneg yn rhan o faes llafur yr Ysgolion Sul.

Yn draddodiadol, clodforid yr Ysgolion Sul am eu dylanwad mawr yn cynnal y Gymraeg, a thraethodd cenedlaethau o gystadleuwyr eisteddfodol sir Fynwy ar y testun poblogaidd hwn. Dengys profiad y sir, fodd bynnag, nad oedd y sefydliadau hyn bob amser yn teilyngu'r fath glod. Ni ellir gwadu nad meithrin y plant yn yr iaith Saesneg oedd y peth amlwg a synhwyrol i'w wneud o ran rhoi iddynt gyfle i ehangu eu gorwelion, ond yr oedd yr athrawon Ysgol Sul, ac eraill a ddadleuai fel hyn, yn camgymryd wrth feddwl y gallent gadw'r Gymraeg yn y capel hefyd. Wrth agor y drws i'r Saesneg yn yr Ysgolion Sul, ni fynnent ragweld yr effaith a gâi hynny ar eu capeli ymhen blynyddoedd. Daeth emynau ac adroddiadau Saesneg yn rhan o ddiwylliant yr Ysgolion Sul mewn sawl ardal yn y sir. Yn ei adroddiad i'r *Tyst Cymreig* ym 1871, gresynai'r gohebydd at y ffaith fod plant y Cymry yn adrodd Saesneg yng Ngŵyl De Ysgolion Sul Aber-carn:

> Y mae fy ngwaed yn berwi wrth feddwl na adroddwyd un dernyn yn yr iaith Gymraeg. Gwarth! Pa ryfedd fod y Saesneg yn ennill tir yn Sir Fynwy pan fo'r Cymry eu hunain yn ei chodi i fyny?[29]

Erbyn diwedd y ganrif yr oedd llawer o gapeli wedi medi cynhaeaf eu polisi o hyrwyddo'r Saesneg. Wrth i'r genhedlaeth ifanc ddod yn aelodau cyflawn, yr oeddynt naill ai'n ymadael neu'n pwyso ar y genhedlaeth hŷn i droi gwasanaethau'r Sul i'r Saesneg ar eu cyfer. Ym 1890 rhoddai Wesleaid Tredegar y bai ar y Cymry eu hunain am sefyllfa wannaidd capeli Cymraeg y dref:

> Pe buasai'r Cymry ... wedi cyflawni eu dyletswyddau tuag at y plant, ni fuasent mor analluog i siarad y Gymraeg ac ydyw naw o bob deg ohonynt; ni fuasai Saron, Elim, Adulam a Siloh mor wag ag ydynt; ni fuasai cymaint o addoldai Saesneg ... ym mha rai y mae y Cymry yn aelodau, y rhai na ddeallant Gymraeg na Saesneg yn iawn.[30]

Ni ellir cyffredinoli ynglŷn â'r trawsnewid iaith yng nghapeli Cymraeg sir Fynwy. Gwahaniaethai amgylchiadau o ardal i ardal, ac yn wir ymysg y gwahanol enwadau o fewn yr un dref. At ei gilydd yr oedd yn broses a symudai o'r dwyrain i'r gorllewin, gyda chapeli'r Bedyddwyr a'r Annibynwyr yn dueddol o fod yn barotach i newid eu hiaith na'r Methodistiaid Calfinaidd, ond y mae eithriadau

---

[29] *Y Tyst Cymreig*, 28 Ebrill 1871.
[30] *Tarian y Gweithiwr*, 17 Ebrill 1890.

hefyd yn niferus iawn. Daliai rhai capeli eu tir, gan ymwrthod ag unrhyw newid; ond i'r mwyafrif, mater o amser ydoedd cyn i'r gwasanaethau droi bob yn dipyn i'r Saesneg (er y gallai'r broses hon barhau am gyfnod o ddeng mlynedd ar hugain neu ragor). Yr hyn a oedd yn gyffredin i brofiad pawb oedd eu bod yn gorfod wynebu ar y naill law y bwlch a fodolai rhwng agwedd dwy genhedlaeth at y Gymraeg, ac ar y llall y gwrthdaro rhwng crefydd ac iaith.

Dadleuai'r mwyafrif fod angen wynebu realiti. Gan na ellid atal y cyfnewidiad, eu dyletswydd oedd trosglwyddo'r etifeddiaeth grefyddol a moesol 'i'r rhai a fyddont yn Saeson Cymreig'.[31] Mae'n debyg y byddai llawer o flaenoriaid y capeli Cymraeg wedi cytuno â'r Parch. J. Glyn Davies, Casnewydd, a fynnodd, '... pan ddelo crefydd ac iaith i wrthdrawiad ... yr olaf a ddylai ildio'.[32] Ond yn wyneb y gred fod perthynas gyfrin ac arbennig rhwng y Gymraeg a chrefydd, nid oedd yn bosibl dewis heb gefnu ar ryw elfen ddyfnach nag iaith hyd yn oed. Roedd rhaid dewis, ond mewn gwirionedd nid oedd dewis yn bod. Teimlai llawer na fedrent ildio heb ddinistrio un o hanfodion yr etifeddiaeth y ceisient ei throsglwyddo.

I'r rhai a deimlent felly, yr oedd y Gymraeg yn bwysicach na dim arall. Mewn cyfnod pan oedd gwahaniaethau enwadol yn fwy ystyrlon i'r aelodau nag ydynt erbyn hyn, fe gefnodd nifer o gynulleidfaoedd sir Fynwy ar ddiwinydd-iaeth eu henwad er mwyn cadw'r Gymraeg. Ar yr union adeg yr oedd cynulleidfa eglwysig Aber-carn yn trosglwyddo'u heglwys i ofal y Methodistiaid Calfinaidd, yr oedd Annibynwyr capel Tabor ym Maesycwmer yn gwneud yr un modd. Gadawyd Tabor i'r Saeson a sefydlwyd capel newydd (Zoar) yn hytrach nag ildio i bwysau Undeb yr Annibynwyr a oedd am droi Tabor yn achos Saesneg.[33] Ym Mhont-y-pŵl sefydlwyd achos Cymraeg cyd-enwadol yn y 1880au,[34] a dig-wyddodd yr un peth rhwng y ddau ryfel byd yng Nglynebwy pan sefydlwyd capel Noddfa.[35]

I'r rhai, fel Arthur Mynwy, a ofnai fod 'y sêl yn diffodd' am fod y 'cynulliadau bastarddol o Gymraeg a Saesneg yn pylu yr awyrgylch addolgar oedd mor nod-weddiadol o'n cyndeidiau',[36] yr unig obaith wrth i'r capeli droi i'r Saesneg oedd ceisio trosglwyddo nodweddion yr 'ymdeimlad crefyddol Cymreig' i iaith arall. Mae'n ddiddorol fod y bardd Crwys, a fu'n weinidog ym Mryn-mawr rhwng 1898 a 1914, yn egluro:

> ... mai yr hen eglwysi Cymreig sydd wedi myned yn eglwysi Saesneg yw eglwysi cryfaf ... Mynwy erbyn hyn. Gallasant gario trosodd i'r oruchwyliaeth newydd ryw arddeliad, hwyl ac afiaith nas ceir yn gyffredin mewn eglwysi Saesneg ...[37]

[31] *Y Diwygiwr*, Gorffennaf 1868.

[32] J. Glyn Davies, 'Yr Eglwysi Saesneg yng Nghymru' yn T. Stephens (gol.), *Cymru Heddiw ac Yfory* (Caer-dydd, 1908), t. 54.

[33] NLW, C.M.A. 14702–3.

[34] *Tarian y Gweithiwr*, 3 Ionawr 1889.

[35] Tystiolaeth lafar Miss Sarah Ann Jones (93 oed), Brynteg, Glynebwy, recordiwyd Ebrill 1979. Ceir copi o'r tâp yn Adran Dafodieithoedd Amgueddfa Werin Cymru, Sain Ffagan.

[36] *Tarian y Gweithiwr*, 2 Medi 1886.

[37] W. C. Williams (Crwys), *Pedair Pennod* (Llandysul, 1950), t. 59.

Dywed T. Glanville Jones yr un peth wrth egluro llwyddiant capel Tabernacle, Aberteleri.[38]

Felly, yr oedd y cysylltiad rhwng crefydd a Chymreictod yn parhau i fod yn elfen yn ymdeimlad crefyddol addolwyr sir Fynwy hyd yn oed ar ôl colli'r Gymraeg. Mater o farn ydyw a gyflawnwyd proffwydoliaeth Cadeirydd Cymanfa Undeb Annibynwyr Cymraeg sir Fynwy pan ddywedodd ym 1905: 'When the Welsh language expires, the spirituality and sacredness of religion will expire at the same time'.[39] Yn ystod yr hanner can mlynedd blaenorol profwyd bod cysylltiad agos rhwng y Gymraeg a chrefydd. Erbyn 1905, y capeli oedd yr unig sefydliadau cymdeithasol (ac eithrio yn Rhymni yng ngogledd-orllewin y sir) a gadwai'r Gymraeg yn fyw o gwbl. Y capel, yn wir, oedd noddfa olaf yr iaith mewn llawer man. Ond wrth ynysu'r Gymraeg fel hyn yr oedd crefyddwyr sir Fynwy wedi gwadu i iaith y nefoedd le teilwng ar y ddaear. Ni fu'n bosibl iddynt gadw'r iaith i grefydd heb i ddylanwad y Saesneg, a oedd mor gryf ym mhob maes arall, dreiddio i'r hafan hon hefyd. Pan gyhoeddwyd adroddiad Comisiwn Brenhinol 1908–10, dangoswyd mai Rhymni oedd yr unig ardal lle y goroesai sefydliadau crefyddol i'r un graddau ag o'r blaen.[40] Yno yr oedd eglwys Gymraeg ffyniannus yn ogystal ag wyth o gapeli Cymraeg llewyrchus iawn. Dyma hefyd yr unig ardal yn y sir lle'r oedd y genhedlaeth ifanc yn cynnal yr iaith.[41] Yng ngweddill y sir yr oedd y sefydliadau crefyddol Cymraeg yn dirywio wrth i'r iaith gilio.

Dangosodd astudiaethau gan gymdeithasegwyr iaith ei bod hi'n bosibl i iaith leiafrifol oroesi mewn cymdeithas ddwyieithog os neilltuir un agwedd ar fywyd ar ei chyfer, ac y'i defnyddir yn arbennig at y gweithgarwch hwnnw. Ond er i'r cysylltiad rhwng y Gymraeg a byd crefydd fod yn fodd i gynnal, ac i roi pwrpas cymdeithasol i'r Gymraeg, ni fu'n ddigon i sicrhau ei dyfodol yn sir Fynwy yn y bedwaredd ganrif ar bymtheg. Nid oedd byd crefydd yn fyd cwbl uniaith, ac yr oedd y ffaith mai gan y Saesneg yr oedd y pŵer ym myd addysg, diwydiant a masnach yn allweddol mewn cyfnod pan oedd newidiadau cymdeithasol yn raddol leihau dylanwad y sefydliadau crefyddol. Nid oedd y ffaith fod perthynas mor agos rhwng y Gymraeg a chrefydd bob amser yn fantais i'r naill na'r llall yn y sefyllfa oedd ohoni.

I'r rheini a fagwyd yn Gymry Cymraeg crefyddol yn sir Fynwy profiad poenus oedd colli'r iaith o'r capeli. Erbyn y 1920au yr oedd rhai ohonynt yn dechrau sylweddoli fod yn rhaid i'r gymdeithas gyfan gymryd cyfrifoldeb wrth geisio trosglwyddo'r Gymraeg i'r plant, ac na fedrid ei chynnal drwy'r capel yn unig. Dyma a ysgogodd Evan Price (Ieuan Gorwydd), gweinidog ac aelod blaenllaw o Gymreigyddion Glynebwy, i gyfansoddi'r penillion a ganlyn ym 1922:

---

[38] T. G. Jones, *Tabernacle Calvinistic Methodist Church, Abertillery* (Cardiff, 1954), t. 20.

[39] *Y Tyst Cymreig*, 25 Ionawr 1905.

[40] *Royal Commission on the Church* . . . PP, 2, *Minutes of Evidence*, tt. 335–50.

[41] J. E. Southall, *The Welsh Language Census of 1901* (Newport, 1904); *Census of England, and Wales, Population Tables* (County of Monmouth) PP 1902 (Cd. 1361), Language Spoken; *Census of England and Wales, Population Tables* (County of Monmouth) PP 1914 (Cd. 6259–11), Table 33, Language Spoken.

Mae'r iaith Gymraeg yn marw a'r Beibl yn ei llaw,
A'i phlant yn llawn mursendod ffôl, a'u Saesneg bras di-daw.
Nid gormes llan na chapel yw'r achos, medden nhw,
Ond pawb o'r Cymry yn eu tai'n baldorddi—'How do ye do'.

Hen Feibl mawr y teulu gornelwyd yn ei gell
Mae 'Whist' a 'Bridge' y Saeson balch yn gampau can mil gwell,
Rhaid bod yn goeg ffasiynol, mae'r cwmni'n caru 'show',
A dim Cymraeg i'r aelwyd mwy—'It's out of date you know'.

A wnaiff cartrefi Ebbw roi nodded i'r hen aeg
A siglo crud pob baban bach drwy ganu'r hen Gymraeg?
Ond cychwyn gyda'r aelwyd, fe'i cedwir rhag pob cam,
Wna'r hen Gymraeg ddim marw mwy, na Beibl mawr fy mam.[42]

Erbyn 1922, fodd bynnag, yr oedd ef a'i fath yn lleiafrif bychan iawn yn nhrefi'r sir.

---

[42] *Cymru*, 62 (1922), t. 212.

Ritualism, Railwaymen and the Poor: the Ministry of Canon J. D. Jenkins, Vicar of Aberdare, 1870–1876

CHRISTOPHER B. TURNER

THE Revd Peter Williams, in a contribution to J. Vyrnwy Morgan's *Welsh Religious Leaders in the Victorian Era* (1905), passed this judgement on the influence of the Oxford Movement in Wales:

> The Oxford Movement has never touched the Welsh mind. It did appeal to the sympathy of some of the Welsh clergy—good and earnest men, and strong in their love for *the Church*—who perhaps had come into contact with the originators of the movement in their undergraduate days at Oxford. Such men were Dean Lewis of Bangor; Constable Ellis, Llanfairfechan; Canon Jenkins, Aberdare; and G. Arthur Jones, Cardiff. They made the attempt to raise the *altar* by lowering the pulpit. They have but few followers amongst the Welsh people. The successful leaders of the Church in Llandaff were all Evangelical men, and they have left their mark on the Church in the diocese.[1]

Whilst it is true that disciples of the Oxford Movement were relatively few in Wales, later writers were better placed to acknowledge that its influence was greater than that suggested by the Revd Williams.[2] His statement was in any case rather too dismissive of the contribution made by individual Welsh clerics and it largely ignored the significant impact of Tractarian theology in particular Welsh parishes. The parish of Aberdare, for example, could in itself stand as a lasting tribute to the principles of theology and Church ceremony on which the Tractarians, and more especially the Anglo-Catholics of a later generation, had based their philosophy. A succession of Tractarian incumbents from 1860 onwards had ensured that Aberdare was perceived as an inherently High Church parish. For the people of the parish itself, no vicar could have been more highly regarded than Canon J. D. Jenkins, who held the parish from 1870 until his death in 1876.

---

[1] P. Williams in J. V. Morgan (ed.), *Welsh Religious Leaders in the Victorian Era* (London, 1905), p. 100.

[2] For example, H. L. James, 'Yr Hen Lwybrau', a series of articles for *Yr Haul*, (1932–4). Also D. E. Evans, 'Dylanwad Mudiad Rhydychen yng Nghymru', *Journal of the Historical Society of the Church in Wales*, 6–10, (1956–60), esp. 7, (1957), 92–100.

The living of Aberdare had been in the patronage of the marquis of Bute since 1846, when it had been purchased from the dean and chapter of Gloucester. The second marquis, however, had died in 1846 and patronage was therefore held by trustees until the third marquis came of age in 1868. Twelve other parishes in the diocese of Llandaff were in the gift of the Bute family, but of these Aberdare was the poorest. The fixed endowment was only £29 per annum, to which were added annual payments of £75 each from the Bute estate and Queen Anne's Bounty. Such a financial inducement was likely to attract only the most committed incumbents to an industrial parish which, by 1871, had a population of 37,774.[3] The situation of all the Bute parishes was thrown into confusion when the young marquis, on reaching his majority in 1868, immediately announced his conversion to the Church of Rome. This effectively denied him his right of patronage but, rather than allow this to lapse, he appointed 'quasi-trustees', personal friends and members of the Church of England, to represent his interests. Canon Jenkins, who had known the marquis as a young scholar at Christ Church College, Oxford in 1866–8, was promptly appointed a trustee and he acted in this capacity until his death.[4]

The appointment of Jenkins to the parish in 1870 could hardly be seen as representing any break with tradition. He was only the latest in a line of incumbents who had been influenced, in varying degrees, by the Oxford Movement and its theological derivatives. The succession had first been established when, in 1859, the evangelical vicar, the Revd John Griffith, had moved from Aberdare to become rector of the neighbouring parish of Merthyr Tydfil. His replacement was the Revd Evan Lewis, a native of Llanilar, near Aberystwyth. Lewis was a graduate of Jesus College, Oxford, one of the spiritual abodes of the Tractarians. On his appointment, Lewis immediately set about changing the traditional form of service at St Elvan's Church by introducing Gregorian chants and choral singing.[5] This particular emphasis on chanting had been developed by Lewis whilst he was curate at Llanllechid, Caernarfonshire, between 1847 and 1858. In the middle decades of the nineteenth century, Llanllechid was regarded as a training-ground for Welsh Tractarians, under the sympathetic guidance of Bishop Christopher Bethell. Lewis's elder brother, David, who was also a graduate of Jesus College, served as curate to J. H. Newman and eventually followed the cardinal into the Roman Catholic Church. Evan Lewis left Aberdare in 1866 to become first rector of Dolgellau, and then, in 1884, dean of Bangor.[6]

The new vicar of Aberdare was the Revd H. T. Edwards, yet another graduate

[3] See G. O. Evans, *A History of St John's Church, Aberdare* (Aberdare, 1982), pp. 78–9, and T. J. Dyke, 'Memoir of the late Rev. John David Jenkins, DD', in Jenkins's own *Passages in Church History* (Oxford, 1879), pp. xviii. T. J. Dyke, Medical Officer of Health at Merthyr Tydfil, was a half-brother to Jenkins and his brief memoir is, unfortunately, the only biography of Canon Jenkins. There is also an entry on Jenkins, by W. W. Price, in *DWB*, p. 435.

[4] The Rt. Revd Sir David Hunter Blair, *John Patrick, Third Marquis of Bute, KT 1847–1900: A Memoir* (London, 1921), pp. 102–3.

[5] H. L. James, *The Life and Work of the Very Rev. Evan Lewis MA, 1818–1901* (Aberdare, 1904), p. 8.

[6] Ibid., pp. 5–6; also *DWB*, pp. 551–2.

of Jesus College. Edwards continued the form of church service initiated by Lewis, but his overriding concern was with church provision in the parish. In 1867 he published a tract entitled *Church Extension in Aberdare*, in which he urged better provision of churches and, as an essential corollary, better pay for curates. He pointed out that curates received 'on average smaller remuneration than the workmen in the collieries and ironworks'.[7] Edwards persuaded local colliery owners to contribute towards the restoration of St Elvan's, and the building of a new boys' school and an iron church in the outlying village of Cwmaman.[8] Although less easy to categorize as a Tractarian sympathizer, he does not seem to have attempted any change to the practices instituted by Evan Lewis. In 1869 Edwards was appointed vicar of Caernarfon and later dean of Bangor.

The people of Aberdare generally seemed to accept, or at least tolerate, this 'High Church' approach with little comment. Judging from the local press, it was the Revd John Griffith, rector of Merthyr and a leading spokesman for the dominant evangelical faction within the diocese, who had most to say on such matters. Griffith insisted that the Church should demonstrate a far greater concern for the condition of the working classes and place less emphasis on worthless ritual. He mockingly dismissed the idea that working men 'are to be converted henceforth by carrying wooden crosses, by seeing young gentlemen in copes and chasubles, and by a procession of gorgeously arrayed priests'.[9] Griffith was in almost perpetual correspondence with the bishop of Llandaff, Alfred Ollivant, urging him to be constant in his defence of the diocese against the 'catholic menace from within'. It was understandable, therefore, that much attention should be focused on Aberdare when H. T. Edwards announced his departure. The issue was magnified because this was to be the first appointment to a Bute living in the diocese since the third marquis's conversion to the Roman Catholic Church. As one of the Bute trustees, Canon Jenkins was known to be in sympathy with the Catholic wing of the Church of England. Given his close association with the marquis and his impeccable Oxford background, no one could have doubted that, in the parlance of the day, the new vicar of Aberdare was a 'ritualist'.

John David Jenkins was born in Merthyr Tydfil in 1828. He was the son of William David Jenkins, who allegedly could trace his ancestry back to Iestyn ap Gwrgant, last prince of Glamorgan. His mother was Maria, widow of Thomas Dyke, druggist of the town.[10] His early education took place at Taliesin Williams's school at Merthyr, and from there he obtained a place at Cowbridge Grammar School. Such was his academic progress that in 1846 he was able to enter Jesus College, Oxford. As an undergraduate, reading Literae Humaniores, he tried on several occasions for the Pusey and Ellerton Hebrew Scholarship. He was unsuccessful but, on the last occasion, the eminent Dr E. B. Pusey presented him with a donation of books, to the value of £10, as a reward for

---

[7] *Cardiff and Merthyr Guardian*, 3 May 1867.

[8] R. O. Roberts, 'The Life and Work of Dean Henry Thomas Edwards 1837–94', Trans. Caernarfonshire Hist. Soc., 40 (1979), 135–60 (p. 142).

[9] Revd J. Griffith, *Re-union with Rome; Convocation and Ritualism* (Merthyr Tydfil, 1868), p. 18.

[10] *Tarian y Gweithiwr*, 17 November 1876.

his sound knowledge of Hebrew.[11] Pusey, perhaps the most prominent Tractarian of his day, clearly influenced the young Jenkins and, probably with his support, Jenkins was elected in 1851 to the 'King James the Second Missionary Fellowship'. Under the terms of the fellowship, he was required to take holy orders and 'proceed to such one of Her Majesty's plantations as the Bishop of London, for the time being, might appoint'. Jenkins obtained his BA in 1850, with a disappointing third class honours, but in the following year he achieved his overriding ambition when the bishop of Oxford ordained him as a deacon.

Throughout his years at Oxford Jenkins was in direct contact with Pusey and other Tractarian sympathizers. Despite the lack of his own writings there is pictorial evidence which demonstrates his theological outlook. In 1852 he was the subject of a portrait by the Pre-Raphaelite painter William Holman Hunt, and the men were said to be constant companions at this time. The painting, entitled *New College Cloisters*, depicts Jenkins wearing garments wholly representative of contemporary Tractarianism or 'Puseyism', as opponents preferred to call it.[12] Notably, his robes were those which would be worn only by an avowedly High Church priest at the communion service, and he wears a stole of black silk over the surplice, a recently revived pre-Reformation tradition. The setting of the painting in the cloisters has monastic undertones and, together with the Gothic ambience, reflects contemporary, if not early, Tractarian philosophy. In 1852 Jenkins was appointed curate to the Revd Alfred Hackman at St Paul's, Oxford. St Paul's was itself a Tractarian Church which had been endowed by Thomas Combe, who was also responsible for commissioning Hunt's painting of Jenkins. Indeed, the painting may have been a parting gift to Jenkins who, in November 1852, was to take up his missionary fellowship in South Africa.

While serving as curate to Hackman, Jenkins compiled a book of sermons which highlighted many of his early theological ideas.[13] Typically, the sermons were composed for the various 'feast' days, but they were, in essence, fairly simple homilies stressing the need for constant prayer, pure thoughts and fear of God. One sermon, however, dealt with the need for personal confession. Jenkins considered it perfectly acceptable that, if a man or woman could not soothe their guilty consciences, then they should confess it to a priest who had the power to absolve them in Christ's name. There is no explicit encouragement to regular confession, but even such guarded support would have agitated evangelicals within the Church, who regarded the ceremonial practices at Oxford as ominous indications of unwelcome trends in doctrine.

Jenkins took up his missionary fellowship in Natal, South Africa, early in 1853.[14] He was immediately placed under the direction of the Revd James Green, rector of Pietermaritzburg, to whom Jenkins was to dedicate his book, *The Age of the Martyrs*, in 1869. The diocese of Natal was created in 1853 and

---

[11]   T. J. Dyke, 'Memoir', pp. ix–x; *Crockford's Clerical Directory* (1870), p. 384.

[12]   J. Bronkhurst, 'William Holman Hunt', *The Pre-Raphaelites* (London, 1984), pp. 105–6. The painting is now owned by Jesus College, Oxford.

[13]   Cardiff Central Library MS 2929, Manuscript Sermons of J. D. Jenkins, Fellow of Jesus College, Oxford.

[14]   Dyke, 'Memoir', pp. xiii–xiv.

its first bishop was Dr J. W. Colenso, a Cambridge mathematician. Colenso was to place himself at the centre of one of the enduring theological controversies of the nineteenth century because he consistently questioned the literal accuracy of certain biblical passages. He claimed, on the basis of his own mathematical calculations, that the early books of the Old Testament could not be regarded as wholly accurate. It is known that Jenkins, together with James Green and others, vehemently objected to Colenso's views and his claim to authority. Colenso was particularly unpopular because of his strident condemnation of ritualist practices in his diocese, and he was particularly critical of the wearing of 'gorgeous-coloured vestments'.[15] The bishop of Cape Town, Robert Gray, on the other hand, was a convinced Tractarian determined to exclude Colenso's heretical and divisive teaching from South Africa. Bishop Gray was later congratulated by sympathizers 'for the noble stand he had made in defending Catholic truth and discipline and in upholding Church authority against any surrender to Erastian aggressiveness'.[16]

It is evident, therefore, that Jenkins continued to demonstrate his fullest support for ritualist practices while in South Africa. There, too, he emphasized another trait of character which was to become his hallmark, an abiding compassion for the less fortunate. As a missionary in Natal, Jenkins served as chaplain to the 45th Regiment and Battery of Field Artillery, and contemporaries recalled many instances of his kindness and concern:

> His influence for good was boundless, and while he tried to get a half-tipsy soldier unnoticed into barracks at night, he would the next day, by loving remonstrance, induce him to take the pledge of total abstinence.
>
> He also worked with me well with the soldiers' wives, supporting my endeavours to induce them to save their money, and make and mend for their children, instead of spending it in folly, and alas, in many cases in drink.[17]

Jenkins was made canon of the cathedral church at Pietermaritzburg in 1856, but continued to act as chaplain to the armed forces before, in 1858, he was forced to leave South Africa through ill health. It was this illness which led to his early death in 1876, for he was suffering from the incipient stages of cancer of the liver. His final act before leaving Natal was to donate the £250 he had received as military chaplain to the dean and chapter to support studentships in divinity. This generous gesture was made in spite of continuous financial difficulties of his own.

In 1859 Jenkins returned to Oxford where he obtained a number of academic posts, including that of dean of Jesus College in 1865 and, later, bursar of the same college.[18] He devoted time to literary pursuits, mainly the completion of *The Age of the Martyrs* (1869), a history of the early church. But he also indulged his love of languages by travelling widely in Europe. As a result he was able to add French and German to the Welsh, English and ancient languages with

[15] G. W. Cox, *The Life of J. W. Colenso, DD, Bishop of Natal* (2 vols., London, 1888), 1, 105–7.

[16] J. Embry, *The Catholic Movement and the Society of the Holy Cross* (London, 1931), pp. 29–30.

[17] Dyke, 'Memoir', p. xiii; see also *Yr Haul*, 28 (1926), 162–8.

[18] J. Foster, *Alumni Oxoniensis*, 2, 748.

66

Canon John David Jenkins, MA. Oil painting entitled *New College Cloisters* by William Holman Hunt. (*By permission of the Principal and Fellows, Jesus College, Oxford.*)

which he was already familiar. In the 1860s he occasionally stood in for friends as army chaplain to the household troops in London and Windsor, but the greater part of his time was spent ministering to the sick and poor among the railway workers of Oxford and their families, and so great was his commitment to this task that he became widely known as the 'Railwaymen's Apostle'.[19] This activity was related to his links with the 'Societas Sanctae Crucis' (SSC) or 'Society of the Holy Cross'.[20] The society, founded by a group of ritualist clerics in the 1850s, included Pusey, but the first master of the society was the Revd C. F. Lowder. The primary objectives of the SSC were to resist the enemies of the Church and spread the gospel of Christ by mutual sympathy, constant prayer, counsel in difficulties and works of charity. For Father Lowder, the twin ideals on which the society was founded were a defence of true faith, by which he meant a return to pre-Reformation ceremonial, and missionary work. He maintained that the Church must assume a more missionary character and seek to adapt Catholic practice to the altered circumstances of the nineteenth century.[21] The SSC was attacked by some as a secret society which sought to undermine the Protestant Church by the sinister introduction of Catholic ritual. Singled out for particular opprobrium was the society's support for the priestly right of absolution, as put forward in its manual *The Priest in Absolution*.[22] Critics also pointed to the advocacy of celibacy as evidence of Roman Catholic menace, and this feature of the society's beliefs may explain why Canon Jenkins remained unmarried. The historian of the SSC took a different perspective. Writing in the less disapproving 1930s, he viewed the SSC's approach as a means of attracting the masses, especially the industrial masses, by placing the best aspects of Evangelicalism in a Catholic setting. His strategy for successful evangelization was:

> The Lord's own Service held at a convenient hour, the simplicity and tangibility of the sacraments, practical devotions, simple meditations, litanies, lantern services, religious tableaux, classes of instruction all the year round, regular visiting, individual interest, augmented by the work of Catholic nurses, midwives, dispensaries and social gatherings, all these and other efforts made the Catholic movement, as interpreted by the priests of the SSC, a living power.[23]

In practical matters, members of the society, such as Lowder and Father A. H. Mackonochie, organized the St George's Mission, which was a concerted attempt to fuse ritual practices with direct social concern in the slum districts of London. The mission was to achieve some success, though Mackonochie in particular was constantly subjected to persecution and even prosecution by the evangelical Church Association, a group established to maintain the Protestant

---

[19] Dyke, 'Memoir', pp. xvi–xvii.

[20] This section is based on B. M. Lodwick, 'The Oxford Movement and the Diocese of Llandaff during the Nineteenth Century' (Univ. of Leeds M. Phil thesis, 1976), pp. 165–8; also Embry, *Catholic Movement*, pp. 2–10.

[21] Embry, *Catholic Movement*, p. 2.

[22] See W. Walsh, *The Secret History of the Oxford Movement* (London, 1899), pp. 46–79.

[23] Embry, *Catholic Movement*, p. 403.

ideals of faith and worship.[24] Canon Jenkins's contribution to this missionary initiative was to serve, alongside Father A. H. Stanton, another slum priest working from St Alban's, Holborn, as a clerical superior of the Railway Guild of the Holy Cross. The purpose of the guild, founded in 1872, was to promote the Catholic faith among railway employees. Again, critics were loud in their accusations of popery, especially as the guild produced a manual in which was described a form of blessing for the Cross and Cords, and this came to represent the badge of the guild.[25]

How much of Jenkins's involvement with the SSC would have been known to the people of Aberdare is difficult to judge. What is indisputable is that those people who did care must have realized that their next vicar was a man who had retained a close connection with the leaders of the Catholic revival in Oxford throughout the 1850s and 1860s. His influence on Church ceremony was readily apparent. In November 1871 he organized one of a series of Aberdare Valley Church Choral festivals at which 'The Psalms were chanted to single Anglican Chants and the Canticles to Gregorians'. The choir wore white surplices, while the clergy were similarly attired and wore their university hoods.[26]

Jenkins had preached his first sermon at St Elvan's in March 1870. This was some time later than had been expected but was probably due to illness rather than to press speculation that the marquis of Bute was having second thoughts about confirming the appointment.[27] It was a relatively short time, however, before the new vicar began to allay what suspicions there might have been. In November 1870 the *Aberdare Times* could report that, on the occasion of the consecration of the local cemetery, 'our parish is now blessed with a vicar who is a kind and genial man, and it was pleasant to see him with a number of Nonconformist members, joining together in giving a hearty welcome to the Bishop of the Diocese. We trust the worthy Canon may live years amongst us to serve the parish.'[28] His relations with local Nonconformists were generally very good, except when Nonconformist sensitivities were severely exposed, as was the case with the formation of the Aberdare School Board. As vicar, Jenkins had been centrally involved in the formation of a committee to set up a school board, but the Nonconformist grouping, led by the Baptist potentate, the Revd Thomas Price, did not see fit to appoint Jenkins to the newly formed board.[29] They were understandably keen to keep the Church out of state education as much as possible.

The vicar's initial difficulties were not confined to his relations with Nonconformists. Although the Church had made remarkable advances in the parish since 1850, problems, not least financial ones, remained. The improvement in Church provision was largely due to the unceasing efforts of the Revd John Griffith, who was vicar from 1847 to 1859. In 1852 the building of St Elvan's

[24] See O. Chadwick, *The Victorian Church* (2 vols., London, 1970), 2, 308–11.

[25] Walsh, *Oxford Movement*, p. 258.

[26] *Aberdare Times*, 4 November 1871; 1 June 1872.

[27] *WM*, 26 March 1870.

[28] *Aberdare Times*, 19 November 1870.

[29] Ibid., 8 April 1871.

Church was completed and it was able to complement the provision offered by the dilapidated parish church of St John's. In other parts of the parish, St Fagan's was built at Trecynon (1854) and St Lleurwg's at Hirwaun (1858). Interestingly, one of the subscribers to the building of St Lleurwg's was listed as the Revd J. D. Jenkins. In 1864 the Revd Evan Lewis had secured the erection of St Mary's in Aberdare itself, for the specific purpose of holding Welsh-language services.[30]

Nevertheless, the situation which Canon Jenkins inherited was far from encouraging. New churches had been built but the population of the parish had risen massively and provision remained inadequate. In 1841 the population was 6,471 but, with the expansion of the sale coal industry, the parish had attracted large-scale immigration and in 1871 the population had reached 37,774.[31] Nor can it have escaped the attention of the vicars of Aberdare that, in comparison with that of the Nonconformists, Church provision was meagre. Before the building of St Elvan's, the only available provision was at St John's, a mere 179 places, all of which were impropriated. By the 1860s, moreover, St John's had fallen into considerable disrepair, many of its structural problems, such as a collapsed roof, being the result of coal-mining operations in the immediate vicinity.[32] Canon Jenkins therefore identified his first objective as vicar to be the rebuilding of the parish church. He sought to raise the necessary money by public subscription and arranged a Vestry meeting in October 1870 to consider the condition of the church. This, however, had to be postponed due to poor attendance.[33] When a committee was finally formed, Jenkins stated his objectives as not simply the repair of the parish church but also the clearing of the substantial debts of St Elvan's and St Mary's. The latter church had encountered problems when the Revd Evan Lewis had accepted the living at Dolgellau before he had finished collecting money for the building. In fact, he had been forced to sell some of his own furniture to reduce the debt, but the problem remained even in 1870.

The restoration of St John's took place between 1871 and 1876 at a total cost of £900. The canon was anxious throughout the restoration that the church should be returned, wherever possible, to its original Gothic design. It was re-opened for public worship on 24 June 1876 (St John's Day) and the vicar's influence was immediately apparent. Several windows had been replaced with five pairs of ogee-headed lancets, said to be the exact pattern of the 'original Gothic'. The chancel was enlarged, the one window in the east wall replaced with a three-lancet window with painted glass, depicting the Crucifixion. This window was dedicated to the Wayne family, local industrialists and contributors to the restoration fund. The church was also re-roofed and the pews were replaced

[30] Aberdare Central Library, Church in Wales MS, RCH1/19/1–4; also I. G. Jones, 'The Building of St Elvan's Church, Aberdare', *Glamorgan Historian*, 11 (1975), 71–81; idem., *Communities: Essays in the Social History of Victorian Wales* (Llandysul, 1987), pp. 88–101.

[31] *UK Census*, 1841–1871, Parish of Aberdare. The registration sub-district of Aberdare increased from 9,332 to 40,305 over the same period.

[32] Evans, *St John's Church*, p. 48.

[33] GRO, Parish of Aberdare, Vestry Minute Book, P/61/2, 1 October 1870.

with seats.[34] Yet, not for the first time, Canon Jenkins came into conflict with a member of the coal-owning élite of Aberdare. At the time the restoration committee was established, the vicar's churchwarden was William Thomas Lewis, mining engineer and agent to the marquis of Bute, but also the owner of collieries in the Rhondda. Although Lewis, as a member of the committee, had contributed £21 to the church fund, he was clearly unhappy at the way in which the canon had authorized the money to be spent and complained of a lack of consultation. Canon Jenkins, in an unusually vociferous statement, defended his right to authorize expenditure as appropriate. Lewis apparently objected also to the style of the improvements and tendered his resignation as churchwarden. The Vestry expressed its sympathy with Lewis, but the church was completed to the satisfaction of the vicar.[35]

It is difficult to understand why the canon's presence in Aberdare and his conspicuously 'catholic' approach should have provoked so little antagonism among the Nonconformist groupings under the influential leadership of men such as the Revd Dr Thomas Price, Calfaria (Baptist) and the Revd David Price, Siloa (Independent). It may have been that they regarded the town as a Nonconformist stronghold and perceived no direct threat in the eccentric actions of the canon. More likely, they were won over by his 'saintly' character which, judging by contemporary opinion, was acknowledged by all sections of the community. As early in his ministry as July 1870, the *Aberdare Times*, published by J. T. Jones, a leading Nonconformist, had referred to Jenkins's 'well-known kindness and liberality' in providing a tea for the children of the local National Schools.[36] He had shown considerable kindness to an unmarried pregnant woman at a time when the respectable sections of Aberdare society had proved less charitable.[37] He also worked regularly with Nonconformists in the promotion of local Friendly Societies. He was a subscribing member of the Odd Fellows, Ivorites, Alfreds, Foresters and True Britons within months of his arrival in the town.[38] His stated view in supporting Friendly Societies was the desirability of making the working man more provident and independent. So deep was his involvement with them that he was called to give evidence to the Royal Commission on Friendly Societies which reported in 1874. In his submission, he stated that members of the various societies in Aberdare were mainly colliers and ironworkers, but that there were no exclusions:

> The Clubs serve as a meeting place for friends as well as a benefit society, and are conducted with thorough soberness and propriety. The energy of existing members to induce others to become partakers of the benefits seems to me a most valuable element of strength.[39]

---

[34] *Aberdare Times*, 26 February 1876; 1 July 1876.

[35] GRO, Parish of Aberdare, Vestry Minute Book, 1 May 1876; *Aberdare Times*, 6 May 1876.

[36] *Aberdare Times*, 9 July 1870.

[37] Ibid., 27 August 1870.

[38] Ibid., 1 October 1870; 12 November 1870.

[39] *Report of Royal Commissioners appointed to inquire into the Friendly and Benefit Building Societies*, xxii, Pt. II (1874), 28.

He believed emphatically that the efforts of working people themselves were better than patronage from gentry or clergy. Jenkins's support for the societies brought him into close contact with local Nonconformist ministers and their relations on this front were most cordial. This was demonstrated in 1872, when society members and Nonconformist leaders appointed a committee to present a testimonial to the canon in recognition of his services both to the societies and, more generally, to local workmen and their families. The treasurer of the committee was Thomas Price and the chairman the Revd T. Johns, also a local Baptist minister. The presentation was to be made to the canon 'in token of our sincere appreciation of his genial and affectionate regard for the hardworking and humbler classes of society, his devoted care and concern for the poor and afflicted, and summarily of his thoroughly disinterested and impartial goodness'.[40] The presentation was finally made in 1874 'to you as a man, as the vicar of Aberdare, and as the friend of all movements having a tendency to improve the condition and elevate the position of the industrial classes'.[41] With characteristic self-denial, Canon Jenkins asked that the money collected be put towards a library, though it was some years before his wish was finally realized.

The testimonial also acknowledged his important involvement with the South Wales Choral Union. He was chairman of the Union, and Dr Thomas Price its treasurer, in 1872 when 'Y Côr Mawr' entered a competition in London and won a trophy and £1,000, presented by the Crystal Palace Company. The prize was secured on this occasion without a contest, but when, in the following year, the choir met strong opposition it was once more successful. The choir was conducted by Griffith Rhys Jones, 'Caradog', but Canon Jenkins instructed the choristers in the Latin works and he received the cup on their behalf.[42]

Canon Jenkins spent only six years at Aberdare, but during that time it was inevitable that he should encounter the social problems caused by recurring strikes in the volatile coal industry. A particularly bitter and protracted strike occurred in the Aberdare district during the summer of 1871. In response to a wages claim, put forward on behalf of the colliers by the increasingly influential Amalgamated Association of Miners (AAM), the coal-owners had offered a reduction. The owners themselves were well-organized at this time, mainly through the efforts of W. T. Lewis. Inevitably, a strike resulted, but Canon Jenkins was prominent in his efforts to conciliate between the employers and their workmen. The local press, noting his unfailing kindness towards the workmen, declared, 'he is truly the friend of the poor and the needy.'[43]

Another strike took place between January and March 1873, and again Jenkins was to the fore. What was interesting on this occasion was his public stance as compared with that of Nonconformists. Dr Thomas Price, for example, appeared anxious to urge a return to work at all costs.[44] Jenkins, however,

[40] *Aberdare Times*, 3 August 1872.
[41] Ibid., 28 February 1874.
[42] Ibid., 1 March 1873; see also G. P. Ambrose, 'The Aberdare Background to the South Wales Choral Union (Y Côr Mawr), 1853–72', *Glamorgan Historian*, 9 (1972), 191–202.
[43] *Aberdare Times*, 8 July 1871.
[44] Ibid., 1 February 1873.

openly addressed a meeting of the AAM at Newport in April 1873. He referred
to the recent strike at which he had tried to act as mediator, and he spelt out
his view of what might result from the hardship they had endured: 'He hoped
to see the growth of capital in its due and proper proportion whatever that
might be; but, at the same time, he felt still more keenly the exceedingly great
importance of good houses for those who worked, of social progress, and mutual
goodwill.'[45] The meeting thanked the canon for his constant support, conscious
that one of the largest employers in the district and the local Liberal MP, Richard
Fothergill, had asked him to keep out of the dispute. One speaker urged other
religious leaders to follow this example, for 'no truer friend of the mining population of England, Ireland, Scotland or Wales existed in the world than Canon
Jenkins'.

He performed a similar role in the 'lock-out' of 1875. Addressing a meeting
of the AAM at Merthyr in January, he asked the men to consider their position
carefully and warned them that a strike would produce great misery, but he
assured them that 'whatever the result of their deliberations ... his services
would be cheerfully at their command'.[46] He presided over a number of the
union's meetings and seemed ever prepared to join the national leader, Thomas
Halliday, on the platform. Jenkins maintained a high profile in trying to secure
agreement by 'reconciling, if possible, these two conflicting elements, without
sacrificing in any way the self respect of either party'.[47] He was appointed
by the colliers as an arbitrator to preside over negotiations with the employers
and he seems to have been involved in the resolution of the strike and the introduction of the sliding scale agreement.[48]

Throughout the strike, which had also spread to neighbouring valleys, Canon
Jenkins's efforts to relieve distress among the colliers was complemented by
the work of the Revd John Griffith, rector of Merthyr. The two do not appear
to have stood on the same platform, presumably because their theological inclina-
tions were so divergent. Griffith laboured incessantly, on the one hand organizing
soup kitchens and on the other issuing general condemnations of the employers.[49]
But the intensity of Griffith's language would have been viewed by Jenkins as
inappropriate. Griffith was criticized by the local press, who doubted that he
was a genuine friend of the working classes and had never been blessed with
a large congregation of working men.[50] Both men, however, adopted positions
which were different from those expressed by the Nonconformist leadership.
Dr Price argued that no relief, financial or otherwise, should be offered to those
who were intent on prolonging the strike.[51] In Merthyr, Nonconformists, acting

---

[45] *Merthyr Telegraph*, 11 April 1873.
[46] Ibid., 1 January 1875.
[47] *SWDN*, 7 April 1875; 28 April 1875.
[48] Dyke, 'Memoir', p. xix.
[49] *Merthyr Telegraph*, 26 February 1875. Griffith's role in the strike is well documented in W. D. Wills,
'The Rev. John Griffith and the Revival of the Established Church in Nineteenth-Century Glamorgan', *Morgannwg*, 13 (1969), 75–102.
[50] *Merthyr Telegraph*, 19 March 1875.
[51] Ibid., 19 February 1875.

in concert, refused to join with the rector in issuing a condemnation of the employers. They were adamant that the employers' actions were governed by the state of the coal trade, though they could sympathize with the plight of the strikers.

Despite the rector's wholehearted support for the workmen, he does not seem to have attracted the same respect and confidence which was everywhere reserved for Jenkins. At one point during the strike, Jenkins travelled to the Rhondda valleys to meet the colliers and 'at every station, when the train stopped, men, women and children came to the door of the carriage, and seemed not satisfied till they had received a shake of his hand or a kindly word'.[52] Moreover, one of his obituary notices recalled that his compassion for the colliers in 1875 had brought him into open conflict with some employers:

> the rich and autocratic coalowner treated his kindly offices with disrespect, and even insult, and the rev. gentleman sometimes said that there were truer gentlemen and kinder hearts among the miners than could be found among the educated masters.[53]

If the colliers of south Wales believed they had a friend in the canon so, too, did the railwaymen of Wales and England. It has been noted already that he had come into contact with railway workers and understood their problems and aspirations while at Oxford in the 1860s. In the early 1870s he was associated with the attempt to form the Amalgamated Society of Railway Servants (ASRS). The first conference considered a request for admission from the canon and in recognition of his services to railwaymen he was appointed Vice-President, alongside the Liberal MP, Samuel Morley. On accepting this position in 1872, Jenkins was anxious that 'the society would not allow his position to be that of a sinecure. He hoped railwaymen would always claim him as their friend.'[54] He was also active in helping to form an Aberdare branch of the Society, first as an honorary member and later as Chairman.[55] His addresses at local and national level stressed the need for unity among the men, the necessity of providing in health for the times of sickness and old age, and a shorter working day. He gave unqualified support to the proposal to limit the working day and in relation to this he was certain that employers had a duty to their workmen that extended beyond the payment of wages alone.[56] In 1873 the canon was unanimously elected President of the ASRS and he retained this position until his death in 1876, although recurring ill health restricted his ability to attend all the executive meetings. During his presidency the society benefited from his consistent advice to seek 'peaceful co-operation' with the employers. In 1874

---

[52] *SWDN*, 10 November 1876.

[53] *Railway Service Gazette* (hereafter RSG), 17 November 1876.

[54] Ibid., 28 September 1872. For the background, see P. S. Bagwell, *The Railwaymen* (London, 1963), p. 62.

[55] *Aberdare Times*, 11 April 1874.

[56] See, for example, *RSG*, 24 January 1874.

he supported the society's stance on the general election. This involved a pragmatic resolution that the ASRS should vote for any MP, Liberal or Tory, who was prepared to support the Railway Bill as put forward by the society's patron, M. T. Bass, another Liberal MP. The essence of the Bill was a shorter working day, since overwork was said to be the cause of a spate of recent accidents.[57] The defeat of the Liberals in the election ensured that the Bill went no further. Jenkins refrained from making political statements as such, but his views seemed to favour the Liberals. His readiness to speak on the same platform as Thomas Halliday, an unsuccessful Liberal candidate for the Merthyr constituency in 1874, confirmed his political stance on the 'labour' wing of the Liberal Party.[58]

The ASRS, of course, was far from being a radical trade union. Recent writers have viewed it more as a Friendly Society, formed under middle-class patronage, and seeking to improve working conditions by peaceful persuasion rather than direct action.[59] This would have completely accorded with Jenkins's view of the role of trade unions. His opinion was that trade unions were by no means bad for employers, since the men would make better servants if their working conditions were improved. He consistently argued that working men should only demand things that were just, and while they should be straightforward in their negotiations, they should approach their employers with due respect. In his view:

> There was nothing more gratifying than to see every class improving their condition, especially when it was not the result of class pulling down class ... The growth of national prosperity had brought its evils with it, in as much as the proper remuneration of labour had been overlooked ... and employers had no right to make those who served them old men before their time.[60]

Clearly, the ASRS was unlikely to be a confrontational union under such a President, but the union officials were full of praise for Jenkins's skill in defusing difficult situations, especially where allegations of improper ballots were concerned. The General Secretary of the ASRS, Fred W. Evans, wrote this tribute to Jenkins on his death:

> The latter part of his life has been a Chapter of kindly acts and personal sacrifices for the happiness of the working classes, and more especially the railway servants and the Welsh miners, who had long learned to reverence the good man and look to him for kindly counsel and assistance ... Before the society existed our late President was known as the 'Railway Apostle' on account of his ministrations to the sick and dying railway servants, their wives, and families, whom, he quaintly said, had no parish and required someone especially to care for them ... His conduct as Vice President and President of our Society won for him the confidence of all members. He had the greatest faith in the judgement and discretion of the officers and members of the society. It was one of his maxims that the members

---

[57] Ibid., 7 February 1874.
[58] Bagwell, *Railwaymen*, p. 199.
[59] See H. Pelling, *The History of British Trade Unionism* (London, 1963), pp. 76–7.
[60] *RSG*, 7 February 1874; see also 11 October 1873.

knew best the requirements of the society, and their self-government was the only practical and beneficial form.[61]

The general impression was that Canon Jenkins had helped place the affairs of the society on a more organized and stable footing. Destructive confrontations with the employers had been largely avoided and the society had been able to secure a number of concessions from the railway companies.[62] This is not to say that there was a steady increase in membership. During the depressed years of the mid-1870s, membership actually declined. Nevertheless, the society remained in existence and, unlike the AAM, it survived to fight another day.

Canon Jenkins died on 9 November 1876, at the early age of forty-eight. Local newspapers were adorned with typical Victorian tributes, but the warmth which is evident in these notices is unusual for a clergyman who had served only six years in the parish. A recurring theme of the obituaries was his genuine concern for the poor, a concern that was evidently rewarded with the respect and affection of the working classes of Aberdare and elsewhere. One newspaper reminded its readers that at certain times 'as many as a dozen poor women might have been seen waiting at the door of the vicarage, seeking good counsel and pecuniary relief, neither of which were refused'.[63]

The funeral service was conducted by Jenkins's friend, the Revd Griffith Arthur Jones. The business of the town was at a complete standstill from one until four o'clock on the day, and it was said that 20,000 people lined the streets. The service itself was attended by clergymen, Nonconformist ministers, and leaders of the workmen such as William Abraham, 'Mabon', and Fred W. Evans, the general secretary of the ASRS. It must be assumed that those who assembled in this diverse group were not in the least surprised to find themselves at a service in which 'the garments of the clergy were of a somewhat striking description—such as on any other occasion might perhaps have elicited adverse comment, but which under the circumstances were regarded as a not unseemly element of the funereal display'.[64] As a permanent tribute, the ASRS paid for the installation of a stained glass window, dedicated to his memory, at St Elvan's Church.[65]

Although the canon's ministry in Aberdare was relatively short, he was able to influence the affairs of the parish and even of the diocese in various ways. One area of influence resulted from his close association with the marquis of Bute. Jenkins was known to be a regular visitor to Cardiff Castle and to be one of a small number of the marquis's confidants; as one of the Bute trustees, he was instrumental in appointing his friend from his days at Jesus College, the Revd G. A. Jones, to St Mary's, Cardiff. He also appointed, among others, the Revd F. W. Puller to Roath and the Revd John Morgan to Dowlais.[66]

[61] Ibid., 17 November 1876.
[62] Ibid., 1 December 1876 and G. W. Alcock, *Fifty Years of Railway Trade Unionism* (London, 1922), pp. 183–4.
[63] *SWDN*, 10 November 1876.
[64] Ibid., 15 November 1876; *Tarian y Gweithiwr*, 17 November 1876.
[65] *Aberdare Times*, 2 December 1876.
[66] *Tarian y Gweithiwr*, 17 November 1876; J. W. Ward and H. A. Coe, *Father Jones of Cardiff. A Memoir* (Cardiff, 1907), p. 31.

These men were all convinced Anglo-Catholics. In company with such clergy-men, Jenkins adopted a fresh approach to the problems of the diocese of Llandaff after 1870. They seemed prepared to encounter the evils of poverty and bad housing at first hand and to offer direct relief. The Anglo-Catholics were not alone in operating this form of 'outreach', for the Evangelical Churchmen were also active. But, as the *Merthyr Telegraph* had noted in 1873, the Anglo-Catholics had made social concern as essential to their approach as the spread of ritualist practices:

> the Ritualists are no longer timid, modest or squeamish. They go about their work with the boldness of lions, and while the Evangelical Clergy—in Wales especially—are busy throwing stones and dirt at their Nonconforming brethren, the Ritualists are plodding hard, visiting sick and poor, as well as giving instruction to milliners and laundresses about surplices.[67]

The Revd G. A. Jones had argued that Welsh people did not want the Church to offer the same kind of services as the chapels. He thought that working people would be attracted by catholic practices and the reintroduction of 'mystery' into religious faith.[68] But there is no firm evidence that Canon Jenkins increased to any large extent the numbers of working-class communicants in his parish. 'How glad he would have been', it was said on his death, 'could he have drawn them to Christ and His Church; but we must remember how he had to overcome their long prejudice against the Church, and how necessary it was first to gain their confidence.'[69] It was more likely, therefore, that if the Church could claim some affinity with the working classes of Aberdare, it was because Jenkins was perceived as a man prepared to suffer personal privations in his concern for others. As a ritualist, he might have been subjected to persecution, but this did not prevent him from wearing his distinctive cassock around the town. It was said that there was universal regard for the canon's loyalty to Jesus and no one dared abuse Christ's name in his presence. The fact that he was able to obtain the degree of DD, to which he was entitled, by the kind actions of friends who paid the required money reflects his desire to help those whom he considered to be in greater need than himself and the respect which he earned in the community at large.[70]

Not all ritualist clergy could claim the same level of respect. In a most revealing series of diaries, the Revd David Griffiths, a curate of Aberdare, made a telling comparison. Griffiths was far from being a ritualist and his diary for 1880 recorded a litany of complaints against Jenkins's successor, the Revd J. W. Wynne Jones, a ritualist who lacked the canon's concern for his parishioners:

> Visiting the flocks is our weak point. The head of a parish should live in the midst of the parishioners, if he would live in their hearts. This was the secret of the late vicar's popularity—Canon Jenkins. Still he lives in the heart of the

---

[67] *Merthyr Telegraph*, 18 July 1873; see also *Aberdare Times*, 12 July 1873.

[68] Ward and Coe, *Father Jones*, p. 34.

[69] *Merthyr Telegraph*, 1 December 1876.

[70] Thomas Williams ('Brynfab'), *Pryddest goffadwriaethol am y diweddar Canon Jenkins, Aberdâr* (Pontypridd, 1878); also Dyke, 'Memoir', pp. xx–xxi.

people. A Vicarage or Rectory should be an 'open-house' accessible to rich and poor—small and great. A sympathetic soul is a mighty power.[71]

The parish of Aberdare continued to represent the Catholic ideal after the death of Jenkins, and in the 1880s there is some evidence in the bishop's visitation returns that the number of communicants was growing. Ritualist practices such as surpliced choirs and readers and the celebration of 'Gregorian Festivals, Mass Matins and Evensong' were firmly instituted. In 1881 a direct contact with Oxford itself was again established when the Revd R. M. Benson of Cowley led a clergy retreat at Abernant House, formerly the home of the industrialist Richard Fothergill, and he also preached at St Elvan's. Benson was a founder member of the Society of St John the Evangelist, better known as the Cowley Fathers, whose adherents included the Revd (Fr.) F. W. Puller, who resigned his position at Roath in 1881 to join the Society.[72] The Anglo-Catholic tradition of Aberdare vicars was continued by the Revd J. W. Wynne-Jones, the Revd R. B. Jenkins and, as curate and vicar, the Revd C. A. H. Green, later to become the first bishop of Monmouth and subsequently, in 1934, archbishop of Wales. In 1892 the Theological College of St Michael and All Angels was founded at Abernant House and this was to be a training-ground for future priests of the Anglo-Catholic persuasion.

The Anglo-Catholicism which prevailed at Aberdare into the twentieth century maintained a direct concern with the plight of the working classes, whose growth continued as immigration into the area increased. The parish magazine of February 1886 described the particular activities of the Church in this respect, activities which were directly calculated to undermine the social basis of Nonconformist strength:

> The Church of England in Aberdare endeavours to plant her churches in the midst of dense and poor populations, and appoints her clergy, not to minister to a few select, well-to-do people who can afford to contribute to the support of her ministry, but to administer to all whether they attend church or not ... They (the Nonconformists) not only seek to build their chapels in the midst of well-to-do populations, but when the well-to-do people begin to migrate from any given overcrowded locality into a suburban district Nonconformists begin to make arrangements for closing and selling their Chapel that they may build a new one in the rising suburban district with the proceeds. The poor and overcrowded populations are left to the Church to be taken care of.[73]

The success of this approach can be judged by the flourishing Church associations, such as the clothing, shoe and maternity clubs, as well as the coffee tavern movement, which was to prove a relatively successful alternative to the public house. But for all this effort there was only slow improvement in the situation described in the first parish magazine in 1882:

---

[71] UCNW, Bangor MS 1650, Diaries of the Revd David Griffiths, curate of Aberdare, 1877–83, 19 June 1880. For Griffiths, see *DWB*, pp. 1126–7.

[72] This section is based on Lodwick, 'Oxford Movement', pp. 171–80 and O. W. Jones, 'The Welsh Church in the Nineteenth Century', in D. Walker (ed.), *A History of the Church in Wales* (Penarth, 1976), pp. 144–63.

[73] *Aberdare Dawn of Day and Parish Magazine*, 1886.

... the aggregate number of worshippers being about 1,685. There are 590 communicants on the books of the parish, of whom 311 attended monthly. The actual number last Easter was 390, an increase on previous years, but a lamentably small proportion of the professed Church people, to say nothing of the total population of the parish for which the Church is responsible.[74]

Any success which the Church did achieve was due to the respect which local people, despite the Nonconformist preponderance, were prepared to offer it. And it was Canon Jenkins, as much as any of Aberdare's illustrious line of incumbents, who had worked hardest to elicit this response. Jenkins, like other Anglo-Catholic 'slum' priests, had defied his cloistered academic background and was probably closer to the people than the Evangelicals and more in tune with working men's aspirations than most Nonconformists. In many ways his approach was individualist. He does not seem to have adopted the 'missionary' approach of Lowder and Mackonochie, which was simply a more direct form of evangelization. Nor did he necessarily subscribe to the strategy of his ritualist successors at Aberdare, whose promotion of Church clubs and guilds was in reality a novel approach to the traditional quest for an increase in the number of communicants. Jenkins does not seem to have shared totally the prevailing view that social evils were fundamentally the result of a lack of religious faith. For him, it does not seem to have mattered that the working man and his family might not become communicants. In his view, the mission of the Church was designed for the benefit of all sections of society, whether they confessed affiliation or not. Significantly, Jenkins worked more closely with the institutions of working people themselves, the Friendly Society and the trade union, than the majority of his contemporaries. However moderate his opinions on unionism might have been, to be appointed to the presidency of an active and developing trade union was an unique and radical commission for a clergyman. He was by no means a Christian socialist, like F. D. Maurice, but by his conspicuous good works and humility he had secured the trust and affection of ordinary people.[75]

The 1870s were years of transition for Aberdare, as for the valley communities as a whole. The continued expansion of the coal industry and the quickening pace of non-Welsh immigration brought a concentration of new social problems. But in Aberdare, at least, the Church was successful in facing squarely, if not conquering, the challenge presented by second-phase industrialization. Jenkins would have been pleased by the esteem which was accorded the Church by the working classes of the parish. He would also have been gladdened by the knowledge that the ceremonial and ritual aspects of Church service, which he had striven to preserve throughout his life, were to become almost commonplace in succeeding generations. It may have been that by labouring in such close proximity to the working classes, and in such sympathy with their needs, Jenkins had come to realize what Nonconformists and evangelical churchmen had yet fully to comprehend. The advance of secularism among the industrial population,

---

[74] *The Aberdare, Mountain Ash and St. Fagan's Gospeller and Parish Magazine*, 1882.
[75] *RSG*, 17 November 1876.

and the first signs that the Welsh communities were failing to assimilate the increasingly English immigration, meant that it was futile for religious 'outreach' to be directed solely at increasing Church membership by converting the unbeliever. The new challenge for the Church was how to retain its present position and, equally important, how to work for the wider good of the total parish, irrespective of whether the parishioners, especially the poor, were inclined to attend Church services or not.

Voices from the Void: Social Crisis, Social Problems and the Individual in South-West Wales, c. 1876–1920

RUSSELL DAVIES

THE political and religious history of Wales in the nineteenth and twentieth centuries has been brilliantly explored and explained by Welsh historians during the past two decades. The study of politics and religion provides a mass of documentation from which a detailed portrait of society can be drawn, but the social historian must be aware that these are only two aspects of human experience. In order to present a full picture of a society, the social historian needs to penetrate beneath the generalizations in order to capture the particular experience of the individual person. The fears, hopes, anxieties, aspirations, ambitions, loves, hatreds, phobias, neuroses, and desires that were the dominant forces in an individual's life need to be studied so that commonly held concepts can be evaluated. In studying them the historian encounters both the pathos of the human condition and the extraordinary nobility of human suffering, expressions of the timeless problems created by the principal constants of conflict in the condition of mankind—the confrontation between men and women; ambition and ability; authority and the individual; age and youth; and mankind and its God. By examining the particular experience of the individual in the total social context, and by observing as many different experiences as possible, new perspectives emerge to test and question traditional generalizations. The problems of the individual, fraught with compassion, controversy and passion, although given no acknowledgement in the 'official' imagery of Welsh society, are social problems of profound importance which intensified during periods of crisis and dislocation. Their study reveals the savage personal tragedies which lie concealed beneath the superficially placid façades of social institutions. The incidence of bliss reveals that pleasure and happiness, were, like wealth, unequally distributed in society. The family, for example, traditionally regarded as the cornerstone of Welsh society, was also a theatre of considerable tension and violence.

The central role of the happy, contented, Christian family supported on the twin pillars of the authoritative father and the morally-inspiring mother is one of the most forceful images of nineteenth and early twentieth-century Welsh society. Reminiscences and novels such as D. J. Williams's *Hen Dŷ Ffarm* and William Llewelyn Williams's *Gwilym a Benni Bach* present images of peaceful, placid, orderly, happy families in which children respond willingly to the dictates of their parents. In their mind's eye, these authors walked again amongst the loved and loving people who gave warmth and beauty to the first years of their pilgrimage on earth. The visual arts in nineteenth-century Wales, in particular printing, painting and photography, abound with images of the Angel at the hearth and a family at peace. Perhaps the most fruitful and revealing sources for the historian intent on tracing the romanticization of the Welsh family are the popular poems and songs of the Victorian period, and among the most representative of the works which abound in the pages of newspapers and transactions of local and national eisteddfodau was Samuel Roberts's *Y Teulu Dedwydd*.[1] This commenced with the poet's discovery of the contented family:

> Mewn hyfryd fan ar ael y bryn
> Mi welwn fwthyn bychan ...
>
> Y Teulu Dedwydd yno sy
> Yn byw yn gu ac annwyl
> A phob un hefyd sydd o hyd
> Yn ddiwyd wrth ei orchwyl.

The poem is firmly in the romantic pastoral tradition in Welsh poetry which presents a cosy, picturesque, orderly peasantry happily toiling in the green and pleasant native Eden. The secret of the happiness of the family is that, although its members have only a few earthly material possessions, they are in the Lord's keeping:

> ... mae rhinweddol win a llaeth
> Yr iechydwriaeth ganddynt,
> A Christ yn Frawd a Duw yn Dad
> A thirion Geidwad iddynt.

Thus they were kept firmly on the path to their spiritual rewards in Heaven. The fundamental importance of adhering to Christian values and practices in the maintenance of family peace is one of the underlying themes in all the literary works of nineteenth-century Wales which discuss the position of the family. It is the abandonment of such principles by her father which forces little Bell through terrifying ordeals at the hands of the White Slave Traders in H. Elwyn Thomas's *Martyrs of Hell's Highway* (1896). The few volumes which offered some marriage guidance to young couples, such as M. Hopkins's *Cyn ac ar ôl priodi: a'r Fodrwy Briodasol* and Rhys Gwesyn Jones's *Caru, Priodi a Byw*, stressed that of all the qualities a man should seek in a wife the most important was strong religious conviction.[2] 'Ewyllyswyr Da' quoted the scriptures for their graphic warning:

> Na thwyller chwi: ni chaiff na godinebwyr, nac eilun-addolwyr, na thorwyr-priodas, na masweddwyr, na gwryw-gydwyr, na lladron, na chybyddion, na meddwon,

---

[1] S. Roberts, 'Y Teulu Dedwydd', in E. G. Millward, *Ceinion y Gân* (Llandysul, 1983). This also contains a valuable discussion of the broad themes raised here.

[2] M. Hopkins, *Cyn ac ar ôl Priodi: A'r Fodrwy Briodasol* (Denbigh, 1881); R. G. Jones, *Caru, Priodi a Byw* (Bala, 1886). In a similar vein are E. Foulkes, *Y Pwysicrwydd o Fyned i'r Ystad Briodasol yn Anrhydeddus* (Caernarfon, 1860) and J. Jones ('Trefriw'), *Arferion a Defodau Priodasol ymhlith Amryw Genedloedd y Ddaear* (n.d.).

... etifeddu teyrnas Dduw ... bydd eu rhan yn y llyn sydd yn llosgi â thân a brwmstan, yr hwn yw yr ail farwolaeth.[3]

Perceptions and romantic idealizations of the perfect family were not confined to the middle ranks of society, who were keen to advocate marriage because of its role as a force for social control, for these notions permeated the whole of Welsh society. A happy, contented marriage was something which was, justifiably, aspired to by people of all classes. In his very popular 'Dy Fodrwy Briodasol', Watcyn Wyn clearly illustrates the symbolic importance of the wedding ring ('pelydr pur o serch dywyniad') to the ordinary people of Wales.[4] This regard for marriage was not entirely due to the efforts of religious reformers, for there remained a wealth of popular superstition which, for instance, told young girls how to divine future marriage prospects. A plethora of beliefs and techniques existed, ranging from walking backwards three times around a dung-heap or a churchyard while reciting a rhyme to the phallic use of a knife and sheath.[5] But whatever the source of encouragement, the prospect of settled family life had its appeal, and the attachment was seen clearly in popular songs such as 'Y Bwthyn Bach To Gwellt', 'Gwialen Fedw Fy Mam', 'Cartref', 'Gair Olaf fy Mam' and scores of others. Although the tone of these works of popular literature is one of gross sentimentality, the historian, in considering them, should beware of being dismissive or cynical. In their day such works had real meaning and gave genuine pleasure.

But the harsh reality for many people was that happiness was an elusive and ephemeral ideal. Profound pressures and tensions existed in every family. There were tensions in the way parents, in particular fathers, sought to reconcile their authority and the instillation of discipline with the expression of their love and inner feelings; tensions were created by the differing aspirations, ambitions and requirements of husband and wife; and above all, as we shall see, profound tensions were created by financial stringencies. These tensions, and others, were normally contained and suppressed by an arsenal of defence mechanisms which individuals created around themselves. Husband and wife created distinct, separate spheres of influence in which one partner was acknowledged as superior. Many sought solace in palliatives such as drugs and alcohol. Not least amongst these defence mechanisms was humour, a humour often self-mocking but born of a resignation to one's fate. But tensions and frustrations could, and did, become unbearable. The proceedings of the police courts are littered with terrifying accounts of vicious assaults and violent behaviour that took place within the

---

[3] 'Ewyllyswyr Da' (W. Edwards and E. Pryse), *Y Sefyllfa Briodasol. Neu Cyfarwyddiadau a Chynghorion i Wŷr a Gwragedd Er Meithrin a Chynnal Heddwch Teuluaidd* (Newport, 1851), p. 19.

[4] W. H. Williams, *Caneuon Watcyn Wyn* (Wrexham, n.d.), p. 82.

[5] *Bygones*, 29 September 1897; T. C. Evans, 'The Folk-Lore of Glamorgan' in *Cofnodion Eisteddfod Genedlaethol Aberdâr 1885* (Cardiff, 1887), pp. 217–18. Others used more modern methods to obtain a marriage partner. The local press, among advertisements for artificial limbs, eyes and easy-fit steel-less deformity boots—all aids to a bionic utopia—contained advertisements from a young man who sought 'a refined and domesticated young lady of 25' (*Cambrian Daily Leader*, 3 July 1914).

family unit. Wives were abused and beaten, children were abused, assaulted, abandoned, and battered. Brutality, chauvinism and malice were the dark trinity that ruled in many families in south-west Wales at the end of the nineteenth century.

The ruin of the political careers of Charles Stuart Parnell and Charles Dilke as a result of their involvement in divorce proceedings reveals the public opprobrium and stigma which were attached to divorce cases in the late nineteenth century. However, in considering the divorce proceedings which were brought before Welsh courts one becomes aware that, as well as the sense of moral outrage, there was another popular attitude which derived considerable entertainment and fun from the salacious details of the clandestine comings and goings of the defendants. In the case of *Berry* v. *Berry and Carpenter* in 1893, Thomas Isaacs, a Llanelli tinplate worker, achieved considerable popularity among the crowds who packed the court to listen to the accounts of his voyeuristic athleticism in clambering on top of outbuildings to witness the romantic activities of Mrs Berry.[6] During the case of *Blake* v. *Blake and Wadell* (despite the moralistic outbursts of the *South Wales Press*, which rivalled *The Times* at its most self-righteous in the Parnell case) popular behaviour in south Wales revealed far more complex attitudes.[7] The eight o'clock train from Llanelli to London was packed with people called upon to serve as witnesses and others bent on enjoying the trip. The proceedings revealed the claustrophobic environment of gossip and spite that existed in the mining town of Tumble. During the case the details of the love letters sent from 'your sweet curly boy' aroused uncontrollable waves of laughter which swept through the crowded courtroom.[8]

But such cases were exceptions. Divorce was expensive and consequently was not an option available to many people. Historians have been mistaken in assuming that the low number of divorce cases brought from Wales before courts in the nineteenth century is evidence of the cohesion of the family unit. It is not. It is evidence of the inability of people to pay the expensive legal costs involved and suffer the social ostracism that accompanied divorce proceedings. The only option for many people who discovered that they could no longer continue to exist in an environment in which furious hatreds continually clashed was to apply for separation and maintenance orders under the Matrimonial Clauses Act (1878), the Married Women's Maintenance Desertion Act (1886) and the Summary Jurisdiction (Married Women's) Act (1895). That such actions were frequent occurrences in Welsh society is revealed in the fact that the reports of almost a thousand individual cases are available for the administrative county of Carmarthen between 1887 and 1914. The details of cases brought before

---

[6] *South Wales Press* (hereafter *SWP*), 16 June 1893.

[7] For the reaction of *The Times*, P. Magnus, *Gladstone* (London, 1970), pp. 386–91. *SWP*, 27 October, 3 November 1898. It is interesting to note that in each issue of local papers which reported local divorce cases there appeared advertisements for the services of private detectives; see, for example, *SWP*, 12 May 1898. These village Marlowes thrived on the fear and suspicion which were endemic in married life.

[8] *SWP*, 27 October 1898.

local police courts under these acts provide the historian with detailed information about the issues and actions which provoked people to the most extreme
resolution of conflict. An analysis of such cases locates the sources of tension
between the sexes, and reveals the attitudes and expectations which shaped
their relationships. The details of such cases provide a plangent, mournful catalogue of the private stresses and sorrows of ordinary lives.[9]

Several cases which were brought before the police courts of south-west Wales
seemed to confirm the view of contemporaries that the people involved in such
proceedings were members of a degenerate, immoral, drink-sodden underworld
whose worthless, misspent lives revolved around the pub, the lower types of
lodging-houses and the workhouse. Ruth Jones of New Street, Llanelli, had
to deny her husband's allegations that she 'drank gin at night, heard bells and
saw the gates of Heaven'.[10] Susannah Davies of Ropewalk Road alleged that
drink was the cause of her husband Benjamin's violent behaviour; after drinking
sessions he frequently laid out the table for 'my corpse', sharpened knives in
preparation, and wrapped towels around the children's throats and threatened
to strangle them. Among his threats to his wife was the promise, 'I will rip
you up and bottle your blood which I will send to your mother.'[11]

But to blame domestic violence on one cause is too naïve and simplistic.
Drink undoubtedly played an important part in the breakdown of family life,
but it was as much a symptom as a cause of breakdown. Drink served to exaggerate responses to normal disputes and bickerings. A large number of families
from all social groups were split asunder by tensions which were neither caused
nor intensified by one partner's addiction to alcohol. In July 1913 Gwenllian
Lewis of Glanaman took out an order against her husband for his refusal to
pay a maintenance order, awarded to her by a local court, which was £10 16s. 0d.
in arrears. The difficulties encountered in their marriage arose from the fact
that, as a Pentecostal dancer, he believed 'he could not be a disciple of Christ
and serve his wife and children. If he could not worship as he liked he must
give up his religion for the sake of his wife, and he was not prepared to do

[9] The main sources for the evidence discussed in this article are the records of the Carmarthenshire Quarter
Sessions which are housed in the Carmarthen branch of the Dyfed Record Office. The records of the County
Quarter Sessions contain written sentences for the Petty Sessions Divisions of Amman Valley, Carmarthen,
Carmarthen Borough, Kidwelly, Llanboidy and Whitland, Llandeilo, Llandovery, Newcastle Emlyn and
St Clears. These records, which are not complete, provide the bare transcripts of the decision; for the human
story behind each the appropriate issue of one of the county's newspapers has been consulted. Where the
court records make it possible to compare the official transcript with the reporter's press story, the latter
has been found to be reliable. It would appear that one court reporter served several newspapers. In order
to present the details I have concentrated in the footnotes upon the press reports; however, if a reader wishes
to obtain the actual court record, the relevant Quarter Session box should be consulted. In view of the
obvious gaps in the court records, I have resisted the temptation to quantify the incidence of domestic violence.
Further research is necessary in order to avoid what could be misleading statistics. The Government *Volumes
of Criminal Statistics* and *Civil Judicial Statistics* do not distinguish domestic assaults from other assaults.

[10] *Llanelly Mercury*, 12 October 1911.

[11] *SWP*, 15 November 1913.

that.'[12] David Lewis, a butcher of Bryn-teg, Carmarthen, was summoned by his wife Catherine on a charge of grievous bodily assault at Carmarthen Borough Police Court. She appeared in court with black eyes and a 'mutilated face' and alleged that although she had returned with over £25 from Neath and Aber-afan markets, he had beaten her with a horsewhip because she was late. During the case, large crowds from their neighbourhood gathered at the court-room to hear the saga of their marital purgatory. Her statement—'I was struck sense-less, and fell to the ground. I received several blows after I became senseless ... When I came to my senses I found myself upstairs ... He had kicked me upstairs'—was interspersed with bursts of laughter from the crowds. The judge was more sympathetic; David was fined £5 for assault and bound over for six months. The judge also advised the couple to separate.[13]

It is difficult to capture the exact nature of popular attitudes towards wife-beating and inter-family violence. The laughter of those present at the case of David and Catherine Lewis suggests that people derived considerable amuse-ment from the marital unhappiness of others. In some social circles it would appear that wife-beating was an accepted part of married life. In December 1898 two police officers were seriously assaulted by a crowd when they attempted to intervene in a fight between a husband and his wife outside a Llanelli public house. Although some quarrels ventured out from the home into public arenas, most domestic violence was kept within the bounds of the home and there was both a public refusal to acknowledge that the problem existed and a personal refusal to admit to the realities of the abuse. Both attitudes are encapsulated in the warning 'scream quietly or the neighbours will hear'. It was claimed that John Parker, a signalman with the Great Western Railway, refused to let his wife Blodwen out because 'her blackeyes were showing him up'. Evidence of popular attitudes is both fragmentary and contradictory. The popular condem-nation of wife-beaters which found focus in the activities of the *ceffyl pren* conti-nued, even in industrial society, well into the twentieth century. During the case which Mary Edwards brought against her husband, Thomas Charles, at the Llanelli Police Court in April 1895, it was stated that 'effigies of her husband were burnt by people in Pemberton Street', and their neighbours had also physi-cally prevented him from selling the family's furniture.[14] It was clear that his action had gone beyond the bounds of acceptable behaviour. But, if the wife-beater was unpopular, so, too, was the nagging wife. In a culture in which the oral tradition was still the predominant mode of remembrance, proverbs can be seen to represent the distillation of the collected wisdom of that society. Many proverbs offered stark warning against the vituperative loquacity of the female tongue: 'Pwy bynnag sy heb wraig, sy heb ymryson', 'Goreu gwraig, gwraig heb dafawd'. It was even said that dry water and wet fire were as common

[12] Ibid., 16 July 1913.

[13] Ibid., 18 May 1910.

[14] Ibid., 18 April 1895. Among the accusations against him was that his wife had found a bill for 'fancy garters, corsettes, chemises etc.' which were intended for a young lady, and she found something which Mr Howell (her solicitor) said he 'would not like to mention, and he would have to write it on a piece of paper'. Charles was ordered to pay a fine of 10s. for assault and costs of £1 6s. 6d.

as a silent wife: 'Tri peth anhawdd eu cael: dwfr sych, tân gwlyb, a gwraig dawgar'.[15]

The level of violence which existed within many marriages is shocking and the capacity of some women to tolerate years of gross physical abuse is surprising. In analysing the details of separation and maintenance order proceedings, the historian is frequently confronted with the base elemental beast in man. John Emmanuel of Nevill Street, Llanelli, tried to put his wife on the fire;[16] William Jones, a farmer from Carreg Cennen, was committed by Llandeilo Police Court for attempting to use dynamite to blow up the villa in which his wife lived;[17] Margaret Evans of Dunvant stated that her husband Benjamin had 'a curious little habit of leaving dynamite caps about the house near the fire from choice';[18] Mary Ann Lloyd, of Water Street, Carmarthen, claimed that her husband Fred held a lighted lamp above her and her baby's head and threatened to put them on fire.[19] It was inevitable that violence of this kind would lead on occasion to murder. After years of violent and threatening behaviour, David Jones, a sheep farmer of Llandovery, and the son of the Revd John Jones, murdered his wife in 1883.[20] It is understandable that some women subjected to such brutalities followed biblical advice and returned wound for wound, stripe for stripe. Mary Ann Davies of Trostre Road, Llanelli, hit her husband with a poker, and it was a standing joke among Anne Rees's neighbours that they would 'look over the garden wall to see how much crockery was broken' following a quarrel.[21]

The tolerance by married women of the violence inflicted upon them by their husbands is perhaps not so surprising when we realize the profound economic and social disadvantages of women in Welsh society in this period. The overwhelming ideological importance of marriage in all social groups led to the inability of women to admit that their marriage had failed. Beatings had a mental as well as a physical effect. The physical torture had the mental effect of debilitating a wife's capacity to take decisions. Often, the wife's contact with Poor Law authorities and the police served only to increase her feelings of guilt. Any refusal by the wife to carry out the dictates of her husband was interpreted as provocation, and her behaviour was perceived as a threat to the system of male and female prerogatives which underpinned marriage. The main factor which kept man and wife together was the lack of any practical alternative for the wife. A wife had to care for her children. The only place she could turn to was the Poor Law Workhouse and, even when compared with her hostile home environment, this was not an attractive or acceptable alternative. The

---

[15] 'Take no wife, have no strife'; 'You'll find no wife, whatever eyes you seek with,/so good as her who has no tongue to speak with'; 'Dry will water be, fire be wet/Before a silent wife you get' (H. H. Vaughan, *Welsh Proverbs with English Translations* (London, 1889), pp. 171–2, 316).

[16] *SWP*, 18 July 1907.

[17] *The Welshman*, 9 May 1913.

[18] *SWP*, 6 April 1906.

[19] Ibid., 24 December 1919.

[20] Ibid., 14 June 1883.

[21] Exodus 21: 23–5; *SWP*, 1 October 1919; 18 March 1914.

regimentation of workhouse discipline frequently meant that families were split up. Mary Elizabeth Hope absconded from Llanelli workhouse saying, 'I have been a prisoner in the workhouse for two years.' Marina Davies of Pleasant Row suffered nine years of abuse before she was finally forced to confront the alternative.[22] 'Pleasant Row', 'Brynhyfryd', 'Hyfrydle': one continually notices the obscene contradiction between the name of the house and the horrendous, secret brutalities inflicted on the innocent within its walls.

There was a multitude of causes of marital discord, but the most persistent and profound were created by financial stringencies. Interpersonal bonds, which were often stretched taut by disagreements and discord, snapped under financial pressure. Wives deprived of money because of a husband's addiction to drink, his personal intransigence or his abandonment of the family, were forced to live on their wits in order to survive. They took on a multitude of laborious tasks. The experience of several women reveals the centrality of the pawnbroker in the daily lives of the Welsh working class. Any item, irrespective of the personal sentiment attached to it, would be exchanged at local pawnshops. Annie Bourne of Bynea admitted in court that she pawned her wedding ring and the family Bible.[23] Many wives took in lodgers to supplement meagre family earnings. However, the presence of a lodger in a house often served to deepen tensions within the family unit. Many husbands were jealous of the domestic arrangements their wives had to make in order to provide for lodgers, and many resorted to violence as a result of their suspicions that sexual services were secretly offered to lodgers.[24] Some men, however, were anxious that their wives should obtain additional income in this manner. Mary Cottrell of Carmarthen alleged that her husband threatened her at knife-point and urged her to go with other men, something which she steadfastly refused to do.[25] Indeed, many cases reveal in detail that prostitution and venereal disease were widespread in south-west Wales at the beginning of the twentieth century. Louise Williams stated that her husband Henry, a farmer of Dolau Fawr, had brought a common prostitute into their home, kept her there for several months, and frequently forced his wife to share their bed. He also introduced several 'filthy diseases into the house',[26] a charge also made against David Edwin Sheridan Phillips and Frederick Carter.[27] Historians have devoted considerable effort to studying the social impact of major diseases such as cholera, but little work has been done on

---

[22] *SWP*, 23 April 1913. Ironically, not until the profligate waste of life of the First World War were centres such as Lady Howard's 'Marged Fach Welcome Home' established to offer care for mothers and infants.

[23] *SWP*, 25 June 1913.

[24] Ibid., 28 March 1918. Daniel Skinner was accused of assault by Richard Evans, a lodger. In his defence, Skinner replied that although he was quarrelling with his wife 'Evans had no business to interfere between me and my wife' (D(yfed) R(ecord) O(ffice) (Carmarthen), Quarter Sessions Papers (DRO, C.QS) Box 91 (1916). The manuscripts and calendars of the Quarter Sessions do not, unfortunately, provide details of many cases.

[25] *Carmarthen Weekly Reporter*, 18 October 1907.

[26] *SWP*, 3 December 1903.

[27] *SWP*, 21 September 1881; 24 August 1910.

the effects of diseases and infections which had less dramatic effect but which deeply affected many families.

The wives were not the only victims of mental abuse and physical violence within the family. The marriage of Hopkin John, a vagrant, split up on ten occasions in twelve years, and such trauma had profound repercussions on the outlook and attitudes of children. There is abundant evidence of the serious neglect and physical and sexual abuse of children in south-west Wales.[28] In May 1913 the Carmarthen District Branch of the NSPCC[29] reported that, during the course of the previous year, it had investigated 210 cases of cruelty to children, 205 of which were found to be true, affecting 268 offenders and 624 children. The Inspector reported that 168 cases had led to warnings, 19 had been otherwise dealt with, 7 had been dropped, whilst 16 had led to prosecutions and convictions which showed, according to the Society, that 'we are not out to prosecute but to help'.[30] At the Annual Meeting of the Llanelli District of the NSPCC in April 1910, it was stated that the policy of the Society was not to prosecute but to warn offenders. These warnings, it was reported, frequently had beneficial effects.[31] However, there is evidence from Llanelli that, despite the warnings of the courts and the NSPCC officers, neglect of, and violence towards, children continued. William Morris, a former Llanelli and Wales international rugby player, and his wife Elisabeth, were warned in November 1910 for cruelty to their children, and were prosecuted two years later for their persistent neglect.[32] Abuse and neglect of children were not a male preserve. Mary Evans, a 35-year-old widow from Llansawel, was censured by Sir James Drummond at the Llansawel Petty Sessions for her treatment of her three children. It was inconceivable, he said, 'that any beast would treat their offspring so ... [you are] unworthy of the name woman'. For similar offences Mary Phillpot was said to be 'a disgrace to humanity'.[33] Coroners' inquests frequently reveal evidence of the terrible physical neglect of children. Dr W. W. Brodie, the deputy coroner for Carmarthenshire, at an inquest into the death of four-year-old Horace Lloyd at the Llanelli workhouse, was told that on his admission to the workhouse 'Horace seemed to be in a dying condition and looked like a breathing corpse'. At the time of

---

[28] For details of the sexual abuse of children, see DRO, C.QS, Box 86, for a case against John Mayor; and Box 65, a case against David Jones. In the latter case the police evidence is particularly distressing.

[29] The NSPCC was founded in 1884 and was instrumental in securing the passage of the Prevention of Cruelty to Children Acts of 1889 and 1894. The Society organized itself on a federal basis and commenced work in south-west Wales in the early 1890s. See A. Allen and A. Morton, *This is your child. The story of the National Society for the Prevention of Cruelty to Children* (London, 1961), and the Annual Reports of the NSPCC, *passim*. The Society's newspaper, *The Child's Guardian*, does occasionally feature details of Welsh cases. It is difficult to present firm quantitative evidence for the incidence of child abuse because of the unreliability of the official statistics. The Civil Judicial Statistics detail only actual prosecutions, whilst the reports of the NSPCC inspectors, as we shall see, provide evidence that abuse of and cruelty towards children were far in excess of this.

[30] *Carmarthen Weekly Reporter*, 16 May 1913.

[31] *SWP*, 6 April 1910. At the meeting 'a hope [was] expressed that Llanelly, which unfortunately has supplied so many cases of child cruelty and neglect, would give the Society a larger measure of support henceforth than it had afforded in the past.'

[32] *SWP*, 30 November 1910; 3 July 1912.

[33] *Carmarthen Weekly Reporter*, 2 March 1906; *SWP*, 28 June 1916; DRO, C.QS, Box 82.

her death in 1913, Deborah Reed weighed only six pounds, although she was nine months old.[34] The details of the brief, truncated lives of such children are requiems to squalor and cynicism. The reports of the NSPCC inspectors at court proceedings tell of disgusting, verminous households and dirty, diseased, sickly, wild children. Inspector Idris Jones, of the Llanelli NSPCC, stated that he found the children of Henry and Edith Evans frequently on the doorstep of Holy Trinity Church and elsewhere late at night, and that in 1911 he had found them 'living in a pig-sty, not in a house styled as a pig-sty, but in a proper pig-sty'. Though seemingly hardened to the grotesque physical conditions of the homes which he visited, an NSPCC inspector vomited when he encountered an overpowering stench at the home of the Lloyds of Felinfoel.[35]

As with the wives who suffered the indignities of beatings, mothers of the victims of child abuse were forced to take up degrading occupations in order to survive. Mary Ann Jones of Hawkers Lodging House, Carmarthen, obtained a living by calling upon householders and their maids and pretending to tell fortunes.[36] Mary Stewart, and several others, turned to prostitution. When Inspector Jones of the Llanelli NSPCC called at Stewart's home to investigate allegations of cruelty, he found the father drunk, smashing crockery and frightening the children, one of whom was suffering from tuberculosis. Both parents were sentenced to four months' imprisonment with hard labour.[37] In cases of cruelty to children, popular attitudes were clearly on the side of the child. But violence between generations was not confined to the poor; as the editor of the *Carmarthen Weekly Reporter* pointed out, 'cases of cruelty do not come to light in country mansions as we all know'.[38] In 1913 William Rees Howells, a prosperous farmer of Whitland, was sued for a separation order by his wife. Although she had borne his violence for twelve years, she could no longer tolerate marriage to him when he acted violently towards her six children. He was ordered by the judge to separate from his wife and to pay a maintenance order of fifteen shillings. The next case in court was also against Howells. Inspector Batten of the RSPCA charged him for causing cruelty to a pig, and for this offence he was fined twenty shillings.[39] Some cases of child abuse ended tragically in homicide. It appears that many men had very low thresholds of tolerance; they took the most extreme action as a result of the slightest trigger to violence. Unable to cope with stress and strain they simply exploded. In Carmarthen in 1887, and in Llanelli in 1908, three-year-old girls were murdered by their fathers with blunt knives.[40] 'Blind anger' was popularly considered to be the cause. If anger is a factor of such importance in so many forms of interpersonal

---

[34]   *SWP*, 9 March 1910; 5 March 1913.

[35]   Ibid., 28 May 1913; 5 May 1909.

[36]   *Carmarthen Weekly Reporter*, 4 December 1914.

[37]   *SWP*, 11 November 1919.

[38]   *Carmarthen Weekly Reporter*, 31 December 1909.

[39]   *The Welshman*, 7 March 1913.

[40]   The cases are reported in several issues of the *SWP*, the *Llanelly and County Guardian*, the *Carmarthen Journal* and *The Welshman*, December 1887 and September 1908.

violence, then historians need to analyse popular attitudes to loss of temper and examine the strategies which people evolved to cope with stressful situations.

Having considered the violence inflicted by parents on their children, it is not surprising to find that violence and neglect were reciprocated to parents in later life. The Poor Law authorities frequently brought the sons and daughters of elderly parents to court in order to compel them to pay the costs of maintaining their parents. But only a few authorities succeeded in enforcing the court order. In his survey of the *Condition of the Aged Poor* of 1894, Charles Booth noted that, although in east Wales in places such as Merthyr Tydfil, children were willing to provide for aged parents, in west Wales in places like Llandeilo and Aberaeron children revealed a 'callous' disregard for family duties. It is clear that the most relentless, embittered, and persistent current of violence running through the nineteenth century was neither urban nor rural, but domestic.

The details of these individual sagas of misery and despair pose profound questions as to the validity of the real role and importance of several social institutions. In pursuing the details of an individual's life, the historian unearths the fear which underlies human behaviour—fear of illness, economic collapse, unemployment, violence, abuse, neighbours' gossip, vagaries of the weather, disasters at work, vagabonds, the night. These are but a few of the fears that persistently nagged and gnawed at the subconscious of individuals in Welsh society and led to insecurity and anxiety. In reading the popular press of Victorian Britain, one observes with fascination the frequency with which advertisements for instant cures to 'Nervous Debility', 'Mental Anguish' and 'Neuralgia' appear. The statements of mental hospital patients are eloquent, if exaggerated, expressions of the subjects about which common people worried. Religion, commonly regarded as the certain cure for the lonely and insecure, also instilled profound fears—fear of the individual's fundamental wickedness, of the capriciousness of the Devil, of an unsure salvation. These fears were expressed in many of the remarkable outbursts of mass confessions which featured prominently in the 1904–5 Revival services. Such confessions, and the hymns which were popular during the Revival, were not only paeans of praise to man's Creator, they were also expressions of the anxieties and loneliness which many individuals experienced in their disenchanted world.

Tom Ellis versus Lloyd George: the Fractured Consciousness of Fin-de-siècle Wales

KENNETH O. MORGAN

MID-VICTORIAN England, the period between the Corn Laws crisis of 1846 and the passage of the 1867 Reform Act, was once dubbed by W. L. Burn 'the age of equipoise'. To Bagehot, that paradigm mid-Victorian, writing in 1857, these years were 'the day after the feast'. Mid-Victorian Wales, too, appears at first sight to present a deceptively tranquil interlude in the twenty years that followed the excitements of radical Merthyr, Rebecca and Chartism. On the surface, Wales still remained the ordered, deferential society it had been for centuries past, as placid and unchanging as the serene Welsh countryside. Throughout rural Wales, the writ of the landed gentry still ran largely unchallenged. Henry Richard, writing in 1866, could describe Welsh politics, in a famous phrase, in tribal terms—'clansmen battling for their respective chieftains'.[1] And yet, in reality, a new Wales was being born between 1850 and 1870, with its political radicalism, religious revivalism, demographic explosion, passion for educational and cultural advance, and sense of national identity. Victorian Wales was becoming politicized. Episodes like the political evictions at Rhiwlas and elsewhere in Merioneth after the general election of 1859, the explosive growth of a powerful vernacular political press, the rise of native spokesmen like Henry Richard and Michael Daniel Jones, all testified to a new vitality within Wales and to a more dynamic and equal relationship with its English neighbour. In these two crucial decades, the later achievements of Tom Ellis, Lloyd George and their colleagues, those pulsating forces that made Wales in that century of rebirth from 1880 to 1980 an unconquerable stronghold of the British left, were made possible.

It is this vital phase in the modern Welsh experience that has absorbed the attention of my old friend, Ieuan Gwynedd Jones, in a masterly series of articles and studies over the past thirty years. His fascinating first volume of essays, *Explorations and Explanations*,[2] illustrates many of his major conclusions. The centrality of the politics of religion is undoubtedly one, with the Liberation Society forming a pressure group whose appeal by 1868 had transcended the mere cry for Welsh disestablishment. Another is the crucial impact of the

---

[1] H. Richard, *Letters on the Social and Political Condition of Wales* (London, 1867), p. 80.

[2] I. G. Jones, *Explorations and Explanations: Essays in the Social History of Victorian Wales* (Llandysul, 1981).

emergent middle class, not only in major conurbations like Merthyr and Swansea, but in smaller towns like Bala, Dolgellau or Aberystwyth. There is also detectable a powerful working-class presence, often in the unlikeliest of areas. In Merioneth, the local 'shopocracy' of Bala, so dominant in 1859, was by 1868 being outflanked by the slate-quarrymen of proletarian Blaenau Ffestiniog. In Merthyr and Aberdare in 1868, working-class protest, naturally enough, was quite decisive. It was Henry Austin Bruce's inability to satisfy the miners on such matters as the 'double-shift' system that underlay his shattering electoral defeat at the hands of Henry Richard. Latterly, Ieuan Gwynedd Jones has gone on to pursue other, equally seminal, themes, as his second volume of essays, *Communities*, demonstrates. Some marvellously evocative discussions of church building, from Llandaff in the south-east to Llanrhystud on the coast of Ceredigion, have shed much light on social tensions and controls. Surveys of the growth of local public services, covering health and much else besides, have illuminated the dynamics of the growth of a sense of community in the industrial valleys of the south.[3] A fine study of the different value-systems associated with the Welsh and English languages in rhetoric and debate broke new ground in explaining the processes of cultural transmission and its relationship to ideology and the class system.[4]

The broad thrust of Ieuan Gwynedd Jones's historical work must be pieced together from a variety of masterly vignettes and local studies. He is too careful (or perhaps too modest) a scholar to spell it out in synoptic or dogmatic form. But the abiding message of his view of modern Welsh political and social development is abundantly clear. His argument throughout is geared towards an evolutionary, orderly, even consensual view of Welsh social change. Class and denominational conflicts existed in abundance but they were neutralized, and eventually resolved, by institutional advance, social cohesion and the encroaching processes of democracy. Other historians have seen in Welsh history tempestuous tides of revolutionary passion and apocalyptic fervour, shot through with an almost existential view of Wales as a concept. Quietly and courteously, and always with impeccable scholarship, Ieuan Gwynedd Jones has registered his dissent. In fact, the real legacy of his reinterpretation of modern Welsh history lies not so much in the frontier period of 1850–70 but rather in the creative *fin-de-siècle* years, perhaps as far as 1914. This is a period which he has not investigated in depth; yet it is here that the implications of his historical argument and approach can most truly be discovered. It is, therefore, wholly appropriate to include in this *Festschrift* an investigation of later Victorian Wales, following on from the cathartic year of 1868. It forms a proper tribute to a master scholar and supervisor. Ieuan Gwynedd Jones is not merely a comrade-in-arms in many a campaign over the past thirty years. Even when past giants such as David Williams, along with several supremely talented living practitioners of our craft, are taken into account, he remains, in my considered judgement, the most important historian of modern Wales that our nation has yet produced.

---

[3] Idem, *Communities: Essays in the Social History of Victorian Wales* (Llandysul, 1987).

[4] Idem, 'Language and Community in Nineteenth-Century Wales', in D. Smith (ed.), *A People and a Proletariat* (London, 1980), pp. 47–71.

The contrasting roles of Tom Ellis and Lloyd George dominate any serious consideration of Welsh public life in what may be called the post-Ieuan Gwynedd Jones era after 1868. These two symbolize, of course, the high noon of Liberal Wales. It is an era seldom studied these days, when so much attention is focused on the decline of Liberalism after 1918, the rise of Labour, and the ordeal of the industrial societies of the coalfield. Much recent research, often of great insight and brilliance, has focused on a Wales in decline. Ellis and Lloyd George, conversely, represent a glorious, if deceptive and brief, era of national awakening, one to which they themselves mightily contributed. It was a period which saw a dramatic cultural, and especially literary, renaissance, with scholars and poets like John Morris-Jones, Owen M. Edwards and T. Gwynn Jones in pivotal roles. It was a time of quite spectacular industrial and commercial expansion in the Welsh coalfield, and the great ports and entrepôts of the south-east, as the recent celebration of the centenary of the port of Barry reminds us. The coalfield provided an irresistible magnet for young migrants from the rural hinterland; in time the countryside too began to share, however modestly, in the new prosperity. Politically, it was a moment of reawakening and rediscovery. Between 1868 and 1914, Wales experienced the heady advent of mass democracy, both at a national and local level. In that process, two towering figures, Tom Ellis of Cynlas in Merioneth and David Lloyd George of Llanystumdwy in Eifionydd, were powerful catalysts. They created much of the national rhetoric; they participated in many of the national achievements. They are key exhibits of Welsh national politics and self-awareness in the *fin-de-siècle* period.

In their very different ways, the two young men created a romantic image of themselves. Two 'cottage-bred boys' (or so it was claimed), they launched a new Welsh hagiography. Years later, this was most powerfully conveyed in W. Hughes Jones's book of 1937, *Wales Drops the Pilots*, where they appear as the spurned leaders of an unhistoric nation, 'prophets without honour', 'men of vision finding their countrymen blind'.[5] Tom Ellis was venerated as the archetypal 'lost leader', a rare charismatic force, 'burning with a peculiar intensity'.[6] His early death from bronchial illness in 1899, at the tragically early age of forty, merely added to the affectionate legend. He was Wales's refugee from the magic mountain, waiting for a Celtic Thomas Mann to rediscover him. Ellis's latest biographer, Wyn Jones, observes of him that 'no man ever loved his country more deeply and expended himself more selflessly on her behalf'. Ellis, we are told, was seen as a 'political Moses' poised to lead his people towards a promised land of equality and freedom.[7]

The young Lloyd George, in somewhat different fashion, also kindled a new myth. His rise to the Chancellorship of the Exchequer in 1908 was depicted by early biographers like Beriah Gwynfe Evans and John Hugh Edwards, both

---

[5] W. Hughes Jones, *Wales Drops the Pilots* (Liverpool, 1937); John Lloyd in *WM*, 29 October 1960. See also Hughes Jones, *A Challenge to Wales* (Liverpool, 1938), written under the pseudonym 'Elidir Sais'.

[6] J. A. Spender, *Sir Robert Hudson: a Memoir* (London, 1930), p. 24.

[7] W. Jones, *Thomas Edward Ellis, 1859–1899* (Cardiff, 1986), pp. 87, 89.

96

Tom Ellis.   David Lloyd George.

(By permission of the National Library of Wales.)

Liberal journalists, as a veritable 'life romance'. It was a saga of the simple country boy who trod the primrose path from Llanystumdwy to Downing Street.[8] By 1914 the Welsh national movement, at least in political terms, was largely identified with him and his programme. At election time at the end of the First World War, he could be hailed as 'the greatest Welshman yet born',[9] though admittedly this hyperbole was soon to dissolve in the harsh realities of the post-war world.

Yet at the same time, Tom Ellis and Lloyd George also embody the frustration, as well as the triumphalism, of the national politics of post-1868 Wales. For all its achievement, the national movement of this period was overlaid with a tragic sense of incompleteness and lack of fulfilment. Nationalism in Wales, unlike the case of Ireland, had not implied separatism or any form of self-government. Wales had by 1914 become more and more firmly bound to England, to the English constitution, the English class system, English capitalism. Several prized achievements appeared by 1914 to be turning somewhat sour—witness the growing disenchantment with the Welsh educational system and the democratic glories of the 'county schools', as the quarrels between Owen M. Edwards and the Central Welsh Board bore witness.[10] Sometimes, these discontents were linked, personally and directly, with Ellis and Lloyd George. Ellis was attacked, even by a friend and admirer like the High Church nationalist, J. Arthur Price, for his decision to take the whipship in July 1892, thereby betraying his principles, in the view of some patriots, for the loaves and fishes of office. It was noted by Tory opponents that Ellis's will revealed that the champion of the poor Merioneth farmers had left his heirs the considerable sum of over £11,000. Lloyd George, in time, was to be even more fiercely condemned for his neglect of Welsh interests when in office, and especially when Prime Minister in 1916–22. Wales was conspicuously not one of the 'little five-foot-five nations' supposedly liberated after years of war by the byzantine deliberations of the Paris peace conference. Llewelyn Williams, an old *Cymru Fydd* comrade of Lloyd George's in the nineties, angrily condemned him as the prisoner of the Tories and a man who had betrayed his country. Assailed both by Labour and the Conservatives, bereft of much of his old Welsh Liberal constituency, Lloyd George had by the late 1920s become a kind of universal scapegoat, the only true begetter of the strange, sudden death of Liberal Wales.

But all these judgements, both eulogistic and hostile, beg many important questions. They fail to explore the essential nature of the Welsh national movement of the later nineteenth century. Even more, they tend to assume an inherent congruence of outlook between Ellis and Lloyd George, at least in fundamental principles. They were, we have been sentimentally told, 'at all times like David and Jonathan'.[11] At times, Cain and Abel might have been a more suitable

---

[8] J. H. Edwards, *From Village Green to Downing Street: the Life of David Lloyd George* (London, 1909); B. G. Evans, *The Life Romance of David Lloyd George* (London, n.d. [1915]).

[9] *Welsh Outlook*, 6 (1919), 6.

[10] For an authoritative discussion of these matters, see G. E. Jones, *Controls and Conflicts in Welsh Secondary Education, 1889–1944* (Cardiff, 1982), esp. Chapter 1.

[11] Hughes Jones, *Wales drops the Pilots*, p. 36 (citing W. Llewelyn Williams).

Biblical analogy. At all events, a more searching analysis of *fin-de-siècle* politics might lead one to emphasize the differences rather than the similarities between these two remarkably gifted young Liberals. The contrasts between them provide, at least in some respects, a key to the story of modern Wales, and to the political consequences of the historical themes analysed by Ieuan Gwynedd Jones.

The origins of Ellis and Lloyd George show important differences from the outset. Tom Ellis was manifestly a leader of a new kind, the first to thrill the national emotions in overtly political terms. He was born and brought up on a farm at Cynlas, near Bala in north-east Merioneth, that cradle of revivalist Nonconformity. In 1859, the year of Ellis's birth, a massive religious revival galvanized the chapels. In that same year, following the victory at the general election of David Williams, a Liberal landowner from Penrhyndeudraeth, several local tenant farmers were evicted from their holdings on straight political grounds.[12] Among them were four relatives of Tom Ellis himself. A generation later he told the Land Commissioners how these grave events had sent 'a thrill of horror' throughout the countryside.[13] At Bala, too, Ellis came early under the spell of the radical nationalist and Independent minister, Michael Daniel Jones, the very embodiment of the folk consciousness of *y werin*, and a guru for the politically alert younger generation.

Ellis then went on to study at the new 'college by the sea' at Aberystwyth, even then increasingly caught up in intense national ferment. Here, he met gifted young fellow nationalists like the future Liberal MPs, Ellis Griffith and Samuel T. Evans, and the great historian, John Edward Lloyd. Here Ellis first conceived a new vision of organic nationalism within Wales, not so much political as fired by the stimulus of continental folk-culture, of literature, music and decorative art, and by the cult of the countryside as the custodian of the essential national virtues. He was, then and later, very much an agrarian politician. His vision of Young Wales was primarily cultural, literary, philosophical, spiritual. So it was to remain throughout his life. It is highly indicative that in the mid-1890s, when he was Liberal Chief Whip and a major parliamentary figure at Westminster, Ellis should devote himself to studying the works of that mystical seventeenth-century Puritan, Morgan Llwyd.

Yet the young Tom Ellis was not just an inbred, parochial figure. He was, above all, a man who moved out. To be precise, he moved out to New College, Oxford, in 1880; after graduating there (without great distinction) in 1884, he moved on to London to serve as the private secretary of the radical Liberal millionaire MP, Sir John Brunner. Both at Oxford and in London, Ellis added new dimensions to his nationalist creed. At the former, he absorbed the moral ethic of Ruskin, the educational passion of Matthew Arnold (without the freezing fog of the 'Celtic twilight'), and especially the social compassion of the tragic figure of the young Arnold Toynbee, a penetrating critic of the new industrial

---

[12] For this election, see Jones, *Explorations and Explanations*, pp. 83–165.
[13] *Evidence to the Welsh Land Commission*, 1 (PP [1894] C.7439), qu. 16,912.

order and its injustices. Many new themes thus emerged, all to be absorbed somehow in Ellis's nationalist credo. He responded to the social philosophy of the Fabians and their intense commitment to local government and popular participation. He was deeply influenced by the dawning New Liberalism, professed by the neo-Hegelian and Darwinian disciples of T. H. Green, with a more positive attitude towards the state and citizenship. Ellis warmed, too, to the heady vision of that social imperialism increasingly influential in Oxford in the early eighties. This applied not only to Benjamin Jowett's Balliol but also to Ellis's own New College, where the proconsular Alfred Milner was a recent fellow. No fewer than nine of the eleven founder members of Milner's 'kindergarten' in South Africa were New College men, including Brand, Kerr and Curtis. Empire thus became another key to Tom Ellis's ideas of Welsh nationality, indeed its culmination and fulfilment. It was this complex, eclectic philosophy that he brought with him to late Victorian Welsh politics when elected MP for Merioneth in the election of June 1886.[14]

David Lloyd George, by contrast, was neither aesthete nor intellectual. He experienced a more obviously political and partisan upbringing. Born in 1863 and soon to lose his schoolmaster father, his earliest memories were of the great Welsh Liberal election victories in the *annus mirabilis* of 1868. His childhood and early manhood were caught up in disputes with local clergymen, magistrates and landowners; even in his little Anglican primary school in Llanystumdwy, Lloyd George was a strike-leader and rebel. He went on to become a solicitor in Porthmadog, the very prototype of the self-made, small-town, middle-class politician so central to the Wales of the 1880s. In such episodes as the famous Llanfrothen burial dispute, he became the embattled young champion of the Nonconformist tenantry against an outworn social ascendancy. Even within the fragmented world of Welsh Nonconformity, he was an outsider, since he was brought up by his shoemaker uncle as a Campbellite Baptist, a radical offshoot of the old Dissent; in this and other respects, he matched the Quaker Bright and the Unitarian Chamberlain within the Nonconformist firmament. In the late 1880s, though still only in his mid-twenties, Lloyd George rose very rapidly to political prominence. He was active in the anti-tithe campaign in south Caernarfonshire. He took part in local journalism and tried with some friends to found a new quasi-socialist newspaper, *Udgorn Rhyddid*, the trumpet of freedom.[15] He served as the 'boy alderman' on the first county council elected for Caernarfonshire in January 1889, as part of a huge Liberal majority. Within the North Wales Liberal Federation, Lloyd George represented the most militant of tendencies, threatening national rebellion unless Gladstone and the party leadership paid far more heed to the just claims of Nonconformist Wales.[16] While Ellis had imbibed the social and imperial ideologies of élitist Oxford, Lloyd George was evolving his own particular *Zeitgeist* at home, on the political platforms,

[14] There is an excellent, highly subtle analysis of Ellis's intellectual development in N. Masterman, *The Forerunner* (Llandybïe, 1972); a useful work is R. Symonds, *Oxford and Empire* (Oxford, 1986).

[15] See R. E. Price, 'Newyddiadur Cyntaf David Lloyd George', *Journal of the Welsh Bibliographical Society*, 11 (1976), 207–15; NLW, D. R. Daniel Papers, 2744, Lloyd George to Daniel, 12 December 1887.

[16] NLW, Minutes of the North Wales Liberal Federation, esp. for September–December 1889.

in the chapel vestries and county courts of rural Wales. He was elected to parliament for Caernarfon Boroughs in April 1890—it was a Liberal by-election 'gain' and very far from being a safe seat. At the age of twenty-seven, he was already a controversial and colourful politician and stump orator, feared and admired as few were in Welsh public life.

Following on from these highly distinct backgrounds, it soon emerged that Ellis and Lloyd George had markedly different political outlooks. A mutual friend like their endlessly loyal colleague, D. R. Daniel of Llandderfel, came to appreciate their differences, eventually with painful results in his later life.[17] In a variety of ways, Ellis and Lloyd George, as they made their way through Welsh and British politics, were political animals of contrasting species.

Ellis, for example, was a quintessentially agrarian radical. From Bala to the South African veld, the pure, uncorrupted qualities of rural, farming society were his touchstone of nationality, indeed of a morally wholesome society. For Ellis it was 'in the soil of the country areas, and the slope of the hills, in the remote valleys, that the best sources of a nation's life are to be found. It is there that the cradle of a worthwhile humanity exists' to bring balm and succour to 'the casualties of the unmerciful struggle of the cities'.[18] It might have been William Jennings Bryan, of 'cross of gold' fame, speaking. Lloyd George, on the other hand, was representative not of the farming community but of the emergent professional bourgeoisie of the small towns, of which Cricieth and Porthmadog were prototypes. He was never that much at ease with farmers pure and simple. His father was a schoolteacher, Uncle Lloyd an artisan. Lloyd George's differences with his prospective father-in-law, Richard Owen, a substantial Methodist farmer, added to the myriad social and sexual complications of his courtship of Maggie Owen of Mynydd Ednyfed.[19]

In denominational terms, Ellis was always a loyal Calvinistic Methodist. He was a devout chapel-goer if never a bigot, with some sympathy for the aesthetic and cultural visions of high Anglicans like Arthur Price. Ellis's religious convictions and affiliations were beyond dispute. Lloyd George, by contrast, viewed with scorn and contempt the petty jealousies and social pretensions of the chapels, especially the 'glorified grocers' of the *sêt fawr*, or philistine 'beatified drapers' like D. H. Evans.[20] Although popularly seen as the epitome of the Nonconformist conscience in politics, Lloyd George was in religious terms a critic of the chapels; his creed, *pace* W. R. P. George, was that of at best a deist, perhaps even a free thinker.[21] In personal life, unlike the respectable aesthete Ellis, Lloyd George

[17] K. W. Jones-Roberts, 'D. R. Daniel', *Journal of the Merioneth Historical and Record Society*, 5 (1965), 58–78, is a useful discussion of this forgotten patriot. His extensive papers in the National Library of Wales are a most valuable source for both Ellis and Lloyd George.

[18] Jones, *Ellis*, p. 37.

[19] See K. O. Morgan (ed.), *Lloyd George Family Letters, c. 1885–1936* (Oxford and Cardiff, 1973), pp. 19–22. Lloyd George mused in his diary on 30 August 1887 that Maggie deserved 'something better than a farmer'.

[20] Ibid., p. 28 (Lloyd George to Margaret Lloyd George, 10 June 1890). The phrase 'glorified grocers' (in connection with a proposed reform of the composition of the House of Lords in 1910) appears in L. Masterman, *C. F. G. Masterman* (London, 1939), p. 200.

[21] See W. R. P. George, *The Making of Lloyd George* (London, 1975), pp. 107ff, for a contrary view. Also see B. B. Gilbert, *David Lloyd George, a Political Life: the Architect of Change 1863–1912* (London, 1987), pp. 35–7.

was emphatically no puritan. As most of his biographers have pointed out (usually to a vastly excessive extent), he prefigured the so-called permissive society.

Again, as has been seen, Ellis was always deeply involved with the cultural and literary aspects of Welsh nationality. In this he followed his early model, the youthful Protestant prophet of Young Ireland in the 1840s, Thomas Davis (who also died young, as it happened).[22] Ellis's vision of Welsh nationality always had an essentially literary base, as did that of Llewelyn Williams, as he grappled with the anglicized, philistine, 'howling wilderness' of Swansea and Barry.[23] Ellis frequently addressed Welsh colleges and the Honourable Society of Cymmrodorion on the need to sustain the Welsh language, foster its literature and scholarship, to encourage Cymric traditions in the visual arts, and build them up in architecture and design.[24] In the 1890s he campaigned vigorously (and successfully) for public support for the scholar Gwenogvryn Evans in his work of editing manuscripts of medieval poetry.[25] He pressed for a Welsh Historical Manuscripts Commission, a national library and museum; he urged the University Guild of Graduates to help set these enterprises in motion. Ellis's intellectual powers had their limitations, certainly, but the range of his intellectual interests and ambitions was almost of Gladstonian proportions. They provided the *fons et origo* of his belief in Welsh nationhood. Lloyd George, conversely, although a fluent Welsh-speaker, had relatively little interest in Welsh culture, literary or musical, other than the populistic implications of hymn-singing. Unlike Ellis, he very seldom read Welsh (or any other) poetry or literary criticism for pleasure; his awe before the architectural splendours of Rome or Florence did not get much beyond the casual window-gazing of the tourist. Lloyd George's preferred reading matter was inspirational social texts such as Dickens or Hugo's *Les Misérables*, together with romantic novels of the wild west.[26] He acquired knowledge, not through bookish learning, but through personal contact and conversation. His methods of self-education were instinctive, intuitive, inspirational; his favoured companions were 'responsive personalities' of a similar outlook. In this, at least, L.G. was the very model of the impressionable Celtic spirit as Matthew Arnold had misidentified it.

It followed from this that the two young Welsh Liberals contrasted sharply in their response to the contemporary pressure for Irish home rule. Ellis, the disciple of Davis and Mazzini, saw Irish nationalism in almost religious terms as a mass movement for social and cultural liberation. He mingled harmoniously

---

[22]   T. W. Moody, 'Thomas Davis and the Irish Nation', *Hermathena*, 103 (Dublin, 1966), 5–31.

[23]   NLW, Ellis Papers, 2134, W. Llewelyn Williams to Ellis, 19 February 1892; Cardiff Public Library, Cochfarf Papers, W. Llewelyn Williams to Edward Thomas, 'Cochfarf'.

[24]   See T. E. Ellis, *Speeches and Addresses* (Wrexham, 1912), a posthumous publication sponsored by his wife, Mrs Annie Ellis (later Mrs Peter Hughes Griffiths). Particularly relevant are Chapters 2, 3 and 6, on 'Domestic and Decorative Art in Wales', 'A Plea for a Welsh School of Architecture' and 'The Duty of the Guild towards the Literature and Records of Wales'.

[25]   Ibid., pp. 149–50.

[26]   It should be added that Lloyd George also read a certain amount of history during his boyhood, including the work of Gibbon, Macaulay and J. R. Green, though not much later.

with Irish MPs on the back-benches during the so-called 'union of hearts' phase from 1886 down to the Parnell/O'Shea divorce scandal in 1890. He was present, along with Labouchere and William O'Brien, at the meeting in Mitchelstown, County Cork, in September 1887 where the authorities opened fire on a crowd of peaceful Irish farmers, killing three of them.[27] On Irish home rule, Ellis was a fundamentalist, a Sinn Feiner out of his time. Lloyd George, on the other hand, was initially strongly opposed to Irish home rule in 1886. He came within an ace (or, according to one version by J. Hugh Edwards, a misread railway timetable) of joining Chamberlain's Radical Union in that year.[28] Protestant hostility to Rome Rule in Ireland, rather than sectional sympathy for the Orange-men of Ulster, seems to have been the decisive factor for Lloyd George. It is true that by 1890 he was committed to Irish home rule on Gladstonian lines. He was to make at least one good friend among the Irish MPs, 'Tay Pay' O'Con-nor, significantly enough a prominent London journalist and editor. Even so, from the 1880s down to the 'troubles' of the Black and Tans in 1919–20, Lloyd George was never an unambiguous supporter of Irish home rule as Gladstonian Liberals understood the concept. Many of his biographers have misrepresented his views on this very point. He was advocating the separate status of Ulster within the government in 1913–14 and again in June to July 1916; in 1918 he stood firm against its 'coercion'. The basic divergence between him and the Mazzini-like Ellis in the 1880s cast its massive, baleful shadow over British policy towards the Irish nation from 1886 down to the Free State treaty concluded with Griffith and Collins in December 1921. The roots of the Anglo-Irish war of 1919–21 and of the Irish civil war that followed in 1922–3 lay, in some sense, in the complexities of Welsh politics in the 1880s.[29]

Above all, as has already been observed, Lloyd George, unlike Ellis, simply did not move out of Wales at a formative stage of his career. He never went to Oxford as a student, or indeed to any institution of higher education at all. In 1890 his outlook was the more truly local, even provincial. Far more than Ellis could ever be, Lloyd George remained, in his erratic way, essentially Welsh, a political outsider in a manner that Ellis, the confidant of Liberal Imperialists and neo-Fabians like Haldane, Asquith, Buxton and Grey, could never be. There was a personal and philosophical detachment about Ellis's political ideas that contrasted sharply with the inbred enthusiasms of the youthful Lloyd George. The fissure that resulted ran deep through the national consciousness of *fin-de-siècle* Wales.

The political priorities of the two also show significant divergences. Of course, as part of the new wave of young, radical, largely Nonconformist MPs elected between 1886 and 1892, Ellis and Lloyd George symbolized a massive generational

[27] Masterman, *Forerunner*, pp. 62–3.

[28] For a discussion of this question, see J. Grigg, *The Young Lloyd George* (London, 1973), p. 51, n.2. He rightly points out that Edwards suppressed the point in his later versions of Lloyd George's career.

[29] I have discussed Lloyd George's attitude towards Ireland and the Irish more fully in a paper to be published jointly by the British and Irish Academies during 1988.

change in Welsh politics, as dramatic as that when Parnell and his followers supplanted Isaac Butt in Ireland a decade earlier.[30] Along with D. A. Thomas, David Randell, Samuel T. Evans, J. Herbert Lewis, and Frank Edwards, Ellis and Lloyd George represented a younger, more aggressively nationalist movement. They left far behind in their wake, not only veterans like Lewis Llewelyn Dillwyn, Henry Richard and Sir Hussey Vivian, but even heroes of 1868 like Sir George Osborne Morgan. This was truly a new breed of Welsh representatives that dominated the recently-formed Welsh Parliamentary Party, somewhat cautiously led by the Englishman, Stuart Rendel, from 1888 onwards. In this context, Ellis and Lloyd George worked closely together. They were an effective pair of freelance snipers, alarming to Gladstone and Morley as well as to the Conservative government on such matters as the 1892 Clergy Discipline Bill. They appear to have got on well personally. Ellis took his younger Caernarfon colleague on a tour of the more colourful London cafés, and there were theatre excursions as well, with suitable female company. Ellis was a bachelor; Lloyd George's wife chose to remain moored in Cricieth. Ellis was effusive in his praise of Lloyd George's maiden speech in June 1890; the latter responded that Ellis was 'a good sort' and pleasant company despite his already uncertain health.[31]

Yet the main priorities of the time were seen in significantly different lights by the two men. This comes across clearly if the major themes of Welsh land, local government, education and, above all, governmental devolution are examined in turn.

As regards Welsh land, Ellis took a very broad view of the question. He had a Fabian passion for the statistics for rent returns, and the details of easy credit arrangements for freeholders.[32] But the land question, in Wales as in Ireland, was to him above all a crucial facet of emergent nationhood. Land, indeed, included the labour question as well—'Nationality and labour are our two main principles', he wrote to his Flintshire colleague, Herbert Lewis.[33] The system of landed tenure comprehended the Church establishment, tithe, the very structure of the social order and of the national ethic. A remodelled Welsh land system, on the basis of a small-scale freeholding proprietorship would be the very basis of that peasant democracy from which the new Wales would arise. Lloyd George, however, saw land reform in more dialectical terms, as a form of disestablishment of the landlords, and levelling the gross social inequalities of Welsh rural society. For him, as for many others, the essence of Welsh land was social rather than economic. He was less interested in ideals of freehold tenure and of diffused peasant proprietorship than in taxing the unearned increment on land, urban as well as rural, as advocated by Pan Jones of Mostyn

---

[30] For a fuller discussion of this theme, see K. O. Morgan, *Wales in British Politics, 1868–1922* (Cardiff, 3rd ed., 1980), Chapter 3.

[31] Morgan, *Family Letters*, p. 47, David Lloyd George to Margaret Lloyd George, 5 April 1892, in which Ellis compares, for Lloyd George's benefit, an Egyptian restaurant and cyclorama in London with the real Egypt.

[32] See particularly Ellis's speech in the Commons, 29 June 1888 (*Parl. Debates*, Third Ser., 337, p. 1792ff), when introducing a resolution on agricultural tenancy in Wales.

[33] NLW, Ellis Papers, 2890, Ellis to Herbert Lewis, 31 October 1891.

in *Y Celt*, perhaps even with land nationalization as an objective.[34] Significantly, his main hero amongst the Irish members was not the aloof Protestant landowner, Parnell, but the quasi-socialist land nationalizer and friend of Keir Hardie, Michael Davitt.[35] Lloyd George was more attracted to the single-tax theories of the American, Henry George, than Ellis could ever be. The 1909 Budget with its multiple taxation on the landowner, along with the semi-nationalization of the 'Green Book', *The Land and the Nation*, in 1925, were proposals that could only have come from Lloyd George, never from Tom Ellis.[36]

As regards local government, Ellis saw it as the instrument of populism. He cited Tocqueville's view that local assemblies of citizens 'constituted the strength of free nations'.[37] He took a keen interest in the provisions of the 1888 Local Government Act, which he thought could be developed in the localities so that the Welsh county councils could combine to provide something like a functional Welsh assembly. He was equally excited by the potentialities of the 1894 Parish Councils Act, passed by the Rosebery government while he was Chief Whip. The measure would provide civic training; it would enable local communities to secure and retain their hold over the land; it would offer a forum for the public debate of local issues; it would provide an essential machinery for energizing and elevating the national spirit.[38] The Welsh, Ellis believed, had a natural capacity for local collective association. Theirs was a land of *cyfraith, cyfar, cyfnawdd, cymorthau* and *cymanfaoedd*, all of them concepts which embodied the co-operative ethic.[39] By extension, Ellis took a keen interest during his various travels in the growth of similar self-governing rural communities, such as the Swiss cantons (a famous late-Victorian obsession), the Austrian Tyrol, and the Boer republics in South Africa. His concern with local government was subtle and refined, and voiced with a religious passion.

Lloyd George's view of local government, by contrast, was relatively simple, at least at the conceptual level. He had no specialist interest in the mechanics of local government as the germ of a wider devolution of power. He took no part in the debates on the 1894 Parish Councils Act. Nearer home, his membership of the Caernarfonshire County Council was conspicuous for a poor attendance record; he did not share Ellis's Fabian enthusiasm for highways, allotments and drains. Unlike many other men of the left, Liberal and socialist, from Joseph Chamberlain to Herbert Morrison, Lloyd George did not develop his administrative skills at the local level at all. He became interested in local government only when it could be used as a political lever. Hence his extremely shrewd decision in December 1902 to transfer the powers of the Welsh local authorities

[34] P. Jones-Evans, 'Evan Pan Jones—Land Reformer', *WHR*, 4 (1968–9), 143–59.

[35] Lloyd George noted in the early 1880s that Michael Davitt was his 'most admired character in real life' (George, *Making of Lloyd George*, p. 113).

[36] The 1909 Budget included a 20 per cent tax on the 'unearned increment', payable when land was sold and when it changed hands after death. The 'Green Book' included a form of quasi-nationalization, 'cultivating tenure', for all land deemed to be productive.

[37] Ellis, *Speeches and Addresses*, p. 167.

[38] Ibid., pp. 165ff.

[39] Ibid., p. 22.

under the 1889 Intermediate Education Act to the new local authorities constituted under Balfour's new Education Act—a vital move in welding together
the 'revolt' of the Welsh county councils against the Balfour Act.[40] Lloyd George
henceforth found himself at the head of a nationwide rebellion by all the Welsh
local authorities (with a handful of backsliders) in 1903–5, and threatened with
mandamus writs by central government. But here his concern with the potentialities of local government was far narrower in concept and more purely partisan
than was ever the case with Ellis.

It followed that much the same could be said about education, another of
Ellis's abiding passions. A product of Aberystwyth and Oxford, as has been
noted, he was a major architect of the Welsh Intermediate Education Act of
1889. The precise degree of credit to be allocated to Ellis, Stuart Rendel, A.
J. Mundella, the Tory Education Minister, William Hart-Dyke, and others,
has been a subject of some historical debate,[41] but perhaps this is of secondary
importance. There is no doubt that Ellis was enormously interested in the Act
and the social potentialities of the secondary education system it created. He
saw the new 'county schools', which by 1914 numbered well over a hundred
in all the Welsh counties (including Monmouthshire for this purpose), as the
creators of a new educated élite, intellectually superior, but instinctively in tune
with the new democracy. Liberal *littérateurs* like Morris-Jones he saw as para-
digms of the new kind of social and intellectual leadership that would emerge.
Ellis was zealous in turning the funds of Welsh educational charities to good
purpose; he was active in rescuing such famous old local academies as the grammar school at Botwnnog.[42] Equally, he was deeply involved, first in reinforcing
the new fledgeling college at Aberystwyth, and then, in 1893, in encouraging
the drafting of the charter for the federal University of Wales, which was then
composed of the colleges at Bangor, Aberystwyth and Cardiff. The clerical delaying tactics from the Anglicans of St David's College, Lampeter, were dismissed
with some ruthlessness. Ellis was intimately connected with the work of his
friend, Arthur Acland, a resident in Caernarfonshire, the Minister for Education
under Gladstone in 1892–4, in this and other contexts. When the Aberystwyth
Old Students' Association came into being in 1892, Ellis was its natural first
president, as he was later for the new University of Wales Guild of Graduates.
Both of them he saw as active pressure-groups for scholarship and the arts.
Here was a politician of no ordinary kind, one who saw higher education as
the key to a wider, participatory view of democracy, a Welsh Greece to England's
Rome.

Lloyd George, on the other hand, was unusually detached from the movement
for higher education, on which so much of the national endeavour of *fin-de-siècle*
Wales was expended. Arthur Humphreys-Owen, another Liberal MP closely
connected with Welsh education, noted that Lloyd George, having had no formal

---

[40] NLW, Herbert Lewis Papers, Herbert Lewis's diary, 11 November 1902.
[41] See J. R. Webster, 'The Welsh Intermediate Education Act of 1889', *WHR*, 4 (1969–70), 290–1; K.
O. Morgan, '"The Member for Wales": Stuart Rendel (1894–1913)', *Trans. Cymmr.*, 1984, pp. 160–1.
[42] NLW, Daniel Papers, Ellis to Daniel, 24 August 1891.

literary education himself, was 'unable to see the needs of the educational system. He regards it simply as a political scaffolding.'[43] Lloyd George stood largely outside the Welsh higher education crusade of the nineties, the campaign for the intermediate schools, the creation of a Central Welsh Board and inspectorate, the founding of a University of Wales, all with their class-collaborationist and consensual overtones. He became decisively involved with Welsh education only in the purely political context of the 'revolt' against the 1902 Balfour Education Act which has just been described, and in subsequent unsuccessful attempts to build on that movement by creating some kind of Welsh council of education.[44] It is certainly the case that, later on, Haldane, amongst other Cabinet colleagues, managed to broaden Lloyd George's interest in education in the 1910–14 period, and that education, including technical instruction, was one of the prospective beneficiaries, along with health and housing, of his abortive budget of 1914.[45] The Fisher Education Act of 1918 was given every encouragement by the Prime Minister, who himself saw the historian, H. A. L. Fisher, as another Guizot or Morley.[46] Nevertheless, it remains true that Lloyd George's lifelong attitude to education as a social and political priority was less ardent than that of Tom Ellis. As late as the Cabinet discussions on the cuts proposed by the Geddes Committee in 1921, the Prime Minister was zealous to economize by raising the age of school entry and cutting back on further education, including the day continuation schools.[47] He had received little formal education himself, and it had not done him any harm. His stance was that of the self-made, self-taught man, to be contrasted with the arid abstract learning of the schoolmen. In this sense, Lloyd George differed, not merely from Ellis but also from Herbert Lewis, Humphreys-Owen, Samuel Evans, Ellis Griffith, Llewelyn Williams and most other major figures in *fin-de-siècle* Welsh Liberalism. Even the coal-mining tycoon, D. A. Thomas, himself a Cambridge graduate with a decent degree in mathematics, championed the need for technical education. In his philistinism, Lloyd George stood almost alone.

Finally, there was the supreme political priority of Welsh home rule. As an MP from 1886 onwards, Ellis moved steadily towards the need for Welsh self-government, as a political, perhaps spiritual, necessity. His mystical experiences beside the temple at Luxor in Egypt merely deepened this commitment. His speech at Bala on 18 September 1890 was a passionate statement of the need, not merely for the wider recognition of Wales in political, religious and cultural terms, but for a Welsh assembly, elected on a broad democratic basis by all adult Welsh men and (be it noted) women as well.[48] His involvement with

[43]   NLW, 79466C, no. 704a (Rendel Papers), A. C. Humphreys-Owen to Lord Rendel, 18 June 1905.

[44]   Morgan, *Wales in British Politics*, pp. 198, 223–6; L. Wynne Evans, 'The Welsh National Council for Education', *WHR*, 6 (1972–3), 49–88.

[45]   E. Ashby and M. Anderson, *Portrait of Haldane at Work on Education* (London, 1975), pp. 116–19.

[46]   BL, Add.MS 50905, f. 211, C. P. Scott's diary, 30 November–1 December 1919.

[47]   PRO, CAB 27/165. Report, Proceedings and Memoranda of the Cabinet Committee appointed to examine Parts I and II of the first interim report of the Committee on National Expenditure: proceedings of 26 January 1922.

[48]   *Baner ac Amserau Cymru*, 24 September 1890.

the current movement for Irish self-government gave his concern for Welsh home rule additional overtones. A subsequent visit to South Africa in 1891, during which he talked with personalities as varied as Cecil Rhodes and Olive Schreiner (though, apparently, with no black people), no less than his reveries beside the Nile, merely strengthened a passionate affirmation of the need for self-determination. For Ellis, an elected assembly would 'form the highest embodiment of the national unity and the main instrument for fulfilling the national will and purpose of Wales'.[49]

Lloyd George's early Welsh nationalism was no less genuine and determined. It dominated his election address in the by-election for Caernarfon Boroughs in April 1890. At the same time, Lloyd George's outlook was markedly free from Ellis's commitment to cultural nationalism (including the sacred cause of the Welsh language). Lloyd George became deeply involved with the *Cymru Fydd* movement only in 1894–6, when he saw it primarily as a political instrument for uniting Welsh constituency parties and thereby putting pressure on the Liberal party leadership and the London-based party machine.[50] The self-governing Wales that Lloyd George ardently championed from 1894 onwards had highly political objectives—disestablishment, land reform, temperance and somewhat vaguely-conceived labour policies among them. It flowed from his inability to persuade his parliamentary colleagues to support him in his attempted 'revolt' against the Liberal Party leadership in April to May 1894, when four Welsh Liberals announced their independence from the party whip owing to the delays in introducing a disestablishment bill. On the other hand, Lloyd George's courage in championing *Cymru Fydd* in the 1894–6 period is beyond dispute; he came far closer to entering the political wilderness than Ellis ever did. It can also be argued that Lloyd George's campaign for some kind of national assembly was more realistic and practical in form than Ellis's inspiring oratory. Lloyd George worked specifically within the hierarchies and power structures of Liberal Wales, north and south. Conversely, his tactics could also embrace a wide range of allies, including some High Church disestablishers in early 1895.[51] They might help get disestablishment (more specifically disendowment) out of the way, to leave the way clear for Welsh home rule. The future coalitionist and architect of new forms of inter-party liaison from 1910 onwards can certainly be discerned in Welsh politics in 1895. In this sense, and some others, Ellis was far the purer—though not necessarily the more effective—Liberal of the two.

For both Ellis and Lloyd George, the events of July 1892 marked a turning-

---

[49] Ellis, *Speeches and Addresses*, p. 184.

[50] For the *Cymru Fydd* crisis, see Morgan, *Family Letters*, pp. 77–95; W. George, *Cymru Fydd: Hanes y Mudiad Cenedlaethol Cyntaf* (Liverpool, 1945); and Gilbert, *David Lloyd George*, pp. 120ff.

[51] This refers to Lloyd George's indirect involvement in the so-called 'Bangor scheme' of January 1895, in which J. Arthur Price and four other Welsh High Churchmen advocated a compromise settlement over Church endowments for the sake of Welsh home rule: see E. E. Owen, *The Early Life of Bishop Owen* (Llandysul, 1958), pp. 179–81.

point. Welsh members, with disestablishment and other major demands heading their programme, were in a rare position to put pressure on Gladstone and the new Liberal government. After all, the Welsh numbered thirty-one while the government's majority was barely forty. There was also the offer of the position of junior whip to Tom Ellis. This was a crisis not only for him personally but for his friends also, and for the Welsh national movement as a whole. Ellis, as we have noticed already, was attacked by J. Arthur Price, then and later, for 'grasping the Saxon gold',[52] but he took his prime loyalty to the Liberal Party for granted. He pointed to the Welsh disestablishment measures of 1894–5, the University of Wales charter, and the royal commission on Welsh Land as evidence of his effectiveness within the charmed circle of government. Lloyd George was not so sure: later on, he was to speak of the party making Ellis its 'doormat' (long before Arthur Henderson commandeered the term!).[53] The example of the Irish Nationalists was a beguiling one, showing how resolute independence could be made to serve the national cause. Lloyd George seems initially to have endorsed Ellis's decision to accept the whipship in July 1892, as a way of securing greater political pressure on behalf of Welsh causes. It would also ensure that a somewhat aged government, headed by an octogenarian, had some new radical blood.[54] Equally, he endorsed Ellis's succession to Marjoribanks as Chief Whip in March 1894. But Lloyd George himself proved to be a persistent rebel against the whips, Ellis included, in the 1892–5 parliament. This included the highly contentious circumstances in which the Rosebery government fell from office on 20–21 June 1895; in this episode, Ellis's later loyal defence of Lloyd George's role was more ardent than Asquith and others felt was justified by the facts.[55]

Overall, the effect of Tom Ellis's becoming a whip in July 1892 marked a clear rift between him and his old political comrade-in-arms, David Lloyd George. The latter emerged all the more strongly as a Welsh freelance, a *mauvais coucheur* and a permanent headache for the party leadership. Ellis was a loyalist now, essentially a Welsh-speaking but London-based politician. His main friends were Englishmen like Acland, Buxton and Robert Hudson. This most essentially Welsh of politicians was imperceptibly drifting from the Wales of his own day, with its harsh internecine and interreligious conflicts, and clashes of interests. He was becoming something of a stranger in his own honoured land.

The gulf that had now opened up between Ellis and Lloyd George became very apparent during the *Cymru Fydd* crisis of 1894–6. Ellis, like Llewelyn Williams, saw *Cymru Fydd* as the institutional agent of a wider cultural movement. He was distant from the movement in 1894–5 to unite the Liberalism of north

---

[52] UCNW, Bangor Library, Lloyd Papers, 314, 449, Price to J. E. Lloyd, 14 October 1892. This view is curiously echoed in H. Spender, *The Prime Minister* (London, 1920), p. 54, no doubt reproducing Lloyd George's own views.

[53] Morgan, *Family Letters*, p. 151, Lloyd George to Margaret Lloyd George, 10 January 1908. The more celebrated 'door-mat', of course, was Arthur Henderson in August 1917.

[54] NLW, Ellis Griffith Papers, 385, Ellis to Ellis Griffith, 25 August 1892.

[55] BL, Herbert Gladstone Papers Add. MS 46022, f. 94, Lloyd George to Ellis, ?April 1894; NLW, Ellis Papers, 74, 'private', Asquith to Ellis, 30 November 1895.

and south Wales and subordinate both to the Welsh home rule cause. This was not simply because he was Chief Whip, but because he saw *Cymru Fydd* under Lloyd George's aegis as a narrowing, pedestrian, even philistine kind of national self-expression. It was a caricature of the ideal of *Cymru'n Un*. Ellis would have agreed with Llewelyn Williams in seeing it as the kind of limited, stereotyped creed that Parnell/Redmond nationalism had become in Ireland, far removed from the cultural idealism of Young Ireland in the 1840s (or, indeed, of Sinn Fein a few years later).[56] Ellis was much upset by the freelance tactics that Lloyd George adopted against his own party comrades in the later months of 1895. He regarded the collapse of the *Cymru Fydd* League after the fiasco at Newport in January 1896 without emotion.[57].

Lloyd George, by contrast, saw *Cymru Fydd*, as it spread throughout Wales, as an instrument of power and control. He managed to capture the North Wales Liberal Federation as part of the base for his new all-Wales movement. The Liberals of south Wales, however, were far more resistant, partly on linguistic grounds. The Newport meeting saw their mercantile, English-speaking spokesmen howl Lloyd George down. The essential conflict between Liberalism and nationalism was starkly revealed. In a narrow sense, *Cymru Fydd* under Lloyd George failed because of the social and linguistic divisions between rural and industrial Wales. Wales was not a unity in 1896 any more than it had been in the Age of the Princes centuries earlier. Perhaps it never could be. But in reality, the fragility of *Cymru Fydd*, as a basis for Welsh self-government, had emerged clearly in every single Liberal association and club throughout the land. Ellis, the idealist, continued to hope that the vision of *Cymru Fydd*, for all its practical difficulties, could provide the stimulus for a wider nationalist upsurge, as in so many continental countries. If there could be Pan-Slavism, why not Pan-Celticism? Lloyd George, the clear-headed realist, had no such illusions. He knew that the cause of Welsh separatism was lost, at least for his generation. After a mild resurgence of the cause in 1897–8,[58] he withdrew from the Welsh home rule campaign almost as rapidly as he had leapt on to the bandwagon. In consequence, devolution in any serious sense was no longer a major theme in Welsh politics. Nor was it to be for a further seventy years, until the startling revival of Plaid Cymru and the appointment of the Crowther/ Kilbrandon Commission in the later 1960s breathed new life into the apparently defunct cause of home rule for Wales.

After 1896 Ellis and Lloyd George still found it possible to collaborate, for instance in resisting the Unionist government's Agricultural Rating Act of 1896 or the Education Bill of 1897. Ellis was largely concerned now with his organizational work as Chief Whip, and especially with trying to promote the involvement

[56] UCNW, Bangor Library, Lloyd Papers, 314, 592, Llewelyn Williams to J. E. Lloyd, 21 September 1894.

[57] For a discussion of this point, see T. I. Ellis, *Thomas Edward Ellis: Cofiant*, 2 (Liverpool, 1948), 260–1. Also see T. E. Ellis's speech at Aberdyfi, *SWDN*, 4 February 1896.

[58] Morgan, *Wales in British Politics*, pp. 170–1.

of trade unionists and other working men within the Liberal tabernacle.[59] His premature death in April 1899, shortly after his marriage, released passionate outpourings of national emotion. Lloyd George himself expressed them with a deeply moving address at the unveiling of Ellis's statue in Bala, a few years later. Yet in practical terms, Ellis had already become a symbolic figure in his native land. Lloyd George, for his part, gradually turned away from his preoccupation with Welsh affairs, especially after the wider horizons opened up by his prominent role in opposing the South African War. For the next forty years after 1902, years which included a brilliant six-year premiership, he was concerned above all with social reform at home and international conciliation overseas. His commitment to Welsh objectives remained, though with a fainter emphasis, down to the eventual passage of Welsh disestablishment in 1919, amidst a general sense of anticlimax, even plain boredom. But he was moving away from Wales, as Tom Ellis had done before him. He kept his old base in Caernarfon Boroughs where, until 1941, Dame Margaret was ever present to hold him firm to the grand old causes. But political operations in London and the alternative ménage with Frances Stevenson, eventually located in Churt, were testimony to changing allegiances and shifting values. The rise of socialism and organized labour within Wales after 1918 left him bereft. He failed to engage with the priorities of the new post-war world, dominated by the confrontation of capital and labour, rather than by the time-worn issues of his rural youth. The most magnificent and strident of one-man bands, he had, long before the final decline after 1931, become almost as much of an anachronism within the Welsh scene as had the stylish literary politics of Ellis in the past.

Tom Ellis and Lloyd George, comrades in many battles, really represented very different approaches towards the Wales of their time. Ellis was a rare kind of philosophical nationalist, a Mazzini rather than a Cavour, with close affinities to the folk-consciousness of central and southern Europe in the mid-nineteenth century. Lloyd George was a political radical of a remarkably flexible type, whose vision of national identity began with class and social conflict where Ellis would emphasize organic unity. Ellis's nationalism was based on the inheritances of the folk, Lloyd George's on the imperatives of the state. The one looked back to Heine and Goethe, the other had affinity with Bismarck and Theodore Roosevelt. They were contrasting legatees of the political transformations which Ieuan Gwynedd Jones has explained to us, children of the brave new world released by the electoral revolutions of 1868 and, later, 1885.

Which of the two, it may be speculated, was the more appropriate agent for the national aspirations of late-Victorian Wales? In the past, the present writer tended to be drawn more strongly to Tom Ellis. He was manifestly a lovable man, an intellectual, an idealist, a gentle, chivalrous personality, without fear and without reproach. Many contemporaries thought he was too pure for this world—witness his attempts to excuse Lloyd George's flagrant indiscipline

---

[59] Masterman, *Forerunner*, pp. 230–2.

against his own whip in June 1895. The apostle of Mazzini and Kossuth is surely a deeply attractive, compelling figure to whom Welshmen of all shades of opinion must still be drawn. On the other hand, Ellis was basically a consensus man, who sought to celebrate and amplify the organic unity of his people. As such, he naturally appeals to middle-class academics who, by their training and background, tend to revere continuity, consensus and the Greek liberal virtues. Ellis himself, however, was not without ambiguity or guile on key issues. Over the land question, the extent to which he himself favoured a peasant proprietorship, or alternatively preferred some form of common ownership, was not always clear. On imperial matters, he was less outspoken than modern-day liberals might wish towards the Boer republics, with their clearly discriminatory attitude towards the black majority visible even in 1891. Over the Jameson Raid inquiries in 1896–7, Ellis was less than outspoken, perhaps the result of the admiration he had conceived for Cecil Rhodes when they met. Again, the Bala speech of September 1890, with its inspirational call for self-government, was also less than precise, and was never adequately followed up. It is noticeable that Ellis never quite formulated that kind of message again when he returned to Wales from southern Africa.

Ellis, then, had his grey areas, too, like all other politicians. Accounts which exaggerate his Gandhi-like saintliness do his memory a disservice. Lloyd George was a stronger character, tougher, harder, more ruthless, with a more obvious capacity for supreme leadership. (He could also, contrary to many assessments, be a good friend, as men like Herbert Lewis and C. P. Scott of the *Manchester Guardian* bore witness over the years.[60]) Whether Tom Ellis, if he had lived, would have held major office in the Liberal governments of 1906–14 is a nice question for counter-factual debate. On balance, after a quarter-century of reflection the present writer is now inclined to feel that, warts and all, the more realistic figure of Lloyd George may have been rather more appropriate for his generation. His view of Welsh nationality focused on schisms, conflicts, class tensions and fractured sensibilities endemic in the divided, schizophrenic Wales of his day. Further, he had the ambition and drive to harness them, on behalf not of personal ambition alone, but also of wider social and international objectives. In a hard, brutalizing world, Lloyd George, the disenchanted man of action, rather than Ellis, the noble man of vision, might have been what Welsh Liberalism and the nation as a whole required.

But it is perhaps wrong to try to choose between them in so arbitrary a fashion. Really, Wales needed them both. Each was central to the national renaissance of the *fin-de-siècle*. Ellis and Lloyd George were, above all, great democrats who applied their very different talents, temperaments and philosophies to promoting national equality for their countrymen. They did so without stirring up class war, without revolution, without the violence and bloodshed that continue to scar the national experience of Ireland down to the present day. They redefined the national identity with permanent results. They contributed mightily to what

---

[60] The Herbert Lewis Papers in the NLW and the Scott Papers in the BL are a valuable corrective to many wild criticisms by later writers.

the present writer, in a literary conceit, once termed Wales's Antonine Age.[61] Together and separately, Ellis and Lloyd George grasped many of the opportunities first elaborated in the mid-century, on which Ieuan Gwynedd Jones has written with such grace and understanding. They enabled their Wales to come to terms with its past, and to contemplate a more fulfilling and creative future.

[61] K. O. Morgan, *Rebirth of a Nation: Wales, 1880–1980* (Oxford and Cardiff, 1981), p. 123, referring to the 1900–14 period.

Amateurs and Professionals in the Cultures of Wales

PETER STEAD

AS he looked back on the lives of those 'Great Welshmen' of his era, Sir Thomas Hughes declared there were two paintings that he would like to have seen commissioned and then exhibited in the National Museum: one would be of the young David Lloyd George being taught the rudiments of mathematics by his uncle, the 'saintly old village shoemaker', and the other would be of Joseph Parry, the musician, who would be shown as a young steelworker 'stripped for his exhausting toil, lying prone on the iron floor of the great rolling mill, chalk in hand, intent on working out the melodies that were flooding his soul'.[1] Both paintings would indeed have been highly appropriate images to commemorate the lives of those nineteenth-century Welshmen who rose from humble origins to positions of distinction and the way in which those individual lives had been so much a reflection of the values of a whole people. The image of the young man who was destined to become Prime Minister would have served as a reminder that, ultimately, nineteenth-century Wales became a distinct political reality characterized by a firm commitment to democratic and radical values and by a belief that fitting parliamentary representation would give to Wales both a new dignity and a greater degree of social justice. But Thomas Hughes spoke for many of his fellow countrymen when he suggested that another image was needed which would have commemorated both the artistic talent which Wales had produced in the modern era as well as that quite remarkable enthusiasm for artistic creativity and participation which had been shown by so many ordinary Welsh men and women. For, whilst Wales was to become famous for its politics, there was to be a tendency for even the Welsh themselves to forget that political activity had always existed alongside other pursuits, and that there would never have been a distinct Welsh voice in politics had it not been for the enormous participation of the people of Wales both in Nonconformity and in those activities that we would now regard as the arts.

Taken together, as they must necessarily be, Nonconformity and those artistic pursuits had throughout the nineteenth century constituted a remarkable culture, a culture that had become totally synonymous with a new definition of Welshness itself. In a period dating from about the middle of the previous century there had been considerable social and economic changes, but the people of Wales

[1] T. Hughes, *Great Welshmen of Modern Days* (Cardiff, 1931), p. 116.

had reacted to those changes by committing themselves fully to a new religious
adherence and by ensuring that, along with religion, there were many other
diversions and entertainments. The theology of Nonconformity was determined
by preachers and hymn-writers, and the occasions, opportunities and modes
of the various entertainments were largely determined and organized by a group
of scholar-patriots; nevertheless, what was absolutely of the essence in both
areas of activity was the degree of popular participation.[2] A traditional rural
society had undergone dramatic change but the people themselves had responded
by evolving an associational life which not only made dislocation bearable but
was ideally suited to take advantage of the new opportunities offered and the
new energies released. For the duration of the nineteenth century, Wales was
to be characterized more than anything else by the way in which both its agricultural and industrial areas sustained this genuinely popular culture, a culture
that has been variously described as 'peasant' or 'working-class'.[3] It was a
culture that had been shaped by the people, it belonged to them and it was
one that was almost exclusively articulated in the Welsh language. This was
the traditional language of the people, but both Nonconformity and the new
pattern of artistic entertainment had given that language a new vitality and
a deeper spiritual and cultural hold. As Professor Ieuan Gwynedd Jones has
reminded us, all the meaning of life, all the values that the Welshman cherished
most and which lifted him above the ordinary and mundane, everything which
reminded him of why he and his community were special, were to be found
in that very language of his faith, his poetry and his music.[4]

The new power of the language was the key to the culture and it ensured
that congregations and audiences would be fascinated by the spoken and, increasingly, by the printed words of both preachers and poets. All the while the language
was intensifying and refining the faith and, almost miraculously, the complex
poetry of an ancient aristocracy became, in the words of Professor T. J. Morgan,
'the accomplishment and plaything of shepherds and quarrymen and coal-
miners'.[5] All the while, too, the great preachers and poets were achieving a
heroic status within the popular mind, a status which had been initially ensured
by the quality of their art but which was confirmed as their personalities, and
even their abbreviated or bardic names themselves, became respectively the
symbols and the catch-phrases of the culture. Rivalry was intense, with each
denomination and each congregation developing its own loyalties, whilst for
the poets the competitive eisteddfodau, which had been held in public houses,
but which had now been given a new lease of life first by the literary societies
and then by the chapels themselves, ensured that there would be a continuous
supply of new heroes. The rivalry operated at every level and served to bind
the people, even the most isolated and humble communities, in a national culture:
poets competed within the chapel, within the village, within the valley, within

---

[2] P. Morgan, *The Eighteenth Century Renaissance* (Llandybïe, 1981).

[3] T. J. Morgan, *Peasant Culture* (Inaugural Lecture, University College of Swansea, 1962); I. G. Jones,
Communities: Essays in the Social History of Victorian Wales (Llandysul, 1987), pp. 139–57.

[4] Jones, *Explorations and Explanations* (Llandysul, 1981), p. 233; idem., *Communities*, pp. 105–38.

[5] Morgan, *Peasant Culture*, p. 12.

the county and then for the highest honours. Every village had its practitioners and there was often some sympathy for their view that rivals in the larger centres of population were conspiring to deny them the recognition they deserved. Abercynon, for example, was proud of William Henry Dyer ('Mabonwyson'), a poet who always felt that he was competing against a clique of rivals from nearby Pontypridd; it was his view that the 'Clic-y-Bont' would always hand the prize to one of their number, and by way of revenge he developed a nice selection of carefully chosen insults for 'Brynfab', 'Dewi Alaw', 'Ap Myfyr', and others. In reference to the Graig shopkeeper 'Dewi Wyn o Esyllt', he suggested that 'all his stock is in the window'.[6] It was a tough business, but for the really talented there was fame to be achieved and great prestige to be earned. The winners of chairs, especially those awarded at the National Eisteddfod, became the most respected figures within the culture and they were given every opportunity to acquire celebrity status. The whole nation thrilled at the story of how a vast audience had acclaimed the success of Evan Rees at the International Eisteddfod held as part of the Chicago World Fair in 1893, but this was only one of twelve chairs to be won by the former Aberdare collier and railwayman who, as 'Dyfed', was to be Archdruid for seventeen years.[7] Such was the great demand for verse that the Revd William Thomas of Ynys-ddu in Monmouthshire, the highly respected poet 'Islwyn', found that he was required to be the poetry editor of seven different newspapers or journals.[8]

The preachers and poets were the custodians of the language and therefore of the culture as a whole. They lived quite humbly in their communities, yet there were ways in which they inevitably stood apart. Undoubtedly they were public entertainers, but their roles also required that they spent hours in solitary reflection; their writing would be done in the relative privacy of their homes and, ultimately, for all their popular following, their sermons and poems were rather esoteric compositions fully appreciated by only a minority. It is always the fate of custodians to become conservative, and it was inevitable that the poets especially would be more and more associated with the glories of the past rather than with the capability of the language to reflect more progressive ideas. Cultural leadership gave way to a more detached respect as the masses became more and more aware of what writers, both great and small, were doing through the medium of English prose. For most of the nineteenth century the Welsh language had held its supremacy even in the coalfields of the south, and indeed many of the presses that had turned out the sermons and the verse had been located in Merthyr and Aberdare, but such was the complexity and intensity of Welsh literary life that it was inevitable that first the poets, and then the preachers, would be thought of as the leaders of a sub-culture rather than of the nation as a whole. The men of the word had been mighty men but, as the century unfolded, things were always moving against them. In this respect there was a particularly marked contrast with music, which always had

---

[6] T. Evans, *The Story of Abercynon* (Cardiff, 1944), pp. 64 ff.

[7] Hughes, *Great Welshmen*, pp. 42 ff.

[8] W. J. Townsend Collins, *Monmouthshire Writers* (Newport, 1945).

the capacity to be more genuinely popular and which served to bind people into what was still almost exclusively a Welsh-language culture by appealing to those who were not entirely able to follow the finer points of theology or strict metre or alliteration, and especially to those—and this became an increasingly important factor—who were not fully confident of their ability in the Welsh language itself. Music gave this culture a mass dimension, and what was crucial in this process was the way in which social and technical changes were to allow and encourage music-making of a communal kind. At the end of the eighteenth century the traditional songs of the peasantry had been taken up by both the hymnologists and the scholar-patriots and so, as the new industrial villages emerged, both congregations and other assemblies found that there was music to be sung. To a unique degree, that distinctive Welsh culture of the nineteenth century owed its identity to the sheer pleasure which ordinary people took in performing and listening to music, and that applied especially to choral music.

Mass participation was all-important but, as was the case with religion and poetry, there were always commanding figures to provide leadership and inspiration. Of course in the field of music there was the added advantage that the most accomplished performers could be exported, especially to London, where their achievements could serve as general reminders of the excellence and legitimacy of the culture and so ensure that Wales was regarded favourably. Throughout the eighteenth and nineteenth centuries Wales sent its musical talent to London to entertain royalty and the fashionable theatre-going classes, and all that was asked was that these musicians should repay the land of their birth and their inspiration by returning to perform and to adjudicate at the National Eisteddfod. The early model careers were those of the harpist Edward Jones ('Bardd y Brenin'), who had gone to London from Llandderfel in the 1770s, and the composer John Parry ('Bardd Alaw'), who took the same route from Denbigh in 1807; both men regularly returned to visit eisteddfodau and both made it their life-work to collect and arrange Welsh melodies.[9] Later they were succeeded by others and especially by two men who both owed their early prominence to eisteddfod successes and who both came to think of themselves as being in some way responsible for the general musical standards of every eisteddfod, and even of Wales as a whole. Brinley Richards, who was born in Carmarthen in 1819, the son of a church organist and music-shop proprietor, became an outstanding student and teacher at the Royal Academy of Music, and by mid-century he was both a fine pianist and a prolific composer.[10] Only a few years younger was John Thomas, a native of Bridgend who went to the Royal Academy and who, as 'Pencerdd Gwalia', Harpist to the Queen and Professor of Harp at the Royal College of Music, became the most revered authority in Welsh musical life.[11] These great figures were always there in London to encourage the harpists, the composers and increasingly the singers who

---

[9] There are excellent entries on the musicians of Wales in S. Sadie (ed.), *The New Grove Dictionary of Music and Musicians* (London, 1980). For Edward Jones, see the entry by Owain Edwards, vol. 9, p. 698 and for John Parry the entry by P. Crossley-Holland and N. Temperley in vol. 14, p. 245.

[10] Ibid., 15, p. 842.

[11] Owain Edwards, ibid., 18, p. 779.

were trying to emulate their success and who were able to pursue their studies by virtue of scholarships provided by wealthy patrons or public collections. Thomas Hughes remembered William Davies ('Mynorydd'), the Merthyr-born sculptor and musician, father of the mezzo-soprano Mary Davies, regularly visiting the Royal Academy of Music and the Royal College of Music, 'ferreting out lonely and home-sick Celts' and inviting them to his weekly 'At Homes' where they would always be expected to join in the music-making.[12] The Welsh network was always there to help the talented, just as there were now distinguished and inspired teachers in most Welsh villages. Joseph Parry himself went to the Royal Academy in 1868, supported by donations made in both America and Wales; by 1874 he was Professor of Music at Aberystwyth and, when funds ran out at the College, he opened his own Academy of Music at Swansea.[13] The avenues to success were well established, but such was the nature of the culture that no composer, soloist or professor was ever likely to forget his debt to the realm of popular music in Wales or to disavow his responsibility in nourishing this remarkable phenomenon.

In the villages of nineteenth-century Wales, and especially in the industrial villages, there occurred a spontaneous eruption of music-making and especially of choral singing. The organizational structure was provided by the chapels and the eisteddfodau, and the urge for group participation and the basic artistic impetus came from the workpeople themselves; there was often whole-hearted support from the influential and prosperous classes, and all the while there were new technical innovations and aids which encouraged even wider participation and allowed even better levels of performance. The quite massive extent to which the Welsh valleys were alive with the sound of music and song can only be fully appreciated by local historians, for they are best able to appreciate that fascinating and clearly crucial chronology which saw each village start its own choirs, open musical stores selling pianos, harmoniums and printed sheet music, form its own bands eager to secure the very latest and best brass instruments, and then acquire teachers of tonic sol-fa who taught the notation which ensured an even wider participation in choral singing. As the century proceeded so the pattern of local activity widened and became even more diverse and, as well as the eisteddfod and the *cymanfa ganu*, there would be a full calendar of sacred and celebrity concerts, male voice choirs and choral societies, and even in some areas operatic groups and choral festivals. The local historian is also the person best qualified to recognize the way in which, amidst what Professor T. J. Morgan described as that 'jungle of choirs and anthems and choruses from oratorios' which seemed to cover every valley, there was always a tendency for each community to take a special pride in occasional manifestations of local excellence.[14] For the people of Merthyr there was the glorious knowledge that the Cyfarthfa band had gone to the Crystal Palace in 1860 and proved that it was the third best of over sixty bands who had all been seeking

---

[12] Hughes, *Great Welshmen*, p. 31.

[13] E. K. Evans (ed.), *Cofiant Dr Joseph Parry* (Cardiff and London, 1921).

[14] Morgan, *Peasant Culture*, p. 8.

fame; at Aberdare they were so proud of Griffith Rhys Jones ('Caradog'), born in Trecynon and conductor of both the very successful Aberdare United Choir and the great 'Côr Mawr' of 456 voices which had sung at the Crystal Palace in 1872, that they paid for a statue which was to stand in the centre of the town.[15] In the Swansea Valley the great oratorios were performed with a regularity and passion which made it seem as though they had been especially composed for that community, whilst in Maesteg it was never doubted that the local chapels produced the best singers in Wales, a conviction founded upon the successes of the Nantyffyllon Children's Choir and the reputation that locally-produced composers and singers gained throughout the world.[16] Gilfach Goch was the home of poets and musicians, but its citizens' greatest object of pride was the brass band which came second at the Crystal Palace in 1907 and whose Band and Musical Institute stood as a symbol of how this small and isolated mining village had become a civilized and nationally known community.[17]

To absorb this local detail is to be overwhelmed by the sheer level of participation and by the superfluity of events. It is difficult for the historian to retain any kind of objectivity in the face of such enthusiasm, and it is important above all that he senses the enormous amount of pleasure and satisfaction that the people of Wales derived from their music-making. It was not just a matter of choral singing, for in almost every village there were the well-established maestros, the composers and cantatas and hymns, the brilliant violinists, the very highly qualified teachers of the piano, the acclaimed soloists; and who is to deny that amongst such people the appreciation of all that was finest in nineteenth-century music was as keen as it was in any other part of Europe? The local geniuses were often regarded as being a little eccentric, but the busts of Beethoven and the terraced houses that were named after the composer were not there as any kind of affectation. In every community there was an opportunity for young people to respond to what was best in music, exactly as Wyn Griffith did when he stood by his father's piano and listened as he had never listened before to Bach's B minor Mass: 'the music sounded rich and massive, chords soaring and falling, the bass patterned endlessly in a swoop upwards and a slow decline.'[18] Griffith himself went on to learn the piano and the cello, as did so many other young Welsh people but, of course, a far greater number responded to music by joining choirs or simply by becoming regular members of an audience, and it was always this group or even mass participation which contemporaries identified as the unique quality of the musical life of Wales. It is precisely at this point that so many commentators become patronizing and begin to discuss choral singing in sociological rather than aesthetic terms,

---

[15] For Merthyr, see the excellent article by Huw Williams, 'Brass Bands, Jazz Bands, Choirs: Aspects of Music in Merthyr Tydfil', in Joseph Gross (ed.), *The Merthyr Historian*, 3 (1980), 98–111. For Caradog, see Anon, 'Aberdare: A Descriptive and Historical Sketch' (1885), reprinted in *Old Aberdare* (Cynon Valley Hist. Soc., I, 1976).

[16] B. Richards, *A History of the Llynfi Valley* (Cowbridge, 1982).

[17] K. O. Pritchard, *The Story of Gilfach Goch* (2nd ed., Newport, 1973).

[18] Ll. W. Griffith, *Spring of Youth* (London, 1935), p. 63.

losing sight both of the sheer pleasure derived from the singing and of the level
of accomplishment which was achieved; such commentators see the achievement
only in terms of how industrial workers collectively and harmlessly organized
their leisure. At times one suspects that there are many scholars who find it
difficult to come to terms with enthusiasm, and surely it was enthusiasm which
accounted for so many of the comic excesses which came to characterize the
Welsh choral scene. English historians of brass bands, having recovered from
the realization that the first genuine brass band in Britain was formed not in
the north of England but rather at the Blaina ironworks in south Wales, have
been quite prepared to concede that the brass band movement, and especially
its competitions, were always accompanied by the same kind of loyalty and
enthusiasm that characterized the behaviour of football supporters, and certainly
much of their analysis can be applied to the ways in which the Welsh regarded
their choirs.[19] In the 1920s the young Wynford Vaughan Thomas was taken
to many a choral competition by his distinguished father, the composer David
Vaughan Thomas, and he remembered the way in which everything came to
a climax with the 'Battle of the Parties'; there would be 'a fierce loyalty' to
one favourite 'party' or choir who would respond by attacking the music 'as
if they were exacting revenge' for the great defeats of Welsh history.[20] Passion
was needed to sustain the choirs and to give them that extra incentive to win,
and so it was not surprising that a complicated and often bitter politics ensued
in which there were to be many splits, betrayals and reunions.[21] The supporters
became as tense as the choristers and the scenes that accompanied the adjudi-
cations did as much as anything to divert attention from the music. When,
much to the surprise of many of his friends, the composer Samuel Coleridge-
Taylor agreed to act as an adjudicator in Wales, he was warned by Dr Turpin,
the Principal of Trinity College of Music, that he should not 'undertake that
job at any price', for Turpin's own adjudication had led to his hat being knocked
off and he had escaped only 'with great difficulty'.[22] Coleridge-Taylor himself
saw his excursions to Wales as a form of dangerous living for, writing in 1904
to an American contact, he made some interesting revelations:

> Please don't make any arrangements to wrap me in cotton wool. I am not that
> kind of person at all. I do a great deal of adjudicating in Wales among a very
> rough class of people; most adjudicators have had bad eggs and boots thrown
> at them by the people, but fortunately nothing of the kind has ever happened
> to me yet. I mention this so that you may know that my life is not spent entirely
> in drawing-rooms and concert halls, but among some of the roughest people in

[19] C. Bainbridge, *Brass Triumphant* (London, 1980) and A. R. Taylor, *Brass Bands* (London, 1979). Both
writers gingerly examine the claim that Blaina came first. See also the entry on Bands by Clifford Bevan
in S. Sadie (ed.), *The New Grove Dictionary of Musical Instruments* (London, 1984), I, p. 138.

[20] W. V. Thomas, *Madly in All Directions* (London, 1967), p. 211.

[21] E. E. Edwards, *Echoes of Rhymney* (Rhymney, 1974), p. 76, for an example of a local historian reporting
the splitting of a choir, but the politics of music was most memorably commemorated in the feature film,
The Valley of Song, which starred Clifford Evans.

[22] W. C. Berwick-Sayers, *Samuel Coleridge-Taylor: Musician* (London, 1927), p. 119.

Wales welcomes M. Laurent de Rille.

M. Laurent de Rille, the eminent French musician, was one of the adjudicators at the International Male Voice Competitions which commenced at Cardiff on Boxing Day, 1903. (*From J. M. Staniforth, Cartoons, by permission of the Western Mail.*)

the world, who tell you what they think very plainly. Yet I have four more engagements among them for next January![23]

Clearly there was some roughness but more often there was simply a pride and, with that, a tendency to detect prejudice amongst others. Outsiders were often alienated by the sheer competitiveness of Welsh singing but it is fascinating to trace the way in which all the parochialism and pettiness of a peasant culture served to fuel a quest for excellence and a desire that one choir, one chapel, one village or one part of Wales should be thought of as being an adornment to the culture. The adjudication of the chief choral event at the National Eisteddfod held in Cardiff in 1884 provided an illustration of the particular rivalry which existed not only in music, but in every aspect of Welsh life, between the north and the south. The announcement was to the effect that the Penrhyn Choir was not only the best choir but in an altogether different class from the south Wales choirs, and so it transpired that 'the transports of the people from North Wales were a sight to see'; 'some among the audience threw their hats in the air, while others mounted the benches and gave way to extravagant demonstrations of delight.'[24]

This was indeed, as Dr K. O. Morgan has concluded, a 'populist' musical culture in which the choice of music, the kinds of interpretation and the mode of performance were determined well down the pyramid of musical accomplishment.[25] It was not, however, a totally parochial culture for it was thrilled by much of the new music that it discovered: neither was it an uncritical culture, for there were many moments when home truths had to be confronted. At the Cardiff Eisteddfod of 1884 the fifty-pound prize for a cantata on the subject of 'The Crusader' was not awarded and neither was the five guinea prize for an anthem, even though there had been thirty entries; but most devastating of all had been the comments that were made about those south Wales choirs which had failed to come up to the standard set by Penrhyn. The chief adjudicator, Sir George Macfarren of the Royal Academy of Music, was quite critical, but it was left to the correspondent of the *Daily Telegraph* to make clear why the choirs of south Wales had failed: they had not been trained by educated musicians, the boy altos had not blended well, and there was a general assumption that volume was a virtue in itself, with the result that unrestrained vehemence had led to disaster. All in all the south Wales choirs had demonstrated that 'enthusiasm, even when combined with a measure of uncultured aptitude is not enough'.[26] Over and over again in those last years of the century, highly trained adjudicators from both home and away were to insist on higher standards and were to urge the musicians of Wales to compete in a higher league: their efforts ran parallel with those of leading scholars, who were by that time attempting to improve the literary standards of the eisteddfod.[27] Nobody was more

[23] Ibid., p. 154.

[24] *Trans. National Eisteddfod of Wales, Cardiff* (1884), p. 433.

[25] K. O. Morgan, *Rebirth of a Nation: Wales 1880–1980* (Oxford and Cardiff, 1981), p. 19.

[26] *Trans. Nat. Eisteddfod* (1884); the *Daily Telegraph* was extensively quoted in the *Transactions*.

[27] Morgan, *Rebirth of a Nation*, pp. 97–9; A. James, *John Morris-Jones* (Cardiff, 1987).

outspoken than 'Pencerdd Gwalia' himself who, when judging the chief choral event at Aberdare in 1885, had praised the 'religious fervour' of the singing but suggested that the boy contraltos had strained too hard, and urged the necessity of an orchestral rather than a piano accompaniment so that the singing could be better supported and rhythm and key maintained.[28] He returned to this theme in 1886 when he called for the formation of an orchestra in every town and declared that, whilst tonic sol-fa had encouraged singing, it had held back the development of instrumental playing.[29] By this time the whole debate was widening and there were many who shared C. Francis Lloyd's view that 'we are, in the matter of music, at least fifty years behind the times'.[30] There were now constant calls for greater emphasis on instrumental and orchestral playing, a broadening of the repertoire, a better organized musical education in Wales, and the commissioning of new works by Welsh composers.

In time the improvements came, and in the first decades of the twentieth century the University, the Council of Music and, above all perhaps, two very talented musicians, Walford Davies and David Vaughan Thomas, both of whom believed that Wales could achieve so much more, worked hard to establish instrumental and orchestral music and the full contemporary European repertoire as the foundation of Welsh music.[31] The urgency and novelty of these later achievements only seem to confirm, however, the general criticisms that were made at the end of the century. For all the talk of the Welsh being a musical nation, the sad truth seems to have been that their skills were very largely the minor ones of being able to sing four-part music with enthusiasm. It was generally accepted that there were no great Welsh composers, that there was no orchestral tradition and that, even with choral music, the Welsh possessed, in the words of Wyn Griffith, an 'interpretive and not a creative' faculty.[32] It is highly desirable that Welsh historians should be able to judge the alleged musicality of the nation with some degree of objectivity, but a great disservice is done if all those contemporary criticisms are accepted as the final judgement. We must retain some sense of scale and a sense, too, of what was possible in a largely peasant and working-class society. In 1920 L. J. Roberts argued that much of the criticism was 'ill-informed and unfounded' and he asked his readers to remember that the population of Wales was only half that of Yorkshire and a quarter that of London. He took pride in the choral achievements and stressed that much of Wales was still pastoral.[33] Even as he made his criticisms in the 1890s, 'Pencerdd Gwalia' had often struck a more positive note, and

---

[28] *Trans. National Eisteddfod of Wales, Aberdare* (1885), pp. lxxix ff.

[29] J. Thomas, *Welsh Music* (a paper read to the Incorporated Society of Musicians, 1896).

[30] C. F. Lloyd, 'The Present State of Music in Wales', *Trans. Liverpool Welsh National Society*, eighth series (1892–3), p. 110.

[31] For Sir Henry Walford Davies, see Hugh Ottoway's entry in Sadie, *Grove Dictionary of Music*, p. 280 and his own *Music in Wales: Memorandum on Music in Schools* (National Council of Music in Wales, 1921). For Dr David Vaughan Thomas, see *DWB* (1959), p. 944, the *Herald of Wales*, 22 September 1934, and his own articles, 'Welsh Music and Modern Tendencies' in *Welsh Outlook*, May 1914, and also 'The Welsh Festival', ibid., January 1920.

[32] W. Griffith, *The Welsh* (Harmondsworth, 1950), p. 118.

[33] L. J. Roberts, 'The Outlook for Music in Wales', *Welsh Outlook*, March 1920.

Martyrs of the Arena.

The victors at the Cardiff International Male Voice Competitions (December, 1903), the adjudicator being M. Laurent de Rille, the eminent French musician. (*From J. M. Staniforth, Cartoons, by permission of the Western Mail.*)

he could speak of how Welsh choirs were carrying all before them, of how so many young musicians were winning scholarships to the best academies and even composing works of note. So many of the criticisms that were made originated from plain frustration that Wales was not fulfilling its potential, given what had already been achieved. Certainly there was considerable pride in the regularity with which individual chapels and local societies were performing the major choral works of the time and in the quality of the soloists who were hired, many of whom were now Welsh singers who were London-trained and London-based. From the 1880s onwards the National Eisteddfod concerts were a remarkable feature: at Aberdare in 1885, for example, the Aberdare Choral Union and the Eisteddfod orchestral band combined with soloists to put on two miscellaneous concerts, a performance of Handel's *Samson* and also of Mackenzie's dramatic oratorio, *The Rose of Sharon*, for which there was an audience of well over 5,000.[34] For the chapel and the eisteddfod the miscellaneous concert and the oratorio represented the maximum use of resources, but in the last years before the war festival organizers went even further. The programme of Cardiff's Triennial Festival held in 1902 ought to stand as a symbol of what could be achieved: between the Wednesday and the Saturday a full orchestra and choir and a group of some fifteen soloists gave eight concerts. There was a performance of Mendelssohn's *Elijah* and Berlioz's *Faust*, but in the other concerts there was orchestral music by Mozart, Brahms, Wagner, Beethoven, Elgar and Tchaikovsky. The organizers were also able to announce that all the railway companies that ran services into Cardiff would be offering both cheap excursions and special reductions for ticket-holders.[35]

A glance at any contemporary programme indicates the enormous popularity of the song. At that Cardiff Festival, Wagner's overture song *Die Meistersinger* was followed by a rendering of 'Hiawatha's Song' by Coleridge-Taylor, and Schumann's Piano Concerto in A was followed by the 'mad scene' solo from Ambroise Thomas's *Hamlet*. When John McCormack came to a Grand Concert in Swansea's Albert Hall in 1908 it was to sing 'I Hear You Calling Me', 'Mountain Lovers', 'Ah Moon of My Delight', as well as to join with the Swansea and District Male Voice Society to sing Beethoven's 'Where is He'.[36] Such programmes are not to the modern taste and they tend to make so much Victorian and Edwardian music look like village-hall offerings, but well-sung songs were what Victorian audiences not only in Wales but throughout the world wanted to hear, and in most respects the tastes of Welsh audiences were not very different from those in the north of England, in London, or even for that matter in America. In fact these old programmes are a very useful reminder that nineteenth-century Welsh music ought to be assessed within the wider context of the British musical scene. There were distinct Welsh traditions such as that of the harp, the folk-song and *penillion* and there were distinctive Welsh institutions which had created

---

[34] *Trans. Nat. Eisteddfod* (1885).

[35] *Cardiff Triennial Musical Festival: Prospectus 1902.* A letter in the copy to be found in the Swansea Central Reference Library shows that the Librarian wrote to Cardiff to request this Prospectus.

[36] Grand Concert, Albert Hall, Swansea, 16 November 1908. The Swansea Reference Library has a collection of eisteddfod and concert programmes.

a passion for choral singing, but in so many other respects Welsh musicians and Welsh audiences were characteristic Victorians.[37] There were more instrumentalists in parts of England, but it was not that much easier to establish orchestral traditions and the deep-felt need for new English composers paralleled what was felt in Wales. Of course, some very talented English composers were to emerge, some of them with suspiciously Welsh-sounding names and strong connections with the Marches, but there was no basic reason why one of those great British composers could not have been Welsh.

Many people, though, expected more of Wales, for in the second half of the nineteenth century and the beginning of the twentieth it seemed as if the future of classical music would be determined within distinct national idioms in both symphonic and choral music. This was not just a question of great nations, for the Scandinavians, the Czechs and the Hungarians were all to show that folk music and the various traditions of both rural and industrial workers could be used as ingredients in the further development of orchestral, operatic and choral music. It is within that league, rather than as a British region, that many Welsh people have wanted to see their nation judged. The similarities, in particular with Czechoslovakia and Hungary, have led many to believe that in the late nineteenth century a golden opportunity was lost, but at no time did Wales have the social structure and cultural institutions which could have created a national music of international stature. In his defence of Welsh music L. J. Roberts spoke of 'young self-taught vocalists living often in far upland valleys, remote from public road or dwelling'; in so doing he probably went a little too far, but we do need to recall what a peasant tradition of music really involved. We must remember that image of the young Joseph Parry as a steelworker struggling with his compositions, and we need also to recall the reference by J. Spencer Curwen after he had adjudicated at the Merthyr Eisteddfod in 1881, to the fact that in the colliery districts 'there is no gentry to lead or to patronise' the working people who therefore have 'to patronise themselves', and that 'almost all the Welsh singers who have risen to fame have been helped by their fellow-countrymen to an education in music'.[38] Of course, the Welsh gentry and the Welsh industrialists played their part by contributing to the cost of chapels and halls, by acting as patrons to concerts and eisteddfodau, and even by helping to send the talented to the London academies, but what they did not and could not do was to establish towns, or even one city, where all the energies of the Welsh-language and working-class cultures might be focused to create a specifically national culture. The most talented peasants and workers could be sent off to London and all the popular festivals could be maintained and supported, but meanwhile there was no reason at all to

---

[37] For a discussion of the place of Welsh music within a wider context, see M. Owen, 'Welsh Folk Music' in *Trans. Cymmr.*, Session 1897–8 (1899), p. 65. J. Thomas, 'Music and Musicians as Relating to Wales' in *Trans. Liverpool Welsh National Society*, 1st Session, (1885–6), and Daniel Jones, *Music in Wales* (annual lecture of the BBC in Wales, 1961).

[38] J. Spencer Curwen's talk 'Popular Music in Wales' was delivered to the College of Organists and then quoted and analysed in 'The Eisteddfod and Popular Music in Wales', *Y Cymmrodor*, 5 (1882), 285.

challenge the norms of that Englishness to which this regional gentry fully sub-
scribed. That lively peasant culture, which it was always expedient to praise
at the appropriate moments, had really to be kept in place.

There were perhaps opportunities in late Victorian Wales for the development
of other musical possibilities, but the failure to capitalize on these opportunities
confirms that there were formidable cultural barriers. In the second half of the
nineteenth century Madame Adelina Patti was generally regarded as the world's
outstanding operatic soprano, 'the undisputed *prima donna*', and in the 1880s
she came to live at Craig-y-nos, just to the north of the industrial villages in
the Swansea Valley and twenty-two miles from Swansea.[39] Wales was very
proud of its new citizen and during the thirty years she spent at 'this charming
Welsh retreat', Patti established many links with the local people.[40] She played
the Lady Bountiful in the Swansea Valley; she gave charity concerts at Swansea,
Neath, Pontardawe and Mumbles; she opened Swansea's Grand Theatre; and
at her own beautiful little theatre at Craig-y-nos she organized entertainments
which not only required the services of a 'capital little orchestra from Swansea'
but which sometimes consisted of light operas that had been composed by Swansea musicians.[41] All this amounted to an honourable contact with the cultural
life of Wales, but what the world's greatest soprano could not do, even though
her theatrical career continued for ten years after she came to Craig-y-nos, was
to establish a local operatic tradition. Of course, it would have been preferable
had her opera house been built at Neath or Swansea rather than at her home
and it might have been better had she provided full-scale productions rather
than celebrity concerts. The initiative should have come from those gentry families whom Patti first came to south Wales to visit and who were always to
remain her greatest supporters. There was a remarkable moment at the Aberdare
Eisteddfod in 1885 when, following a guest appearance by the singer Eleanor
Rees, Lord Aberdare, President for the day, rose to compliment her on her
singing and on the way in which she was keeping alive the old Welsh airs,
and referred to the lovely Celtic air which ran through Flotow's opera *Martha*
and which he had heard sung memorably by Madame Patti.[42] It was to his
great regret that Patti was not well and had been unable to accept his invitation
to come to Aberdare, but there was no evidence to suggest that Lord Aberdare
was taking steps to set up productions of *Martha* in Wales or trying to establish
institutions which would encourage Welsh composers to create an operatic tradition based on Welsh melodies. Songs and oratorios were considered to be
the music of the Welsh, and opera was altogether too metropolitan and too
exotic for the local middle-class and peasant tastes. That was the way of thinking
even as the Welsh valleys began to send their talent to the opera houses of

[39]   R. Christiansen, *Prima Donna: A History* (London, 1984), p. 111.

[40]   H. Klein, *The Reign of Patti* (New York, 1920) reports fully on Craig-y-nos and at the Swansea Reference
Library there is a collection of local newspaper articles relating to Madame Patti.

[41]   B. Lloyd in *Evening Post*, 18 September 1971.

[42]   *Trans. Nat. Eisteddfod of Wales* (1885), p. lxxvi.

London and America: Ben Davies from Pontardawe was one of the great stars of both the *bel canto* and the new operas staged in London, but when he came home to Wales he came to sing in oratorios and to give recitals. In music everything had its place and the consensus among gentry musicians and social leaders was that different musical worlds needed to be kept apart. In 1880 Mrs Florence Marshall very neatly summed up the outlook of those who organized and sponsored Welsh music when she talked of how the oratorio expressed all the musical aspirations of those provincials whose puritanical inheritance had given them a 'distrust and a dislike of anything theatrical' and for whom the 'opera house is *terra incognita*'. It is also worth recalling, however, that David Frangcon-Davies, one of Wales's greatest singers, could argue that 'the loftier the theme the purer the music' and therefore 'oratorio will continue to hold its own'.[43]

The Victorians did not create a Welsh National Opera and neither did they manage to create a National Orchestra and yet, as we have seen, orchestras always seemed to emerge in Wales when the occasion demanded. W. F. Hulley, who is known to history as the conductor who took his orchestra to Craig-y-nos, led a very full musical life in Swansea. He was organist at St David's Roman Catholic Church, his light operas were performed at the Drill Hall and at the schoolroom in Edward Street known as the 'Bijou Theatre', and his orchestra was in constant demand for amateur operatic and other theatrical occasions, concerts and county balls.[44] These were years when most towns and even some individual chapels could boast of orchestral societies but no amateur musicians were to achieve so much publicity and so much fame as the professional orchestras which played at Llandudno. This north Wales resort became one of the orchestral centres of Victorian Britain and this was almost entirely due to the efforts of a very eccentric former French army musician, Jules Rivière, who, in 1887, was appointed conductor of a twenty-eight-piece orchestra which played on the pier.[45] There was already a musical tradition in the town, but Rivière was to transform the local scene and give the town a reputation that it was to retain well into the next century. At the new and very large Pier Pavilion he trebled the size of his orchestra; he later led a company which opened another large concert hall known at first as Rivière's Concert Hall and then as the Llandudno Opera House. Many subsequently famous musicians came to Llandudno to play for Rivière or even just to learn from him, and Ivor Wynne Jones has very plausibly suggested that it was at Llandudno that the young Henry J. Wood realized that there was no harm in playing classical music with a little show-business flair. Wood has left a marvellous description of the old Frenchman, wearing a velvet jacket with a spray of orchids, sitting to conduct his orchestra facing the audience and holding a bejewelled ivory baton in a hand from which

[43] F. Marshall, *The Nineteenth Century*, 8 (December 1880), p. 926, quoted in E. D. Mackerness, *A Social History of English Music* (London, 1964), p. 186. D. Frangcon-Davies, *The Singing of the Future* (London, 1905) reprinted in M. Frangcon-Davies, *David Frangcon-Davies, His Life and Book* (London, 1938), p. 153.

[44] J. R. John in *Evening Post*, 14 March 1958.

[45] I. W. Jones, *Llandudno, Queen of the Welsh Resorts* (Cardiff, 1975).

dangled a massive blue tassel. But Wood was far more impressed with a visiting orchestra at a pier concert in which Arthur Payne played the Mendelssohn Violin Concerto.[46] Payne became the Musical Director of the Pier Orchestra and throughout the season he provided full programmes of classical music by Gounod, Verdi, Tchaikovsky and other composers at morning and evening concerts; on Sunday there would be a sacred concert. There was plenty of good music at Llandudno but, of course, fashionable resorts could bring together special kinds of audiences and once again they were places apart where unusual things could be tolerated and were almost expected.

Jules Rivière is a useful reminder that in Victorian Wales what we may now think of as artistic culture was not the exclusive preserve of chapels and eisteddfodau, and that alongside the highly publicized and much-vaunted peasant or amateur culture there were entrepreneurs employing professionals to play music similar to that provided at amateur concerts. The disadvantage of professional musicians was that they were expensive to retain, not every town being able to guarantee audiences such as those which would gather at resorts, and they still tended to be associated with theatrical entertainment which was thought of as constituting an entirely separate social activity. In Victorian society generally, however, there were many passions and many different energies and, in those Welsh towns and villages in which there was an urge to participate in amateur culture, there was also a desire for other kinds of entertainment and usually there were professional showmen on hand to oblige. The leaders of Nonconformity and the organizers of the amateur culture were always to be suspicious of the showmen and the diversions they offered. Their entertainment called for only a passive participation and there was no suggestion that audiences would be improved or informed by what they were offered; the amusements were all too often both organized and performed by strangers who had no organic link with the local community nor any sense of responsibility for its well-being. Professional diversions were always associated with passions of an undesirable sort; visiting shows could induce a carnival or holiday atmosphere and would bring crowds together, whilst more permanent places of entertainment were always to be linked with alcohol and women of easy virtue. It was clearly established in Nonconformist Wales that professional entertainment was at best trivial and certainly not respectable, but the desire for something different was great and, perhaps more than anything, it was often sheer curiosity which ensured that those very typical Victorians, the showmen, would not always leave Welsh villages empty-handed. Throughout the century the circuses, travelling fairs and shows came, and later there were the variety and music-hall acts which would appear twice nightly in any available hall. The people of Wales were given every opportunity to see the freaks of nature, the acrobats, the magicians and hypnotists, and even many of the leading singers and comedians in the land. Professional entertainment came in many forms, and south Wales as a prosperous

---

[46] H. J. Wood, *My Life of Music*, quoted in R. Nettel, *The Orchestra in England. A Social History* (London, 1948), p. 220. There are Llandudno programmes in the NLW.

and dynamic area was increasingly offered everything that was best and that was not infrequently to include diversions of a very worthwhile nature.

Professor Cecil Price's research has shown that theatre played an important part in the life of Victorian Wales. Swansea was undoubtedly the most important centre of interest for the local gentry, and the town's role as a fashionable resort had led to the opening of a theatre even before the beginning of the nineteenth century; this created a local tradition that was never to be lost and which developed into greater things.[47] It was remarkable how Swansea became associated with some of the most famous theatrical names of the period: Edward Kean appeared there for two years, most memorably as Hamlet and Richard III, although he was never to forget that he and his family both arrived at and departed from the town on foot; W. C. Macready gained valuable experience in his father's company at Swansea before going on to the metropolis; and at the end of his career, on his final tour, Sir Henry Irving was very struck by the emotional farewell he was given in the town when, at the final curtain, the whole audience stood to sing 'Lead Kindly Light'.[48] The key to Swansea's theatrical tradition was a long line of managers, including such names as William M'Cready, George and Andrew Melville and Billy Coutts, who knew how to plan a programme which blended the staples of melodrama and comedy with other forms of entertainment that could include opera and serious drama. The people of Swansea always had the widest choice, but there were other theatres, at first in the resorts and older eighteenth-century towns and then in the developing ports and Valley towns.[49] Towns without theatres were not forgotten, and the great Victorian travelling companies came fully equipped with their portable theatres, so that in almost every sizeable town there would be opportunities to appreciate a repertoire which was largely melodrama but which also included the plays of Shakespeare.[50] Towards the end of the century the emphasis was shifting away from portable theatres to the permanent houses and, whilst most of the larger towns could still offer variety hall and melodrama, Cardiff was now very clearly the centre for serious theatre. Cardiff's several theatres accommodated the West End shows, stars like Irving, Herbert Beerbohm Tree and Sarah Bernhardt, treats like the Imperial Russian Ballet starring Anna Pavlova, and also great innovators such as the Abbey Theatre from Dublin, which presented the plays of Yeats and Synge, and Mr Lovel's Company, which brought a selection of Ibsen's plays. In the years immediately before the war, there

---

[47] C. Price, *The English Theatre in Wales* (Cardiff, 1948) and *The Professional Theatre in Wales* (Univ. College of Swansea, 1984).

[48] For the early days in Swansea, see D. Boorman, *The Brighton of Wales* (Swansea, 1986). For Kean and Irving at Swansea, see D. Brook, *A Pageant of English Actors* (London, 1950) and for W. C. Macready, see Price, *English Theatre*. Macready, son of the Swansea actor-manager William M'Cready, changed the spelling of his name during the course of his career.

[49] Swansea Reference Library has an excellent collection of newspaper articles relating to the local history of theatre. See especially the obituary of Andrew Melville ('Emm') in *The Cambrian*, 7 August 1896 and fascinating articles on the Melvilles and Coutts by George Long in the *Evening Post*, 2 January 1968 and by W. H. Jones in the *Cambrian Daily Leader*, 10 October 1929. See also A. Jones, *The Story of the Grand* (Llandybïe, 1983).

[50] C. Price, 'Portable Theatres in Wales, 1843–1914', *NLWJ*, 9 (1955–6), 65–92.

was live theatre throughout urban Wales, and Cardiff was as exciting a place as any outside London.[51]

The people of Wales acquired a taste for melodrama and many of them would have been familiar, courtesy of Mr Barton, John Hord and Frank Benson, with several of Shakespeare's tragedies. They were discovering that life in urban society was always to involve choice, that one could select entertainments and even, to a certain extent, life styles. Certainly in the ports, and even in some of the Valley towns, variety and melodrama were to develop their own regular audiences, but for most serious-minded families, those with aspirations to respectability and with chapel connections, a visit to a theatre could only come as an occasional event which would not in any way interfere with loyalties to amateur activities. Shakespeare was very rewarding, but he still really belonged to melodramatic actors and showmen, and in any case many chapels and villages were now developing their own amateur dramatic societies and they remained the clear priority. Within society, then, some kind of truce was achieved between the very different worlds of amateur and professional entertainment, and for many years not even Shakespeare's plays could prompt the Welsh into thinking that cultural distinctions were absurd and artificial. Professional drama had its own place within the culture, but what is especially fascinating is that within the diet offered to music-loving Wales by the showmen there was not an inconsiderable amount of opera. In the early 1840s Swansea's theatre-goers were able to see Weber's *Der Freischütz*, Bellini's *La Sonnambula* and Donizetti's *L'Elisir d'Amore*.[52] The evidence suggests that this season was a little too formidable for local taste, but in later decades touring companies were to make a considerable impact not only in Swansea but also in the Valley towns. In the 1860s it was the Lyric Opera Company which had successful seasons in Merthyr; by the 1890s the Turner Grand Opera Company was offering the people of Swansea *Tannhäuser*, and found that operas like *Carmen*, *Il Trovatore* and *Faust* were known 'note by note' and top notes were eagerly awaited and loudly cheered; later still there were memorable performances in Swansea and Cardiff of *Tales of Hoffman* by the Quinlan Grand Opera Company, as well as visits by the D'Oyly Carte Company which helped to create a keen local interest in the works of Gilbert and Sullivan.[53] Above all, though, Welsh audiences came to associate opera with the name of Carl Rosa. This company, which had been formed in the 1870s, introduced many new works to London audiences, but it was as a touring company offering very well-produced if slightly popularized productions to the provinces that it was to be chiefly remembered.[54] The Carl Rosa

[51] M. Stephens (ed.) *The Oxford Companion to the Literature of Wales* (Oxford, 1986), p. 152, where the contributor on 'Drama' calculates that in 1912 'there were thirty-four theatres in Wales' and 'about as many halls holding dramatic licences'. At the Cardiff Public Library one can consult E. Deehan, *Cardiff Theatres: Old and New* (Cardiff, 1986) and *Notes on the Theatres of Cardiff* (South Glamorgan County Libraries) whilst there is an excellent collection of pre-1914 Cardiff programmes in the NLW.

[52] Price, *English Theatre*, p. 112.

[53] The visits of the Turner Company to Swansea are memorably recalled in the *Herald of Wales*, 16 May 1931. See also programme collections at Swansea and Aberystwyth.

[54] E. W. White, *The Rise of English Opera* (London, 1972).

Company appeared in Swansea and Cardiff, but it also toured the Valleys and the resorts and it was hardly surprising that the company acted like a magnet for ambitious Welsh singers. The two most famous south Wales singers of the era, Pontardawe's Ben Davies and Cymer's Tudor Davies, sang with the Carl Rosa, but in truth most valleys could boast of singers whom they had contributed to the company.[55]

Edwardian Wales was a busy and sophisticated society and its citizens had plenty of choice. Individual voices like that of the Revd Thomas Phillips of Bloomsbury Chapel continued to warn of the dangers of some popular amusements and in particular there was to be growing alarm at the impact of the new films on young people but, in general, all the various cultural activities existed alongside each other in a carefully regulated and finely balanced equilibrium.[56] It was in the first decade of the century, however, that the first significant steps were taken to ensure a broadening out of the Welsh-language culture so as to allow scope for some of the enthusiasms that had been aroused by the professionals. The crucial area of breakthrough was drama for, first amongst the students at the University College at Aberystwyth and then in the Welsh National Drama Movement, a new indigenous drama was first created and then presented.[57] At last there were opportunities to see plays about life in Wales written in both English and Welsh and presented in London as well as Wales by companies of a professional standard. Amongst the new playwrights were W. J. Gruffydd, T. E. Ellis, D. T. Davies, and most prominently J. O. Francis, whose 'Glamorgan play' *Change* was particularly well received in the West End and Wales.[58] *Change* was the story of a collier's family in which there were three sons, an invalid, a minister in training and a Socialist: during the course of the four acts the minister abandons his training and the invalid is killed by the troops as he tries to get his Socialist brother away from a demonstration; racked by guilt, the Socialist forfeits his political career and seeks solace in drink in Australia.[59] With such powerful material now being staged in Cardiff, it was not surprising that a major debate ensued with Abel J. Jones posing the question 'Does Wales Need the Drama?', to which the readers of *Welsh Outlook* responded with strong feelings; nor was it surprising that Welsh villages wanted to see these plays for themselves, with the result that there was a great mushrooming of amateur theatricals.[60] The leaders of Welsh cultural life had

---

[55] Many local historians record visits of the Company and name singers who eventually joined them. For example, Edwards, *Echoes of Rhymney*, mentions W. J. Davies, who joined Carl Rosa after successes at several National Eisteddfodau, and Richards, *Llynfi Valley*, notes that Cadivor Davies was the Company's principal tenor.

[56] Phillips discussed 'Church and Stage' in the *South Wales Daily News*, 28 January 1910.

[57] R. F. Walker, 'Entertainment in Aberystwyth' in I. G. Jones (ed.), *Aberystwyth 1277–1977* (Llandysul, 1977), pp. 114–27; the entry on 'Drama' in *The Oxford Companion to the Literature of Wales*.

[58] *Change* was first presented at the Haymarket Theatre in December 1913. The published text was reviewed by W. J. Gruffydd, *Welsh Outlook*, March 1914.

[59] J. O. Francis, *Change*, Welsh Drama Series no. 13 (1914). See also his collected journalistic essays, *The Legend of the Welsh* (Cardiff, 1924).

[60] A. J. Jones, 'Does Wales Need the Drama?', *Welsh Outlook*, 1, 1914.

changed their thinking about drama. Young writers and intellectuals were more interested in plays than ever before and the people within Welsh communities were given a great new interest which would help to sustain them during the Depression.

There was every incentive for the men and women of Wales to commit themselves to a full round of leisure-time activities. All the while, of course, the hold of the chapels and of the Welsh language was being weakened by immigration, cheap transport, education, books, newspapers and magazines, the music halls and their songs, and by new kinds of politicians. For many Welshmen nothing could rival what the chapels and the Welsh language had offered, and they clung to those things with a deepened affection, but in their hearts they knew that, although there were still relatively large congregations and there was still a mass participation in the old musical activities, the real battle was being lost. That equilibrium which had held in the Edwardian years was to survive until the 1920s, but then finally toppled over in the 1930s, a decade that brought first a savage depression and then another great war. Thousands left Wales and amongst those who stayed there was some apathy and also a great passion for English-medium films.[61]

Throughout the years in which the equilibrium held there were many Welsh men and women, whether fluently or incompetently bilingual or just monolingual except when singing Welsh, who were able to maintain their faith and their passion for the old musical traditions even as they became fond of the cinema, of the theatres and smart restaurants in Cardiff and Swansea, and of their excursions or holidays to London and the seaside resorts. For the vast majority there was no real dilemma and nothing had to be sacrificed even if parents and ministers were not always told the full truth. For others, the equilibrium was not acceptable, for the new diversions spoke of a wider world and of opportunities in such a way as to suggest that some things had to be rejected: they could not be amphibious, they had to follow their instincts. Ultimately these questions were resolved privately by individuals who realized how free they were to determine their own values. The historian can learn about how choices were made from his or her own family, by talking to others who lived through these years and, most profitably, by consulting those writers who by the very nature of things experienced the dilemmas in a very special way. Jack Jones was a romancer, a man infinitely amused by the follies, foibles and gossip of the folk, but his writings constitute a significant history of nineteenth-century Wales and above all they reveal his own continual fascination with the manner in which amateur and professional Welsh and English cultural activities interacted and overlapped. His fictional south Wales was one in which the chapel, the choir and the showman had their place alongside the entrepreneurs and the politicians; it was a passionate and divided world and there were many contradictions, as his own career was to show, but the distinctive humour and very strong

---

[61] P. Stead, 'Wales in the Movies', in T. Curtis (ed.), *Wales: The Imagined Nation* (Bridgend, 1986), pp. 161–79.

sense of the interests of ordinary people ensures that the complexity of the culture is captured, as is the fact that this was consciously a world apart in which all the various and diverse sub-sections adhered. He was a native of Merthyr and so he was a man of the live theatre; he was fully aware of how a pride in the achievements of Joseph Parry, and of particular bands and choirs was helping to create both a local and a national identity, and he was aware that both the drama of the chapel, from which he was alienated, and the politics of music were all part of the way in which a peasantry was entertained. The old world is all there but so is the new, for his Cardiff was one in which Oswald Stoll and Marie Lloyd were giving much pleasure, and his Rhondda was one in which an 'illiterate brickyard girl' was a regular theatre-goer and had seen Herman Vezin play Hamlet. Wales indeed had two popular cultures which rested in balance and Jack Jones remains the finest historian of that balance.[62]

Oswald Stoll gave Cardiff several fine theatres and in those theatres the young Ivor Novello Davies discovered his true self. He was the son of Madame Clara Novello Davies, whose pupils were victorious at eisteddfod after eisteddfod, and in his own right he was to win a first prize with a rendering of a Bach aria which prompted 'Pencerdd Gwalia' to describe him as an 'angel'. His destiny, however, lay elsewhere: at the age of five a maid took him to see the blood-curdling *Secrets of Harlem*; at twelve he pawned a family heirloom so that he could attend a Gilbert and Sullivan season; that same year he was given his first gramophone; four years later he had his first song published and he took up residence in London.[63] Rhys Davies was twenty years younger than Novello but he, too, first went to the theatre in the company of a young servant girl: at the Empire Tonypandy the curtains parted to reveal what he described as 'the only fairytale magic I knew in my upbringing'.[64] His first experience was a play about Napoleon and Josephine, but soon the Carl Rosa was in town with *Rigoletto* 'for which prices were doubled'; later in Cardiff there were orchestral concerts before which tea could be taken at the Carlton, whilst beyond there was London where he would see Eleanora Duse and all the talk was of Diaghilev's Russian Ballet. Like Joseph Parry before them, Ivor Novello and Rhys Davies were very much products of the world that Jack Jones has commemorated. As far as north Wales is concerned the commemoration was provided by Emlyn Williams, at first in autobiographical plays like *The Druid's Rest* and, more especially, *The Corn is Green*, which succeeded in theatre and film because of its very apt use of a Welsh setting to deal with the universal theme of how education and travel could convince a young worker that there were other worlds to conquer. In the play a brief visit to Oxford is all it takes to convince Morgan that he had been 'a prisoner behind a stone wall', and he is grateful for 'the leg up' that has enabled him to see 'a new world' in which 'everything had meaning' and

[62] Jack Jones dealt with Welsh music specifically in *Off to Philadelphia in the Morning* (London, 1947) and *Choral Sympathy* (London, 1955); Oswald Stoll and Marie Lloyd play their parts in *River Out of Eden* (London, 1951) and the character Saran recollects *Hamlet* in *Black Parade* (London, 1935).

[63] P. Noble, *Ivor Novello* (London, 1951). For Stoll and Cardiff, see F. Barker, *The House that Stoll Built* (London, 1957), pp. 48 ff.

[64] R. Davies, *Print of a Hare's Foot* (London, 1969), p. 55.

in which he now felt he truly belonged.[65] Later there followed *George*, a very fine volume of autobiography in which we are shown how, for a sensitive and able young lad, the Welsh language of the chapel and of a bad amateur drama group could not begin to compete with the fascination of magazines and the cinema. As a treat he was taken to Chester where 'the spell' of the theatre was first experienced at a performance where 'the Williamses had been swallowed up in the great family Gallery', whilst at school there was the magic that was offered by reading and playing in Shakespeare.[66] So here was another Welshman for whom the call of London was irresistible, but who nevertheless would later find that perhaps his best and most popular writing came when he cast his mind back to how the joys of English and of a wider scholarship had been discovered in a very intense family and community life which had been full of their own humour and warmth.

These writers were not typical. Not everyone could follow in their footsteps and very few felt it necessary to take decisions and to identify priorities so suddenly, but nevertheless they were very much the spokesmen of a generation and they provide us with our social history. In their fictions and autobiographies they personalized and dramatized experiences and crises that were in actuality more generally worked out over a period of at least two generations. Such was their fascination with things English and things theatrical that they could not do full justice to that Welsh-language and chapel-based culture which still meant so much to others and which was to gather new strengths and dimensions later in the twentieth century in ways that they could never have predicted. But there is in their work both a reminder of how special and exciting Victorian and Edwardian Wales had been with its two overlapping cultures and the challenging implication that things might have been easier for them if entertainments had been organized just a little differently. It was inevitable that the preachers and poets would have nothing to do with the showmen, but that should not prevent us from reflecting on the fact that ordinary people themselves tend not to see things in black and white terms or from regretting that Victorian social leaders were unable to make entrepreneurial and organizational skills more readily service the flair that the community as a whole had for the arts. Above all, one must be thankful that so many people were able to enjoy themselves so fully, but if only social leaders had made fewer value judgements then the talent and enthusiasm of ordinary men and women may well have become the foundation of a stunning bilingual urban culture that would have lasted longer and offered the world as a whole just a little bit more.[67]

[65]   E. Williams, *The Corn is Green*, Act III. In its 1950 edition, Pan printed the play along with the two other Welsh plays, *The Wind of Heaven* and *The Druid's Rest*.

[66]   Idem, *George* (London, 1961).

[67]   I was privileged to be present at Professor T. J. Morgan's exhilarating inaugural lecture in 1962, and in the years that followed I enormously enjoyed discussing the points raised in the lecture with Professor Ieuan Gwynedd Jones. More recently I have received quite considerable help from my former teacher Professor Cecil Price and from Neil Evans.

'A Tidal Wave of Impatience': The Cardiff General Strike of 1911

NEIL EVANS

IN the summer of 1911 south Wales exploded into conflict. The Cambrian Combine dispute defied all attempts to achieve a settlement, and in the Swansea Valley a strike at the Tareni colliery was bitterly and violently contested. At the same time the international seamen's strike slowed the export trade and arrested production within the coalfield. This was followed by a national railway strike with its own spectacular confrontation at Llanelli, as well as a host of other less well-known clashes. In the eastern valleys disgruntled workers found Jewish shops a convenient scapegoat for accumulating resentments, and hard on the heels of this came the issues which would produce the national coal strike of 1912. Throughout south Wales there was mounting evidence of working-class militancy and little heed was taken of the proponents of class harmony. It is perhaps tendentious to draw attention to the fact that the proportion of strike deaths was higher in south Wales during that year than it had ever been in the United States, a country notorious for its hard-nosed employers who could readily call on all the resources of the state in order to win disputes.[1] Yet this fact helps us to appreciate the widespread nature of the confrontations of 1911; too often we stress the significance of the events at Tonypandy and, by isolating them in separate compartments, we fail to understand them in their proper historical context.

Remedying this situation will be a larger project than can be undertaken here,[2] but it is hoped to make a contribution towards that end by studying some of the most dramatic events of that tangled and fretful summer, namely the impact of the seamen's strike on the city of Cardiff.[3] By drawing attention to the scenes enacted in Cardiff's dockland and within and without its City Hall, it is hoped to illustrate the tensions of the time by examining a place not usually noted for its militancy. The study is offered in admiration and with

---

[1] R. Jeffreys-Jones, *Violence and Reform in American History* (London, 1978), p. 28.

[2] For recent studies of aspects of this period, see D. Smith, 'Tonypandy 1910: Definitions of Community', *Past and Present*, 87 (May 1980), 158–84; D. Hopkin, 'The Llanelli Riots, 1911', *WHR*, 11 (1982–3), 488–515.

[3] There is a sketchy account of the Cardiff strike in C. Balfour, '"Captain Tupper" and the 1911 Seamen's Strike in Cardiff', *Morgannwg*, 14 (1970), 62–80. M. J. Daunton includes a fine account in his more general article 'Inter-Union Rivalries on the Waterfront: Cardiff 1888–1914', *International Review of Social History*, 22 (1977), 368–76.

affection to an historian (who was once a merchant seaman) who has brilliantly examined the structure of Welsh society in the nineteenth century.

At the height of the 'strike-bound summer of 1911' David Lloyd George came to the Dulais Valley to open a new chapel. He ventured some nervous jokes about the strength of the denomination in south Wales,[4] but he must have felt even more uneasy than when he had, some years earlier, stumped the valleys in the cause of Cymru Fydd, invoking the memory of Llywelyn ap Gruffudd.[5] He now recognized that there was a crisis in the relations between the working class and the rest of society. It stretched from Llanelli, via Tonypandy, to Tredegar and beyond to Manchester, Hull and Liverpool. There was, he declared, 'a tidal wave of impatience' which challenged existing social relations. In the summer of 1911 it engulfed Cardiff.

'Cardiff is a city of contrasts,' observed a visitor from Leicester in that summer. The slums around the docks, he maintained, were as bad as any in London and the alien quarters were 'a serious menace to other parts of the city'. But he showed enthusiasm for other parts—the wide expanses of Queen Street and St Mary Street, the beautiful parks (especially Roath Park) and, to crown it all, in Cathays Park, City Hall, the University buildings and Glamorgan County Hall, buildings which 'even London might be proud of'.[6] Local opinion would have shared the encomium but would have denied the existence of slums. With reservations, even the housing reformers agreed; working-class houses in Cardiff were generally large and well-built, though too expensive for single occupancy, so that overcrowding was a serious problem.[7] But it was clearly a divided city and even the tramways did not forge very effective bonds in this sprawling coal metropolis; the visitor from Leicester found them slow and circuitous. A special correspondent of *The Times*, visiting earlier in the year, passed over the cosmopolitan sailor town with a brief reference to the past and asserted that 'the national spirit of a strong people' had converted the town's wealth into a beautiful city, 'the centre of a country not a region'. Rapid growth in shipping might have produced dirt and a teeming population, but the aspect which Cardiff gave to the world was different. It seemed to be a national capital rather than a provincial town.[8] Such sentiments were the expression of a comfortable middle-class reconciliation of Welsh identity and cosmopolitanism, and it was foisted upon the city as a whole. It is doubtful whether the majority of the population shared this view; in the previous decade most of its inhabitants had voted against

[4] D. Rubinstein, 'Trade Unions, Politicians and Public Opinion, 1906–1914', in B. Pimlott and C. Cook (eds.), *Trade Unions in British Politics* (London, 1982), p. 66; *SWDN*, 30 August 1911.

[5] K. O. Morgan, *Rebirth of a Nation: Wales 1880–1980* (Oxford and Cardiff, 1981), p. 117; idem. (ed.), *Lloyd George Family Letters, c. 1885–1936* (Oxford and Cardiff, 1973), p. 78.

[6] *SWDN*, 15 August 1911.

[7] J. A. Jenkins, *Cardiff and its History: The Town's Claims to the Title Metropolis* (Cardiff, 1905); M. J. Daunton, *Coal Metropolis: Cardiff 1870–1914* (Leicester, 1977), pp. 97–101. Daunton endorses this view with some qualification.

[8] *The Times*, 30 May 1911.

Lloyd George speaking at Seven Sisters in 1911. (*By permission of the South Wales Miners' Library.*)

the compulsory teaching of Welsh, and the bulk of its population was of English extraction and non-Welsh in language. In 1911 not quite seven per cent of the population over the age of three spoke Welsh and most had more pressing concerns than maintaining the sense of Welsh identity and civic pride which had been forged in the previous thirty years. That civic pride had given roots and respectability to an upstart town which gloried in its recent growth but liked to remind a doubting world of its antiquity. Cathays Park and all the other achievements of the Edwardian era seemed to mock the working class. Since the turn of the century, real wages had stagnated and declined and most attempts to form trade unions to ameliorate these conditions had been frustrated.[9] The first acts of the drama of 1911 were to be played out before the dock gates, but the final ones saw a massive convergence of workers on City Hall—a symbol of bourgeois achievement in this divided city.

The parks and open spaces which visitors so prized were themselves areas of dispute. Conventionally they expressed arrival and respectability: 'it would be difficult to find a more neatly dressed and orderly crowd in a cathedral city than is to be seen on the streets, the tramcars and in the parks of Cardiff.'[10] Working-class districts like Splott lacked open spaces; lands acquired by the corporation for parks had subsequently been let for other purposes. People living in the docks area were denied access to the sea both by the docks themselves and by the railway companies which also carved out fiefs on the foreshore. Ratepayers in Splott complained bitterly but found the council reluctant to challenge the powerful interests which controlled the life of the city. When workers' children played in Cathays Park on the site of what was to become the National Museum, they did so to the annoyance of at least one resident of prosperous Park Place, though another resident of that street saw things differently and argued that the distribution of open spaces mirrored the disparities of wealth, privilege and influence:

> many ... of the ... children ... have no such amenities [as those of Park Place]; and if turned out of the bit of unoccupied ground and crushed back into the bare and dusty streets, will have a little ray of sunshine blotted out of their lives ... In the pride of our present 'residences' let us not forget the rock from which all of us, without one solitary exception, were hewn in the past.

Space was becoming politicized.[11] Roath Park, which attracted such admiration, had been laid out in the 1880s as much for profit-making as out of philanthropy. The estate owners gave their land which the corporation, in turn, transformed into parks, around which desirable building plots could be sold.[12] The council had aided the landlords more than they had benefited the public. A sense of

---

[9] For this paragraph, see N. Evans, 'The Welsh Victorian City: The Middle Class and National and Civic Consciousness in Cardiff 1850–1914', *WHR*, 12 (1984–6), 350–87; idem., 'Cardiff's Labour Tradition', *Llafur*, 4 (1984–7), 77–80.

[10] *The Times*, 30 May 1911.

[11] *SWDN*, 28 April; 8, 24, 26, 27 June; 4, 13, 17 July 1911.

[12] *Cardiff Times* [*CT*], 23 June 1894; M.J. Daunton, 'Aspects of the Economic and Social Structure of Cardiff, 1870–1914' (Univ. of Kent Ph.D. thesis, 1974), 1, pp. 255–6.

inherent inequality was expressed in an ironic letter written to the *South Wales Daily News* in July 1911:

> May I ask the Parks Committee if there is anything in Splott Park to equal the scene of destruction one may observe at the entrance to the Recreation Grounds, Roath Park? Whole lengths of protecting wire lay upon the ground, the posts being snapped off at the base, whilst the young shrubs bear evidence of rough treatment. Surely it is a pity to waste ratepayers' money 'on such people'?[13]

Another letter-writer objected that young Cardiff roughs, known as 'nuts', did not remain in their appointed quarters, but hung around Wood Street; it was:

> quite a common thing for pedestrians to have to get off the pavement in consequence of the obstruction caused by groups of 'larrikins' who amuse themselves by insulting respectable people and using language of the vilest description, which must affect the local tradesmen, as it is impossible for decent people to patronise the shops, and on a Sunday these ruffians take entire possession of the street.[14]

The affluent, segregated city was not free of tension, nor were its increasingly rigid boundaries unchallenged. But the behaviour which so disturbed the respectable residents was an inarticulate assertion, lacking any organizational form. It was the labour movement which tried to mount a coherent and sustained challenge out of which an alternative conception of a city community could grow. Council expenditure on fireworks for the forthcoming investiture of the Prince of Wales provided a platform from which to view the faults of the middle-class city. Jimmy Edmunds, a schoolteacher, declared that the city council 'were always ready to go on their knees before the powers of wealth and influence', while a sea-captain, James Griffiths, won some approbation when he argued that 'more loyalty would be shown by spending the money on the relief of poverty on their own doors. If money was to be spent on this Investiture, it could well be done by the philanthropists who locked out their colliers in Wales'.[15] For the workers to gain entry to this world of power and influence they needed some coherence. Cardiff Trades Council represented far too few of them to have much effect. Skilled workers were well accounted for, and some important groups in the docks—like the coal trimmers and tippers—were also organized, but compared with the organization of the middle classes theirs was feeble. The Trades Council was just over a quarter of a century old in 1911; the Chamber of Commerce was not far short of half a century old and it promoted a wide range of causes in south Wales and the world. Cardiff's Coal Exchange dated from 1886 (two years after the formation of the Trades Council) and controlled the world trade in steam coal; in 1910 more than a quarter of Britain's foreign shipments of coal had been directed from this hub of the international trading wheel. The port of Cardiff alone exported almost seventeen million tons, along with almost three million tons in bunkers and another three million tons along the coast. The Cardiff Railway Company, which controlled the Bute Docks,

---

[13] *SWDN*, 7 July 1911.
[14] Ibid., 8 June 1911.
[15] Ibid., 5 May 1911.

was capitalized at more than £6½ million in 1910. The docks were a magnet for other trades—timber-importing, general merchandise, steel production, dry docks, ice factories, patent fuel works and biscuit-making were only some of the enterprises attracted. It was true that the Bute docks were not taking as great a share of the coal trade as their newer rivals at Barry, but this was a segment of the same commercial empire, despite the differences in local government and dock ownership that distinguished Cardiff from Barry. Not all the potential of the area was realized: 'the extraordinary wealth in coal has caused people to shut their eyes to the manufacturing advantages of Cardiff.' The city's rate of growth had declined ever since the opening of Barry Docks in 1889, and in 1911 a local paper was more inclined to see Swansea as the town of the future. Yet the general position was secure; coal, trade facilities, past enterprise and schemes of municipal enterprise all pointed to a better future.[16]

There were, of course, limits to middle-class organization: coal production was not determined by monopoly and cartels. Free competition ruled the industry until the First World War and its monopoly of the world's best steam coal was not exploited since competition within the coalfield undercut all schemes at regulation. The great combines were at war with each other, though coal shipping was very concentrated, with five firms taking one-third of the output between 1882 and 1911. Increasingly these firms were vertically integrated into production. Shipowners, too, organized huge firms, though these tended to be unstable and fortunes were quickly won and lost. The docks and dockside industry were refuges for multitudes of small concerns, a long tail on an imperfectly co-ordinated dog.[17] Employers' organization was therefore extensive though not total; but the area in which it was most effective was in labour relations. There was nothing in working class organization in Cardiff which could compare with it. Although coal-owners and shippers made only occasional forays into a City Hall which was dominated by tradesmen, the fact remained that in 1911 there were no independent representatives of labour in the council chamber to challenge the dominant influence of the affluent.

The root of the industrial problem was the defeat in 1891 of the newly-formed dockers' and seamen's unions by the Shipping Federation. The unions had been wrong-footed into fighting on difficult ground and were crushed by a better organized, more powerful and ruthless adversary, W. T. Lewis, who exercised too great a power in collieries, docks and railways for the unions to have much chance of recovery. All the many attempts to reorganize had enjoyed, at best, only temporary success. For new unionism to spread amongst the casually employed, favourable economic circumstances and a rush of enthusiasm were needed. Union organizers were at times physically excluded from the docks. The Trades Council had taken advantage of the upsurge in industrial strength of 1889–91 to secure some representation on the town council, but its progress had been checked. No new seats were gained after 1897 and some of the four won at that peak were subsequently lost. In 1908, under the influence of the

---

[16] *The Times*, 30 May 1911; *CT*, 6 February, 27 March 1886; *SWDN*, 26 May, 24 June, 5 July 1911.

[17] Daunton, 'Aspects', I, pp. 176–204, 209–13.

ILP, the Trades Council repudiated its erstwhile representatives, whose relationship with middle-class Liberals had become intolerably close. It was naked in the council chamber by 1911 and in the industrial field it was to fail to offer the effective leadership it had provided in the previous upsurge, before the disaster of 1891.[18]

Dock work was largely casual, and a claim by a Bute dock official that only twenty per cent of it was of that nature in Cardiff was over-sanguine. Coal-tippers were permanently employed and had achieved permanent organization (oddly enough in the Amalgamated Society of Railway Servants) from 1898 onwards. Coal-trimmers had also built an organization which survived the erosion of their bargaining position through the arrival of self-trimming ships. Yet it is unlikely that the coal trade, for all its vast volume, engaged a majority of Cardiff's dockers; hobblers, riggers, boatmen and most labourers on non-coal cargoes were casually employed and the whole work-force remained fragmented. In 1911 it was felt that the south Wales ports had 'an army of casuals—men after completing one particular job being quite uncertain as to the next they may pick up'. It was hoped that the new Labour Exchanges would help decasualize the docks and persuade some of the surplus labour into other callings. Meanwhile shelters were provided at the docks to ease the rigours of the waiting which was an inevitable part of the dockers' lot under the prevailing system. In these circumstances it is no wonder that the story of the Dockers' Union in Cardiff between 1891 and 1911 can be briefly told and for present purposes it can be ignored.[19] The position of seamen, the other strategic group, was at least as difficult. Cardiff was a tramp shipping port with a large (and varied) admixture of foreign sailors. In 1904 there were sixty-two foreigners for every hundred British sailors, and wage rates were the lowest in Britain. Generally sailors were amongst the least successful at keeping up with the rate of inflation after 1900; shipowners' organization, steeled by growing foreign competition, made them formidable opponents. Cardiff's shipowners honed their opposition to unions to a fine edge. In 1906 local owners condemned the Shipping Federation (not normally an organization associated with conciliation in this period) for its failure to press home a libel action which would have bankrupted Havelock Wilson, the founder and leader of the union. The union claimed that since 1903 Cardiff had been one of its strongholds, but for such a precarious organization the word was largely meaningless. Frequently it was threatened with dissolution, though it had learned one useful lesson—that it was better to organize foreigners than to oppose them. In Cardiff that was to prove valuable, though in 1911 it was to be combined with making one group—the Chinese—scapegoats during the strike. This lesson, the resourcefulness of its leaders, bluff and a good deal of luck, brought it to the fore in the events of the summer of 1911. If workers

[18] This paragraph is based on unpublished research, on Daunton, 'Aspects', part 4; L. J. Williams, 'The New Unionism in South Wales, 1889–92', *WHR*, 1 (1960–3), 413–29; P. W. Donovan, 'Unskilled Labour Unions in South Wales, 1889–1914' (Univ. of London M.Phil thesis, 1969), ch. 3.

[19] Daunton, 'Aspects', 2, pp. 37–48, 70; *SWDN*, 17 June 1911.

were to assume any significant role in the Edwardian city, it would need a major contribution from the seamen.[20]

Success in a seamen's strike called for the victory of optimistic will over pessimistic intelligence, for the difficulties of organization were formidable. Seamen signed on to individual ships at very different times of the year. There were thousands of bargains to be collectivized and at any one time many British merchant ships were at sea or in foreign ports. An effective strike would require international organization and a large measure of advance planning. In any case, shipowners could avoid local strikes by paying the union rate and then withdrawing it at the next signing-on, when the encouragement of collective action was lacking. As early as 1907 both shipowners and unions were discussing international action. In 1909 the shipowners had established an International Shipping Federation and, at the suggestion of Havelock Wilson, the National Transport Workers' Federation established an International Seafarers' Committee which produced a series of demands. The crucial issues were a minimum wage, to be standard at each port, a conciliation board, a better manning scale for vessels, overtime payments, and an end to the Shipping Federation medical examination, which it was felt was used as an instrument for victimization.[21] Wilson spread rumours of a co-ordinated stoppage and made some preparations in the form of camps for seamen in many ports. Organizers were sent out to the various ports in May 1911, but the shipowners were generally unimpressed. The union was £10,000 in debt, the European unions were even weaker, and the other components of the NTWF were not eager for a strike. Wilson may have thought that in a situation of rising freights, when owners could afford to be generous, bluff would be a vital ingredient in a successful strike. At one stage in his preparations he had believed that huge demonstrations and the sympathy of the President of the Board of Trade would be crucial. He emphasized the co-ordination and international solidarity of the movement, and grabbed some headlines by declaring that the date for the strike was already fixed and that only he knew what it was. In due course he would divulge the secret, but in the mean time he tried to build up the suspense. It was argued that this would be the first real strike, unlike the previous sectional actions, such as the four months' strike in the Bristol Channel in 1903, when blacklegs from other ports had undermined local efforts. In an elaborate joke at the employers' expense, circulars were sent round to shipowners, coal-exporters and docksmen asking for donations for a two-week-long carnival to start on 10 June. The object was said to be to get the men under control and have some fun—the complete opposite of conditions at sea![22] Black humour at the shipowners' expense was likely to be well received. In the months before the strike a series

[20] F. J. Lindop, 'A History of Seamen's Trade Unionism to 1929' (Univ. of London, MA thesis, 1972), p. 129; WM, 10 June 1911; GRO, D/D Com. Cardiff Incorporated Shipowners' Association, Annual Report (1906), pp. 7–8.

[21] SWDN, 18 June 1911; Lindop, 'Seamen's Trade Unionism', p. 137; Modern Records Centre (MRC), MSS 175/7/ITF, Havelock Wilson to H. Jochade, 21 October 1907.

[22] Lindop, 'Seamen's Trade Unionism', pp. 138–40; WM, 9, 20 May, 10, 12 June; SWDN, 21, 24 April, 9, 26, 29, 30 May, 5, 12, 13 June 1911; MRC, MSS 175/7/ITF/2, Wilson to Jochade, n.d.

of issues had arisen in the south Wales ports which inflamed tempers and affronted the dignity of labour. At Newport the Medical Officer of Health complained about the state of the forecastles in many ships. One Cardiff owner blamed the laziness and dirty habits of the British seaman for this state of affairs, while on the other hand Christian Damm of the National Sailors' and Firemen's Union maintained that quarters were too cramped for men to keep them clean. In such restricted space, sweat-sodden clothes had to be dried in close proximity to food. There was a feeling that shipowners cared little for the welfare of seamen; those rejected at the hated medical examination had few opportunities to find other employment. The frequently expressed preference for foreign labour was a particularly hard thing to bear in that imperial age. When Glen Gelder and Co. of Glasgow said that they would 'be quite prepared to pay considerably higher wages to Chinese than to Britishers' because they found them to be superior seamen, they found much support in Cardiff Docks. In fact, relatively little Chinese labour had been signed on in Cardiff—about two per cent of crews in 1910—for the Chinese tended to concentrate in the eastern trades, while the bulk of Cardiff's commerce was with the Mediterranean. Yet it was felt that Chinese were being signed on in increased numbers in 1911 and this provoked a growing hostility in the run-up to the strike. Rumours circulated that 2,000 men could be imported to break any strike in south Wales, a threat calculated to denigrate the strike movement. The *Western Mail*—effectively the shipowners' mouthpiece—offered the view that the men were 'such a medley of races and otherwise lacking in coherence that the intended strike can hardly be expected to affect them to any considerable degree'. Seamen had something to prove and Havelock Wilson could expect a response when he told a crowd at the opening of the carnival in Cardiff that 'they had been too servile to the shipowners and the more they had pleaded, the more they had been trampled on'.[23] But the opening of the carnival proved something of a disappointment to its organizers; only about thirty men followed the Loudon Square Band from the docks to Neptune Park, and placards asking men to 'fall in and follow us' had little effect. The testing time would come with the declaration of the strike itself.[24]

The strike began on 14 June at a mass meeting at Neptune Park in Newport Road. Wilson had made his long-awaited announcement in Southampton the previous night, following rank-and-file pressure there, and the seamen came out port by port, in ragged file.[25] It was not to be a dispute tightly co-ordinated from the centre, but each port fought its own fight simultaneously. The seamen gathered whatever allies they could along the way and the strike proved to be as disordered in its conduct as it had been in its beginnings. In Cardiff there was evident enthusiasm for the cause at public meetings and within days the union was claiming that it had received 700 discharge books, which meant

[23] *SWDN*, 20, 25 April, 16, 19 May; 13 June; *WM*, 27 May; 12, 13 June 1911.
[24] *SWDN*, 12, 13 June; *WM*, 10, 12, 13, 14 June 1911.
[25] This section is based on the *SWDN* from 14 June to 18 July. References are confined to other sources.

that men could not go to sea without reclaiming them from the union. It was at once a dramatic gesture and a practical demonstration of solidarity. There were said to be enough books to fill a kitbag. The first few days, indeed, saw several ships set sail crewed by seamen working at the old rates, but the union's argument that these were sailings for which agreements had been signed before the strike was declared was apparently true, and the stoppage fairly quickly became effective.

Solidarity was encouraged by large-scale picketing of the docks and a degree of violence against those blacklegs who managed to evade the human screen which had been erected. Even the use of maps did not ensure the hermetic sealing of all dock entrances which the union aimed at, but blacklegs had to be nifty and well-protected to run the gauntlet successfully. The greatest drama of all was performed outside the main dock gates. The union office, on the corner of James Street/Bute Terrace and Bute Street, overlooked this strategic location and from its balcony the most accomplished actor in the whole drama played his part and directed operations. Captain Edward Tupper was the chief union organizer sent to Cardiff and his performance from the balcony was to extend over many weeks. Captain Tupper was his stage name, for there is no evidence that he was a captain and definite evidence that he was not the VC he sometimes claimed to be. His background and even his age remain unclear from his own contradictory accounts. Style counted for more than truth and his leadership was a masterpiece of improvization. His vantage-point commanded a view of the Mercantile Marine Offices of the Board of Trade where, in theory at least, sailors were signed on. He also dominated the main thoroughfare which joined the city centre and the docks. Close by were the offices of the Shipping Federation in Mountstuart Square. In the brilliant summer sunshine of June and July, he harangued the assembled crowds and kept his finger on the pulse. He might make a dozen or more speeches in a day and he offered threats and conciliation by turn. He was a bully and a dove of peace, a tribune of the people and a friend of the shipowner and the authorities. Words served the cause and his own ego. He could be a man of the people, ready to take off his jacket to prove it, or a high-born, condescending patrician as the situation demanded. It was a blend which seemed to appeal to sailors used to taking orders from captains and who appreciated the bluff gentry style. His violence was in language rather than deeds and he never challenged the existing system of society. From 1911 onwards Tupper was increasingly the public mouthpiece of Wilson, whose own mobility was checked by the onset of arthritis. Tupper's dispatch to Cardiff may reflect the port's crucial role in any seamen's strike; a 'hard-up' port with ships always available was a plughole down which strikers could vanish in any dispute. Tupper was sent to stop it and secure victory.[26]

The drama in Cardiff was always affected by noises off-stage. News came

---

[26] Balfour, 'Tupper', pp. 63–4, 76–9, is very useful for the biography, but more research needs to be done; Edward Tupper, *Seamen's Torch* (London, 1938). In 1910 Wilson had experienced great difficulty in sustaining wage increases temporarily gained in the Bristol Channel. He described Cardiff as 'our worst port'. MRC, MSS 175/7/ITF/2. Wilson to Jochade, 20 July, 21 September, 4 November 1910.

Captain Edward Tupper addressing a crowd from a balcony in Bute, 1911. (*By permission of County of South Glamorgan Libraries.*)

in of the struggle in other ports in Britain and abroad, and this was vital to the success or failure of the local struggle. The messages were confusing; most ports were quiet, and many owners settled early, particularly the liner operators, who feared losing trade in the run-up to the Coronation. Towards the end of June there were plenty of men available at Rotterdam, but at Amsterdam twenty out of thirty-five steamers were stopped and strikers faced cavalry and baton charges. Nearer home there were also confused tidings. In Liverpool the union quickly won advances against the non-Federation firms; by the end of June the union was making such headway with Federation firms that it bowed to the inevitable and allowed members to negotiate individually. On the very day this happened the dockers sensed a victory and joined the struggle, forcing the employers to promise to negotiate a settlement within a month.[27] In Hull seamen launched an effective strike which became general in the docks after a ship's officer fired on and wounded a striker. Tensions mounted with the privations of the strike and the owners' continued refusal to recognize; the strike spread violently in the last days of June, with many other workers joining in and police baton-charges in evidence. The decay of perishable cargo worth £3,000 forced negotiations which Sir George Askwith, the Board of Trade conciliator, hastily conducted. Despite this there was another eight hours of violence at the docks before a settlement was reached. In Swansea the strike was fairly quiet and the union published regular scores demonstrating the success it was achieving against the Federation in signing on at union rates. By 4 July the *South Wales Daily News* concluded that the strike had ended at Hull, Grimsby, Liverpool and Belfast and was practically over elsewhere. There was violence at Glasgow; at Manchester there were sympathetic strikes before the issue was settled following frenetic negotiations in the City Hall, during which Askwith acted as mediator.[28] How were things in Cardiff?

Cardiff was quite solid and few blacklegs pierced the picket lines. Attacks on those who tried to do so increased in frequency and violence. A seaman was charged with attempted murder and there was a bid to throw a strike-breaker on to the docks. From the beginning of July, when the union was forced to provide strike pay for the first time, the pace quickened. Seamen who demonstrated in Bute Street were allegedly spat upon by Chinese from the upper window of a boarding house. Mayhem followed, with a crowd of about a thousand men, women and children adopting what the press called a menacing attitude, until the police, Tupper and Damm were able to defuse a dangerous situation. The Chinese were not the only blacklegs, but they were the most numerous and conspicuous among them. White seamen (including Greeks) as well as blacks also figured as strike-breakers, yet any split in the ranks was not primarily

[27] H. Hikins, 'The Liverpool General Transport Strike, 1911', *Trans. Hist. Soc. of Lancashire and Cheshire*, 113 (1961), 169–95; E. Taplin, *The Dockers' Union* (Leicester, 1986), ch. 7; MRC, MSS 175/7/ITF/2, Wilson to Jochade, 17–21 June 1911.

[28] K. Brooker, *The Hull Strikes of 1911* (East Yorkshire Local History Society, pamphlet no. 35, 1979); Lord Askwith, *Industrial Problems and Disputes* (London, 1920), ch. 16; MRC, MSS 175/7/ITF/2, Wilson to Jochade, 21 June 1911.

on the lines of British versus foreign or black seamen; blacks were prominent amongst the pickets and many foreign seamen were involved in the attacks on strike-breakers. The Chinese were amongst the newest recruits to the mercantile marine and were not accepted into the union. As the strike became prolonged, so the issue of wider solidarity with dockers and other groups became linked with the prominence of Chinese blacklegs. Early in the strike the Cardiff district secretary of the Dockers' Union had expressed the hope that no action by his members would be necessary, but he had also said that the dockers, ship-repairers and others sympathized with the seamen who were considered to have a just cause. The dockers had recovered some of their strength in south Wales and union leaders were having to restrain militancy. Railwaymen gave vital information on the movement of strike-breakers to Cardiff.[29] Dockers refused to work if Chinese seamen were imported to carry out the jobs of British citizens. Towards the end of June there were signs that the seamen might be winning. Of the 700 discharge books collected, only 45 had been reclaimed, and early in July the NTWF seemed about to meet the Shipping Federation in London, a meeting which would have meant effective recognition of the union. In Cardiff the first sign of a serious break in the shipowners' ranks came when Mr Henry Radcliffe stopped his limousine outside the union offices and summoned Tupper down from his balcony. Tupper, as eager to play Zacharias as any other role, joined him. He returned, claiming to have found a new saviour; his friend, Mr Radcliffe, he declared, wanted a fair deal for seamen. He was exempted from Tupper's more virulent attacks on Cardiff shipowners and there were claims that owners were now stampeding to pay the union rate. In the first week of July, Tupper was claiming that 'peace is in the air. And if you stand firm, victory will be yours.' Perhaps he was encouraged by the successes secured elsewhere and the fact that shipowners in Cardiff found the Shipping Federation's terms for laying up tonnage inadequate. Tupper then went to the office of the shipowner Edward Nicholl and came back hinting at his insider's knowledge: 'If they knew as much as he did they would be delighted—in fact he would not tell them, for fear they would be standing on their heads and clapping their feet.'

The situation was, in fact, more confused than ever and the dispute rapidly approached crisis-point. Tupper and Damm were arguing that unless a settlement was achieved there would be riots such as Cardiff had never seen before. Tupper claimed that he only had to give the signal and the dockers would come out in sympathy. If the seamen were driven into a corner, he claimed, they would fight. The Chinese issue was wound up until the whole city became taut. The memory of the agitations against Chinese labour in the Rand in the 1906 elections was revived and the convictions of local Chinese for brothel-keeping and opium-smoking were played up. Towards the end of June, the Cardiff branch of the ILP condemned the use of Chinese strike-breakers with

---

[29] Donovan, 'Unskilled Labour Unions', pp. 166–71.

lower expectations than white seamen, and found their use more infamous than the conduct of capitalists in South Africa. Within a week, a well-attended meeting of trade-unionists passed a similar resolution and called upon the government to take action, as it had done in South Africa. A couple of days later Tupper was calling for a boycott of Chinese laundries, an action which the Trades Council emphatically endorsed. These actions bolstered morale at a point when the strike was beginning to have serious consequences for the seamen; it was by now almost a month old and apparently little strike pay was available. They also generated some solidarity in sentiment and, though as yet little practical help was forthcoming, the strike remained firm. There were also victories elsewhere to provide encouragement and the Shipping Federation was clearly placed on the defensive, though not defeated. It chose to rally its forces and fight a rearguard action at Cardiff.[30] The attitudes of the Cardiff shipowners were complex and probably influenced by the prevailing economic situation. In 1911 the shipping trade was flourishing after a long period of depression; by the end of the year it would be in a more prosperous state than at any time since the Boer War. Good outward and homeward freights were obtainable, though homeward freights from the major Cardiff markets of the River Plate and the Mediterranean were not as good as for some other areas. The state of trade fluctuated and was reviewed weekly in the local business press. Because of the Cambrian Combine dispute, Cardiff did not share as fully as other ports in the expansion of the coal trade.[31] The novelty of the boom in the summer, and the fact that the port did not enjoy unqualified expansion, account for the divided and wavering response of the shipowners. The decisive moment came with a meeting of the Cardiff shipowners on 11 July. After much discussion it was decided to lay up tonnage, if this was necessary to protect the existing wage-scale. The voices of several large shipowners, moved by fears of civil unrest and the feeling that they would lose the benefits of rising freights if the strike were prolonged, were raised in favour of a settlement. But the more numerous smaller employers were in a hawkish mood and easily outvoted the big owners. The *Western Mail* announced the decision under the heading 'Strike Cloud at Cardiff', and the decision was a bitter blow to the union, which had been aware of the divisions and had sensed victory. Spirits temporarily fell. Tupper had been boasting that all the resources of the union and the 'heavy artillery' used elsewhere could now be concentrated on Cardiff. The Shipping Federation's improved offer and its acceptance by the Cardiff owners represented the same strategy. As was observed at the time, Cardiff was becoming the cockpit of the whole dispute, and within days there were signs that battlelines were being redrawn.[32]

---

[30] GRO, D/D Com., Shipowners' Minutes, 30 June 1911 (Cuthbert Laws to Secretary of Cardiff District, 29 June 1911).

[31] GRO, D/D Com., Cardiff Incorporated Chamber of Commerce, *Annual Reports*, 1907–11. Detailed movements of freights can be followed in the *Cardiff Journal of Commerce* [henceforth *CJC*].

[32] *WM*, 12, 13 July 1911.

Signs of escalating tension were unmistakable. Dockers were refusing to handle ships with scab or Chinese crews; rivet-warmers had come out on strike over their own grievances; coal-tippers were in the midst of long and complex negotiations over Saturday work and overtime payments; and the employers were accused of bad faith in breaking a previous agreement. From the beginning there had been a good deal of rank-and-file sympathy for the seamen's cause which was seen as a test case for union recognition in the port. The leaders of the dockers' union, however, were trying to keep aloof from the dispute and to rely on approaches to the employers to resolve their members' grievances. The combined pressure of the seamen's dispute, the dockers' own grievances, and the determination to ensure the victory of the seamen created tension which was heightened still further by two new factors—the arrival of the blackleg supply ship, the *Lady Jocelyn*, and conflicts over the crewing and unloading of two vessels, the *Foreric* and the steamer *Annan*. The Shipping Federation supply ship, the *Lady Jocelyn*, arrived on 10 July. It was a well-known Shipping Federation tactic to use such vessels from which blacklegs could be supplied as crews in order to win disputes. Tugboats were used to ferry men to the supply ship. Tupper again became the pugilist and offered to fight the owner of the vessel. On 14 July the dock gates were closed to pickets, another echo of past defeats. Two days later a well-organized union raid prevented the embarkation of blacklegs at Swanbridge, near Sully, for the supply ship. The union was now faced with the almost impossible task of picketing a vast stretch of coast from any point of which small vessels could be sent to the *Lady Jocelyn*. The shipowners had tied the Gordian knot. It would take days of riot and a general strike to cut it.

Already there had been fears that Cardiff's police force was not adequately equipped for the tasks in hand, especially when almost twenty per cent of its strength was on loan to other areas to help with royal visits associated with the investiture of the Prince of Wales. Shipowners were pressing the police to clear the crowds congregating outside the Board of Trade offices and to stop Tupper's 'volcanic and uncalled for speeches'. The Chief Constable promised he would do all that he could, as long as it was legal and legitimate. Within a few days pickets were complaining of interference by the police and, when Tupper asked for a hundred men to follow him to investigate a complaint, five to six hundred responded. The Bute Dock gates were closed after Tupper had taken a force of pickets to prevent further Chinese seamen from signing on the steamer *Foreric*. Some boarded the vessel and there were fights, during which missiles were thrown at the Chinese, who were themselves armed with knives and spanners. A crowd of several hundred surrounded the ship and dockers urged the seamen on. Tupper and Damm, arriving in the wake of the crowd which they themselves had summoned, calmed their men. Tippers, riggers, dock labourers, and trimmers stopped work on the vessel until the Chinese were removed. Tupper announced that he would not have peace at any price now, that he was sorry that he had called the crowd off, and that the Shipping Federation vessel the *Lady Jocelyn* was a 'dirty slave dhow'. He offered to fight the owner of the tugboat supplying men to the Federation ship for a purse of £50, and led a crowd of fifty men to his office in Mountstuart Square. The crowd rushed the office but did not find its quarry. Tugboat owners agreed to stop supplying crews and the Chinese were withdrawn from the *Foreric*. Following the action in Mountstuart Square, Tupper was summoned to appear in court on a charge of intimidation.[33]

On the morning of his appearance, 18 July 1911, the *Cardiff Journal of Commerce* sensed trouble. Its political instincts were good, for it proved to be the most critical day of the strike:

> Fears were entertained yesterday that the seriousness of the sailor's strike would become much more pronounced during the next few days. The men congregated outside the union offices undoubtedly displayed a more embittered feeling than has been manifest, added to which there was an unmistakable growing unrest amongst other classes of dock workers. On nearly all sides threats of general stoppage taking place today were heard, chiefly as a protest against the non-recognition of the union by the Cardiff shipowners. It was felt that today would witness something in the nature of a crisis in the struggle, and in view of yesterday's murmurings it would not perhaps occasion a good deal of surprise if many, perhaps the majority, of the dockworkers joined hands with the sailors and firemen at least for one day.[34]

Tupper went from the union offices outside the dock gate to appear in the palatial new law courts, one of the adornments of Cardiff's embryonic civic centre. Five hundred seamen accompanied him and waited all day in the sunny park for him to reappear. As a result, a great many of the striking seamen were away from the docks when trouble exploded. But most of the non-coal dockers had stopped work that morning and it was they who were at the forefront of the conflicts which surrounded the steamer *Annan*.

The *Annan*, owned by a Glasgow firm, plied weekly between Glasgow, Belfast and Cardiff. Dockers refused to unload it and non-union labour was engaged. The most provocative thing about this was that labourers had been obtained from the workhouse during the night. Dockers who had stopped work attacked a warehouse where these labourers were housed, using a crane as a battering ram to gain access. There was something of a playful mood at first, but in the afternoon the violence became more serious. A Bute Docks detective was chased into a warehouse and the crowd lit fires to smoke him out, leaving the building extensively damaged and looted. The fire brigade arrived and their hoses were cut, stones were thrown and eighty extra policemen were drafted into the docks. Battles raged all afternoon and a detachment of police had to fight hard to defend a footbridge. The arrival of Havelock Wilson helped calm the atmosphere but there was dismay at the absence of Tupper, who had been remanded in custody. By then the *Annan* had been cut adrift and at least twenty strikers and ten policemen had been injured. At six o'clock the dock gates were

---

[33] PRO, Home Office Papers, HO 45/210615/10649 (Albert A. Crawley to Home Secretary, n.d.); GRO, D/D Com., Cardiff Incorporated Chamber of Commerce Minutes, 4 July 1911; *WM*, 7, 8, 11, 12, 13 July; *CJC*, 11 July 1911; Tupper, *Seamen's Torch*, pp. 42–3.

[34] *CJC*, 18 July 1911.

closed and the evening crowds in the vicinity were merely sightseers.[35] The merchants Allen Payne and Co., who owned the *Annan*, and the Shipping Federation sent urgent telegrams to the Home Secretary demanding action. The Chief Constable asked for two hundred Metropolitan Police to be sent and they were duly dispatched at 1 a.m. on 19 July, with an extra twenty mounted policemen in attendance. Other policemen—ninety in all—were recruited from adjacent forces, and instructions were given to GOC Western Command that troops might be required.[36]

Wednesday was a much quieter day. Much of the focus of attention shifted to the docks at Newport, to which the violence had spread. Tupper was released on bail and up to 5,000 people came to the docks to greet him. Marching gangs toured the area and brought out most of the dockers who were still in work, against the advice of their union officials. The trimmers' mass meeting to consider the issue, scheduled for the following Sunday, was pre-empted by a pedestrian vote. Sectional meetings seized the initiative. Wilson appealed for a general strike and argued that the issue was now largely resolved—only the Bristol Channel and north-east ports remained to be won for the shipowners to be routed. John Chappell of the coal-trimmers' union claimed that there were twelve men on the Exchange who wanted to use force and involve the city in needless expense. That day and the next the Lord Mayor sought to avoid trouble by withstanding the deployment of the military and by engaging the various parties in negotiation. It was felt that if the *Annan* were unloaded—under police or military protection—there would be a renewed outbreak of rioting and the Lord Mayor's negotiations would fail.[37] By 20 July the Lord Mayor had seen Havelock Wilson and the representatives of the shipowners, and had some proposals to make. The dock strike became complete during that day when the remaining tippers were brought out and non-dock labour became involved for the first time when the patent fuel works at Maindy was brought to a halt. A strike committee had been established the previous day to co-ordinate the grievances of the various sections of labour. Newport and Barry had also been stopped by then, and the shortage of railway wagons threatened to close the whole coalfield by the weekend. Wilson commented that he had never known such solidarity at Cardiff; indeed, only days earlier he had called it a 'blackleg capital'. Tupper insisted that there should be no return to work until all the grievances had been settled. Attempts to stop the trams were unsuccessful, the tramwaymen

[35] PRO, HO 45 (Chief Constable of Cardiff to Lord Mayor, 31 July 1911); *SWDN*; *WM*; *CJC*, 19 July 1911. Tupper claims in *Seamen's Torch* (p. 45) that the riot was the work of seamen angry at his remand. The press accounts show clearly that the seamen arrived back at the dock only after the police had restored order. The trimmers' and tippers' negotiations can be followed in the press and in the Shipowners' Association Minutes.

[36] PRO, HO 45 (Chief Constable of Cardiff to Lord Mayor, 31 July 1911; Allen Payne and Co. to Home Secretary, 18 July 1911; Shipping Federation to Home Secretary, 18 July 1911. Memoranda, 18 July 1911).

[37] *SWDN*; *WM*, 20 July 1911; HO 45 (Lord Mayor of Cardiff to Home Secretary, 19 July 1911; Home Secretary to Lord Mayor, enclosing telegrams from the Shipping Federation, 20 July 1911, and note on file referring to this telegram).

arguing that to do so would risk losing the widespread public sympathy that existed. Wilson claimed that even shopkeepers sympathized with the strike.

The most sinister developments of the day concerned the Chinese. A successful attempt had been made during the day to bring in a Chinese crew under police escort, though the baggage of some of them had been looted in Tyndall Street. Following a mass meeting in Cathays Park where, according to press estimates, 40,000 people were present, crowds attacked all but one of Cardiff's thirty Chinese laundries and inflicted considerable damage. All accounts agreed that youths and women were at the forefront, but the outbreak followed searches for Chinese seamen at the docks. The police were not able to prevent the attacks, which they claimed were co-ordinated and centrally directed; often they arrived in the wake of the destruction, and the crowds found starch a valuable weapon to use against them.[38] This attack brought troops to Cardiff, the Lord Mayor overcoming his earlier reluctance to employ them. He requested them during the course of the riots and they arrived the following morning, just after 10 a.m. Twenty-five officers and over 500 other ranks of the Royal Lancashire Fusiliers were deployed at the disused cattle lairs between Roath Dock and Roath Basin, and a further 250 troops were held in reserve at Newport. The troops in Cardiff were used to guard power stations and gasworks which had been approached by pickets, and to maintain a presence outside the municipal buildings and in Bute Street. The Metropolitans and other imported police were kept at the sharp end as a mobile force. Despite this presence, the strike escalated: the marching gangs of strikers spread the outbreak to non-transport industries—workers at flour mills, breweries and many other of Cardiff's myriad dockside workplaces participated. Women were prominent in this activity and many of them joined the Workers' Union. Employers made many complaints about the use of intimidation during this phase of the proceedings: 'nothing like it had been known by the oldest journalist present,' commented the *South Wales Daily News*. In fact, the strike had now effectively become a general strike of the whole city.[39]

That night crowds attacked the unpopular Metropolitans, who were quartered at the skating rink in Westgate Street. After it was rumoured that there had been attempts to fire the stables, police cleared the streets with more enthusiasm than discrimination. Innocent bystanders and the Wood Street gang of youths were caught up in the mêlée. Police were stoned in Havelock Street and it was some time before quiet—peace would be too much to hope for—was restored. On that night the last remaining Chinese laundry in Cardiff was also wrecked to complete the assault on blackleg labour. On Saturday night there were further clashes with the Metropolitans, whose brutality on Friday had been widely condemned. A crowd estimated at 2,000 people gathered outside the skating rink, booing and jeering. Local patriotism seems to have been more important than

[38] *SWDN*; *WM*, 21 July 1911; J. P. May, 'The British Working Class and the Chinese, 1870–1914' (Univ. of Warwick MA thesis, 1973) chs. 5, 6; HO 45 (Chief Constable to Lord Mayor, 31 July; Major Freeth, Diary of the Cardiff Strike, 20, 21, 22, 23 July 1911).

[39] *SWDN*; *WM*, 22 July 1911; HO 45 (Diary of Events, 20, 21 July 1911). Accusations of intimidation abound in the press and in PRO, HO 45.

political feeling; the police were 'Cockney bastards' reviled for their behaviour. There were more police charges, more vigorous street fighting, and the police were showered with stones gathered from the nearby river bed.[40]

Yet that weekend saw the beginning of the end of the dispute. The Lord Mayor's frantic and protracted efforts at negotiations had already borne fruit when the last major conflict on the streets occurred. At 7.30 p.m. on Saturday 22 July, he was able to announce a settlement of the seamen's dispute; he had met representatives of both sides on Friday and some agreement had been reached. The shipowners' negotiators had difficulty in getting this ratified at their own meeting the following morning since there were continuing objections to recognizing a union which was not registered by the Chief Registrar of Friendly Societies. But the shipowners eventually agreed to accept this proposal which became one of the central planks of Saturday's settlement. Tupper and Damm made concessions on the wage issue, accepting a £5 rate for monthly ships with minima and maxima of £4 10s. and £5 10s. respectively in order to gain recognition. Demands on overtime and for a sixty-hour week were also dropped, but the hated Federation ticket became optional and the medical examination was to be conducted by an officer appointed by the Board of Trade, on Board of Trade premises. Though the seamen's leaders made concessions in the final negotiations, it is impossible to deny them a victory. A fixed-term agreement with binding arbitration, plus wage increases ranging downwards from seventeen per cent (for the monthly-paid men), with provision to vary rates every six months in line with freights, were definite gains.

There was still the more difficult issue of the grievances of the diverse trades who were supporting the seamen. The Lord Mayor broke a Welsh Sabbath to meet the strike committee which had been constituted for the ports of south-east Wales. All the unions involved demanded recognition, no victimization or prosecution for stopping work without notice of any striker, and settlement of the grievances of the various groups involved. These grievances were tabulated, and protests were made at the menacing and insulting importation of police and troops. It was decided not to resume work until the troops were removed. Fifteen thousand people were out on strike in Cardiff itself. The city was threatened with a shortage of bread because the carters were on strike and consequently no flour could be moved in Cardiff. Within a week there was the prospect of famine. Bakers were also sensing that this was the time to remedy their own grievances. Potatoes were also held up by a strike of the women who unloaded the ships, and there was also the possibility of a strike by slaughtermen.[41] Moreover, the action in Cardiff was stopping production in the coalfield and as many as 100,000 were idle. The threat to the coalfield concentrated the middle-class mind; the *South Wales Daily News* observed:

The peace of the district has also to be considered: as thousands upon thousands

---

[40] *SWDN*; *WM*, 22, 24 July 1911; HO 45 (Diary of Events, 22, 23 July; Report of Superintendent Olive, Metropolitan Police, 23 July 1911). For accusations of police brutality, see the press and PRO, HO 45.

[41] PRO, HO 45 (Diary of Events, *passim*); *WM*; *SWDN* 24 July 1911; GRO, D/D Com., Chamber of Commerce, *Annual Report* 1911.

of men are yet idle, as their families undergo privation, what will be the outlook? We have used the term 'solidarity of labour', and it is no meaningless term, as will assuredly be made manifest if one section after another now outside the actual dispute be driven into common cause ... Concession is often the wiser way of winning.[42]

Yet the dispute was not to be quickly solved. On Monday and Tuesday there were disputes over whether or not the railway companies were prepared to grant recognition; the companies argued that the existence of conciliation boards meant that there was recognition at the moment. This was disingenuous, for such boards, while they provided a channel for grievances, did not recognize trade unions. Employers also wanted a return to work *before* the sectional grievances were settled. The most difficult issue, however, arose over the flour mills. The strikers agreed to release flour in warehouses in order to avoid a famine, but they refused to do so for the three flour mills whose workers were engaged in the dispute. Negotiations in City Hall were testily conducted in separate rooms. Flour was released from the warehouses and escorted through the city by pickets wearing white armbands. On Tuesday the strike extended to Port Talbot, threatening the collieries of mid-Glamorgan, along with those already stopped in east Glamorgan and Monmouthshire.[43] On Wednesday the strike committee backtracked on its decisions and allowed perishable goods to be moved by union men as long as they were sold at current prices. There was to be no opportunity to profiteer from the dispute. This had the effect of reopening negotiations and at times there were joint sessions. They continued until 3.15 on Thursday morning and then throughout the day until a strike settlement was announced in the early hours of Friday morning. Work was gradually resumed that evening and on Saturday. Even then not all the difficulties were resolved; the dispute over the recognition of the dockers would drag on throughout the year as the Cardiff Railway Company and the Taff Vale Railway Company had declined to recognize the dockers in the general settlement. The end of the dispute was as ragged as its beginning, and some sections of the workforce would continue to feel aggrieved.[44] But despite such qualifications the overall victory was undeniable. In August there was a mass demonstration in favour of increased labour representation on public bodies. It would be more than a decade before this object was significantly advanced, but a crucial breakthrough had been made. As Tupper observed, 'Cardiff unionism has shown its solidarity' and it was this solidarity which would make it a counterweight to the uneven distribution of power in the city.[45]

[42] *SWDN*, 24 July 1911.

[43] *SWDN*; *WM*, 24, 25, 26, 27, 28 July 1911; PRO, HO 45 (Records of telephone conversations, 25 July 1911; Cummings to Askwith, 28 July 1911. Diary of Events, 25, 26, 27 July 1911).

[44] This paragraph is based on a study of the *SWDN* for August to November 1911; Daunton, 'Inter-Union Rivalries', pp. 372–8 and PRO, HO 45; MRC, MSS 175/7/ITF/3, Christian Damm to H. Jochade, 29 August 1911.

[45] *SWDN*, 28 August 1911.

What had happened at Cardiff? The seamen's strike had quite effectively sealed the port by aggressive picketing and won the wages issue, but had proved incapable of winning recognition from the local shipowners, who were rallied by a Shipping Federation counter-attack. At this point, and when the local authorities seemed to be taking a harder line with the seamen, the long-expressed sympathy of the dock workers and their own grievances led to a general stoppage of the docks. This was later extended to industries around the docks by means of vigorous persuasion. Other workers caught the mood of revolt and joined in with separate disputes. For over a week there was virtually a general strike in the city, which forced large-scale, if far from complete, recognition of the unions involved. During this strike there were three distinct outbreaks of violence. The first, the riot around the steamer *Annan*, was clearly the work of the dockers and it was around this issue that the dispute actually crystallized. In its aftermath the dock strike became complete and was solid by the time of the second outbreak, the attacks on the Chinese laundries. Where lies the responsibility for these is more debatable. Tupper's later claim that he led the crowd can be dismissed; he was addressing a crowd of 40,000 people when the first of the attacks took place, and he was by now too well-known in Cardiff for him not to have been recognized. This attack certainly arose out of the strike—the attempt to bring in a Chinese crew on that day was clearly the trigger—and even the Home Office saw the action as 'provocative'. The issue had been whipped up during the dispute, and Tupper's claim that men taken on board the *Lady Jocelyn* had been drugged may have suggested a connection with opium-smoking. His responsibility was moral rather than direct, unless he actually organized the small group of rioters, and of this there is no evidence on either side. He had little to gain from such attacks at that stage; the dockers were already out and he apparently did not welcome the wider strike which followed the next day. His role in the dispute was to use violent language and encourage aggressive action, but to shun (at least in public) the consequences of this talk. He posed constantly as the conciliator and generally praised the Cardiff police; the major riot in Cardiff occurred while he was in gaol and his claim that it would not have happened had he been there was at least plausible. Tupper needed a militant rank and file, but it served his purpose only when it was on a leash which he gripped. He could then offer his strong arm to the shipowners and police as a necessary restraint and, of course, once the dispute had ended, he would cease to shout 'Seize!' It seems more likely that the attack on the laundries was something which he had provoked and could not control rather than something he himself had organized.[46] The third outbreak of violence was the two nights of stone-throwing and fighting around St Mary Street and Westgate Street, arising from the stationing of the Metropolitan police there. Their widely alleged brutality against attackers and bystanders alike provoked resentment and further

---

[46] Tupper, *Seamen's Torch*, pp. 50–1; May, 'British Working Class and the Chinese', ch. 5; PRO, HO 45 (Chief Constable to Lord Mayor, 31 July 1911, marginal comment 'provocative action' against a reference to bringing in a Chinese crew on 20 July).

trouble. Some of this seems to have involved the street gang which also inhabited the area.

The violence contributed to the atmosphere of apprehension which was an integral part of the stoppage. It prompted fears of social disintegration, facilitated negotiation, and forced a settlement. The prolonged discussions and the expectant crowds in Cathays Park are an indication of the urgency of the crisis. The Lord Mayor was praised on all sides for his role as peacemaker. The unions were probably as keen to defuse the situation as the employers. The general stoppage and the violence sprang from the rank and file, and the strike committee made concessions to end the dispute, despite the power of its position: flour was released from the mills and the railway companies were not forced to recognize the unions. In the end the strike committee was probably as worried as the middle class. Both feared the consequences of escalating violence. Troops and burning buildings were two sides of the same coin; the potential for peace that collective bargaining implied enhanced its value on both sides.[47]

The strike was remarkable for its solidarity and extent. Three of the meetings in Cathays Park were held to have attracted 40,000 or more people. It was claimed that shopkeepers were sympathetic; certainly they never bore the brunt of the anger as did their counterparts in the valleys, though perhaps this might have been because Chinese laundries were a more convenient alternative. The boarding-house masters were a lower-middle-class group whose reaction was crucial and they often evicted sailors who had handed in their discharge books to the union. Despite the fact that some sailors were reduced to sleeping rough, the situation does not seem to have been desperate enough for the boarding masters to become objects of attack. The union did give some strike pay and, as some shipowners were paying the union rate and ships were sailing, the union did not have to maintain all its members throughout the strike.[48] In a sense, it was the shipowners who were isolated in the dispute for, given the division between town and docks which was such a notable feature of the city, they were regarded as hard-faced *nouveaux riches* prepared to sacrifice the prosperity of the community in their stubborn defence of their own prerogatives.[49] The liberal *South Wales Daily News* condemned them throughout, and the house journal of the docks community, the *Cardiff Journal of Commerce*, was frank about the seamen's strength throughout the dispute and failed to express an opinion about the owners' stand. Even the docks community was divided, for the coal-owners had a generation or more of experience in collective bargaining and were probably resigned to it.[50]

There is further, if rather sketchy, evidence of more widespread support for

[47] For general studies emphasizing the spread of collective bargaining and the government's growing role in industrial relations at the time, see K. Middlemass, *Politics in Industrial Society* (London, 1979), pp. 57–67; Rubinstein, 'Trade Unions', pp. 60–1, 63–4, 67–8, 70–4; J. White, '1910–14 Reconsidered', in J. E. Cronin and J. Schneer (eds.), *Social Conflict and the Political Order in Modern Britain* (London, 1982), pp. 85–9.

[48] *CJC*, 30 June; 1, 7 July 1911.

[49] Daunton, 'Aspects', 2, part 5, esp. p. 338.

[50] *CJC*, 28 July 1911.

the seamen. One clerk wrote to the *South Wales Daily News* claiming there was widespread sympathy for the workers' cause among his colleagues. Lionel Lindsay, Chief Constable of Glamorgan, but quite prepared to pontificate outside his jurisdiction in Cardiff, felt that the respectable classes had not played their expected role in the disturbances and had hindered the operations of the police against the 'hooligans' whom he saw as perpetrators of trouble.[51] As was the case in some American strikes of the 1870s, wider community support was with the underdog.[52] Shipowners, Metropolitan police, and troops represented outside interests; they were the unacceptable face of plutocracy. It was significant that the Lord Mayor was much lauded for his conciliation, and City Hall did seem to represent a focus for the reconciliation of interests, a place where Cardiff could solve its problems. A city riven with physical divisions of class and indifference had exploded into anger, but at City Hall reconciliation was still possible.

> The citizens of Cardiff will agree with us that there is no higher function than the peacemaker in these grave issues that could be assumed by the civic head of a local community, and that no service which the Lord Mayor could render the city could be more fruitful of benefit ... (He) ... has been sustained in his efforts by the conviction that the graver the situation the greater the obligation resting on the civic head of the community to apply all his energy, patience and resource to the task of arranging a settlement.[53]

The formal means of such conciliation lay in collective bargaining, an admission of workers at least to some economic and social rights, which would ensure that scarring violence would be the exception and not the normal means by which disputes were settled. A conciliation board might be broad enough to integrate, articulate and salve the wounds of a city inevitably divided by class. In the valleys it was an older system of collective negotiation that was being tested and found wanting and class divisions were becoming polarized in the process; in Cardiff there seemed to be a chance that the introduction of such negotiation would make for reconciliation and avert the prospect of open class war.

The shipowners rather distanced themselves from the Shipping Federation in the course of the dispute, and became prepared to recognize the union even if this meant Cardiff giving the lead to London. They felt the weight of local pressures on the Exchange and in the city and already recognized many dockers. It came to be felt that in the new century recognition could no longer be withheld; the consequences of doing so might be fearsome. A meeting with Tupper and Damm, and their assurances about the financial strength of the union and the unusual power of its executive, along with the knowledge that recognition had been granted at Hull, broke the final resistance. It was a vital breakthrough

51 *SWDN*, 28 July 1911; PRO, HO 45 (Lionel Lindsay to Home Office, 23 July 1911).

52 H. G. Gutman, *Work, Culture and Society in Industrialising America* (New York, 1976; Vintage edition, 1977), pp. 242–8, 254–8; idem., 'The Workers' Search for Power: Labor in the Gilded Age', in H. Wayne Morgan (ed.), *The Gilded Age: A Reappraisal* (Syracuse, 1963), esp. pp. 41–3.

53 *WM*, 13 June 1911.

for the union, for the stoppage at Cardiff had been the most prolonged and bitter of the disputes.[54]

There was a great deal of discussion as to why the Riot Act had not been read in Cardiff and why so much violence had taken place when there were so many troops and police present. In the end, the shipowners never secured the kind of coercive power that would have enabled them to win the dispute. The local authorities held back from calling in troops and generally sought to avoid confrontation. A writer with the pseudonym 'Cardiffian' rejected what he saw as a widespread feeling that the Riot Act should have been read and 500 cavalry commanded to disperse the crowd. The general calmness of the strikers, their own capacity to restrain trouble-makers, and the effectiveness of the local police in handling the situation, were claimed as reasons for moderation. Imported police had not been as sensitive, and this had led to conflict which could have escalated. He concluded—and in a sense so did the key areas of public opinion in the city—that:

> Not by riding roughshod over the people but only by careful consideration and businesslike negotiation can remedy be applied to industrial evils. In ready goodwill, expectant of just treatment, the masses keep order of themselves.[55]

Out of division and disorder came a degree of common purpose. Shipowners had to acquiesce in this, and ultimately they would become one of the key exponents of collaboration with trade unions.[56] The victory which the seamen scored was, at least partly, ideological. One of their key themes in public discussion of the strike was 'liberty' versus 'slavery'. The existing system was slavery because of the power of the owners. Their use of undercutting with foreign and coloured labour and their low wages ensured that only the poorest specimens of British seamen would accept the harsh conditions imposed. Liberty meant higher wages, drawing in better British labour, thereby improving the efficiency and trustworthiness (in the case of war) of the merchant navy. Free men would behave as such, rather than in the drunken and degraded manner of slaves. Such ideas caught on; tippers in dispute with the massive Cardiff Railway Company used the same language on one of their banners: 'Cardiff Railway Co. At Last Slaves Demand Freedom.' Such slogans helped to isolate the shipowners.[57]

Community sentiments proved capable of salving class resentments. Even the hard-line *Western Mail* recognized that there was no general tumult and

---

[54] GRO, D/D Com., Shipowners' Association Minutes, typescript transcripts of meetings of 21, 22 July 1911; Lindop, 'Seamen's Trade Unionism', pp. 144–7.

[55] *SWDN*, 7 August 1911.

[56] B. Mogridge, 'Militancy and Inter-Union Rivalry in the British Shipping Industry, 1911–1927', *International Review of Social History*, 4 (1961) 383–91; N. Evans, 'Regulating the Reserve Army: Arabs, Blacks and the Local State in Cardiff, 1919–1945', *Immigrants and Minorities*, 4 (1985), 68–115.

[57] *SWDN*, 28 August 1911; MRC, MSS 175/7/ITF/2. President's Address to the Annual Meeting of the National Sailors' and Firemen's Union, 1911.

no substantial danger to life and property.[58] There had been anxious moments, as the *Cardiff Journal of Commerce* saw in a clear-headed comment:

> One of the darkest, if not actually the darkest cloud that has ever overhung South Wales ... although of comparatively brief duration, as we have come to regard strikes in South Wales, it was nevertheless one of the most bitter and most fiercely fought in the annals of local disputes. In its general consequences it was withal so totally disastrous as to give rise hourly to feelings of intense apprehension, ... one of the most acute strikes experienced for many years.

Yet the prognosis was optimistic: 'Today we must be content that a crisis of so great a magnitude has been passed, and that a settlement which should prove the forerunner of many years of peace has been arrived at.'[59] In other words, the 'tidal wave of impatience' had not had to batter down tough sea defences and the surplus water had been safely channelled. It no longer threatened the foundations of the city.[60]

[58] *WM*, 11 August 1911.

[59] *CJC*, 28 July 1911.

[60] I am grateful to Martin Daunton, Deian Hopkin, Fred Lindop, Jane Morgan, David Rubinstein and the editors for their help and interest.

The Rise of Labour:
Llanelli, 1890–1922

DEIAN HOPKIN

O N the morning of 23 November 1922, a young election agent stood before an enthusiastic crowd in Town Hall Square, Llanelli, to express his candidate's thanks for a thrilling and epoch-making victory. The candidate himself was too exhausted to speak.[1] At that moment, two strands of history came together, for this was the first Labour victory in Carmarthenshire and the end of a century of Liberalism. Commenting upon the election figures for Wales as a whole in that year, one historian has recently said:

> It was clear that the classes and organizations which had dominated public life since the later Victorian era were in full retreat.[2]

Even as the past was being buried, there was the harbinger of a new future. For the young election agent was James Griffiths who, fourteen years later, was to be elected to succeed the exhausted Dr J. H. Williams as Labour member for Llanelli.

In the general explanations of the rise of Labour in Wales, little attention has been paid to the structure of individual electorates or to the significance of particular election campaigns, the kind of work which Professor Ieuan Gwynedd Jones has pioneered for the nineteenth century.[3] The institutions of the Labour movement have been studied to a small extent, notably the evolution of some trade unions and trades councils, the hesitant birth of socialist parties, the early electoral campaigns of individual figures such as Keir Hardie or John Williams, and phenomena such as the New Unionism or industrial unrest.[4] Yet, none of this has led to a synthesis, and important questions remain to be answered. How did this transformation from Liberalism to Labour take place? How *did* Labour rise to power so rapidly in Wales? Or is the rapidity illusory? Indeed, the question we perhaps ought to be asking of the country which

---

[1] *L[lanelly] M[ercury]*, 23 November 1912.

[2] K. O. Morgan, *Rebirth of a Nation: Wales 1880–1980* (Oxford and Cardiff, 1981), p. 272.

[3] See, for example, the analyses of mid-nineteenth century elections in Cardiganshire, Merioneth and Merthyr in I. G. Jones, *Explorations and Explanations: Essays in the Social History of Victorian Wales* (Llandysul, 1981).

[4] See the special issue on Labour History in *WHR*, 6 (1973). A recent study of the history of the Labour Party in Wales between 1900 and 1914 is P. Stead, 'The Labour Party in Wales' in K. D. Brown (ed.), *The First Labour Party, 1906–10* (London, 1985), pp. 64–88.

produced Rebecca, the radical migrants of Llanbryn-mair, John Frost and the
Merthyr rebels of 1831, is why did it all take so long? Despite a good deal
of research activity in recent years, there is still no general history of the rise
of Labour in Wales; indeed, for most parts of Wales we have no local accounts,
no constituency studies and, with the exception of Aneurin Bevan, very little
in the way of biography. In part this is because the historians of Britain who
have examined the emergence of Labour before 1914 have found very little to
say about Wales. Several historians have cited, almost as a disclaimer, the fact
that the only Welsh delegate to the foundation conference at Bradford in 1893
missed the train and never arrived. Recently, the historian David Howell, in
his magisterial study of the Independent Labour Party in Britain, has paired
Merthyr Tydfil and Leicester as 'ILP Islands'.[5]

There are, of course, special problems involved in studying Welsh Labour
history stemming from the relative scarcity of source material, the difficulty
of extracting information about Welsh trade union branches from general British
records, and the paucity of material relating to the foundation of ILP branches
and the early Labour Representation Committee in Wales. Much of this omis-
sion, certainly at the level of the community as a whole, has been made good
by the appearance of John Williams's *Digest of Welsh Historical Statistics*.[6] Even
so, there are many uncharted territories: problems of language, complexities
of institutional and cultural life in Wales, the special role of religion, as well
as the processes of demographic change which produced such different consequences in north-east and south-east Wales.

The evolution of the Labour Party is a long and complex story, part of which
belongs to the changing mental climate of the trade unions, and part to the
character and structure of the Liberal Party, especially that section which recognized the claims of the working classes. Only a part of the story actually belongs
to the group of people who called themselves socialists, never more than a small
minority. The evolution of the Labour Party was a process of accommodation
by which ever-widening groups of trade unionists became gradually convinced
of the necessity for parliamentary representation; Bradford and Farringdon Hall
are milestones not crossroads. This is not to say that socialists did not often,
even usually, call the tune, but the mass membership of the trade unions, the
thousands of working men, and later women, who voted, were rarely inclined
to call themselves socialists. For the majority, it was a struggle to live, to find
enough money to buy food for their beleaguered families, to provide something
against the all-too-familiar spectre of unemployment or illness. They voted, if
at all, for those who seemed to offer the best deal in the search for the means
of subsistence. Not many had had the opportunity to vote at all, but when
they had done so they had tended to vote Liberal, partly because the Liberals
still seemed to offer something which the Tories clearly did not. When Labour
candidates first presented themselves they were met with suspicion and scepti-
cism, and generally rebuffed. How could a working man, with not very much

[5] D. Howell, *British Workers and the Independent Labour Party, 1888–1906* (Manchester, 1983), esp. pp. 241–53.
[6] J. Williams, *Digest of Welsh Historical Statistics* (2 vols., Cardiff, 1985).

more in terms of skill or resource than the elector himself, possibly achieve that which a well-to-do, powerful and influential Liberal could not. Overcoming the inherent fatalism of the electorate, and that deference which had been inculcated over centuries and which was only partially obviated by religious Nonconformity, was the greatest task facing the pioneer socialists. In the event, the transformation was achieved by replacing oligarchic Liberalism with an even more oligarchic Labourism.

The process was uneven and even eccentric. Between 1892 and 1894 a few branches of the ILP were founded in Wales, as well as a few groups of Fabians. One can perhaps understand why University College of Wales, Aberystwyth, should have produced the first Fabian group in Wales, but why does a group also appear at an early date in Llandysul or, as it was known in Fabian circles, Orllwyn Vale? If Cardiff could produce both a Fabian group and an ILP, why not Swansea?[7] The truth is that participation in a socialist group in the 1890s, and even beyond, was an act of high individualism, at once risky and *outré*. It was, moreover, the impulse of youth rather than the consideration of maturity which led men along that path. Many fell by the wayside; for every socialist who persisted, several more abandoned the quest. Occasionally an institution bred a generation of socialists, such as Ysgol y Gwynfryn in Ammanford or the Theological College at Bala-Bangor.[8] More often than not, however, socialism spread as a result of the zeal and energy of individuals who carried others with them. Historians rarely, if ever, mention them and they are largely forgotten in their own communities, except among the few survivors of their generation. But in their day they were names to conjure with: Llew Francis in Merthyr, John Littlejohn in Swansea, Dan Griffiths and R. Neft in Llanelli, Chris Davies in Wrexham and David Thomas in Caernarfon. These were usually members of the professional classes or, at the very least, skilled and independent artisans: Llew Francis was a hairdresser, Neft a dentist, while a significant number—Chris Davies, Dan Griffiths, John Littlejohn, Edgar Chappell and David Thomas— were teachers.[9] In Swansea, indeed, it was said that the ILP was clearly divided between the 'intellectuals' and the 'workers'.[10] An increasing number of Nonconformist ministers was making an impact in socialist circles and beyond, notably Rhys Huws, T. E. Nicholas, J. H. Howard, George Neighbour and Iona Williams.

If the spread of socialism was the work of individuals, the evolution of Labour was an institutional process. What developed in Wales in the first decade of the twentieth century was a synthesis of socialist idealism and trade union

---

[7] For an account of an early meeting, see B[ritish] L[ibrary of] P[olitical and] E[conomic] S[cience] MSS, Collection Misc 375, 20 August 1892. For the Cardiff branch, see ibid., newspaper cuttings, 1892. For Welsh membership lists for the early 1890s, see Fabian Society Archives (Harvester Microform series), f. 134, 136 and 139.

[8] Watcyn Wyn, *Atgofion Watcyn Wyn* (Merthyr Tydfil, 1907). For an insight into the activities of the school, see NLW, *The Gwynfryn Magazine. Journal of the Watcyn Wyn School in Ammanford* (1903–5).

[9] Material relating to most of these individuals can be found, for example, in the L[abour] P[arty] Arch[ives] and the Francis Johnson Correspondence, both available in microform in the NLW Welsh Political Archive.

[10] S. Awberry, *Labour's Early Struggles in Swansea* (Swansea, 1949), p. 54.

pragmatism, a synthesis which had given birth to the Labour Representation Committee of 1900 and which in Wales produced such rare electoral victories as those of Keir Hardie in Merthyr in 1900 and John Williams in Gower in 1906.[11] In neither constituency, however, was socialism the victor. The electors were voting mostly for the man, and only partly for the idea. In both cases, the determining factor in Labour's success was the degree to which trade unions were prepared to switch their allegiance to the Labour candidate.

One way to examine the evolution of Labour and the conflicts and contrasts between Labourism and socialism is to examine in detail some of the key constituencies. Merthyr has been given a considerable amount of attention, largely because so many key figures in radical and Labour politics—Henry Richard, Thomas Halliday, Keir Hardie—ventured there. It was, after all, the first seat to return a member of parliament sponsored by the ILP. Only recently has attention begun to be devoted to other constituencies—Ogmore, Aberdare, the Rhondda, north-east Wales, and Swansea.[12] The case for studying Llanelli is strong; the mixture of urban and rural sectors, the spread of occupations, the rapid population change, and the particular balance of Welsh- and English-speaking residents make it perhaps more typical of Wales as a whole than many individual constituencies in the coalfield.[13] It was one of the few Welsh constituencies to have a Labour candidate before 1914. Dr J. H. Williams was put forward in 1910 and when he eventually won the seat in 1922 it was to be held for Labour in perpetuity, often returning one of the highest Labour majorities in the United Kingdom. At the level of the local council and county council, too, the Labour Party made remarkable headway in the 1920s and became dominant.

Like many other industrial communities in south Wales, Llanelli was a volatile community which had grown rapidly and where the bulk of the population consisted either of recent immigrants or of first-generation natives. By 1901 the town which a century earlier had been little more than a village of 2,072 people had grown to an urban district of 25,000. In the next ten years the town grew by 25 per cent to 32,000. The rural district, which had grown to 20,000 by 1901, increased by 34 per cent to 27,000, an enormous increase by any standards and one which reinforces the contemporary impression of Llanelli

---

[11] For the Merthyr election of 1900, see K. O. Fox, 'Labour and Merthyr's Khaki Election of 1900', *WHR*, 2 (1964–5), 351–66; for Gower, D. Cleaver, 'Labour and Liberals in Gower, 1885–1910', *WHR*, 12 (1984–5), 388–410; G. D. Thomas, 'Politics in the Gower Constituency: the emergence of a Labour Party 1900–1906' (Univ. of Wales MA thesis, 1982).

[12] See C. Parry, *The Radical Tradition in Welsh Politics. A Study of Liberal and Labour Politics in Gwynedd, 1900–1920* (Hull, 1970); W. David, 'The Labour Party and the "exclusion" of the Communists: the case of the Ogmore Divisional Labour Party', *Llafur*, 3 (1983), 5–15; A. Mor O'Brien, 'The Merthyr Borough Elections, November 1915', *WHR*, 12 (1984–5), 538–66; J. G. Jones, 'Wales and the New Socialism', *WHR*, 11 (1982–3), 173–99; C. Williams, 'The Labour Party in the Rhondda', unpublished paper delivered at Gregynog, March 1987; D. Hopkin, 'Labour in north-east Wales, 1893–1939', unpublished paper delivered at the fiftieth anniversary of the Gresford disaster.

[13] The primary sources for this study are D(yfed) R(ecord) O(ffice), DA/D/POD, papers of the Llanelli Divisional Labour Party; NLW, Douglas and Loti Hughes Collection, papers of the Llanelli Trades and Labour Council and Divisional Labour Party; NLW, James Griffiths Collection.

as a boom town. The town was on the whole prosperous. Rateable values were increasing; between 1895 and 1910 the urban district was able to undertake a substantial programme of improvements, including a new town hall, a new public library, an electric tramway system, a new sewage and water-treatment system, and various other undertakings, while the harbour underwent considerable development in the same period. There is no doubt that the general level of wages was high, but some of this was short-term, produced by the building boom, and the staple industries were susceptible to fluctuation.[14] There is some indication that there were pockets of extreme poverty; this was certainly recognized by the Medical Officer of Health and was cited as one cause of the riots of 1911.[15] The death rate for the urban district was slightly higher than the national average for some of the period under consideration; yet on the whole Llanelli could not be called a deprived area.

It is not possible to be specific about occupations in Llanelli in this period because, before 1921, figures for the town were aggregated with those for the remainder of Carmarthenshire, even though the municipal borough had come into existence in 1913. In 1921, when the population had risen to 36,000 in the borough itself, 5,200 men and 700 women were employed in the metal industry, over half the total for the county as a whole, with a further 670 in building, 1,337 in transport and 500 in textiles. Tin-plate manufacturing dominated Llanelli, though it was nothing like as dominant as mining was in the Rhondda or even in certain communities of rural east Carmarthenshire. Indeed, in the areas which eventually formed the Llanelli constituency, it was mining which was growing fastest, with almost 25 per cent more men employed in 1921 as compared with 1911, in total about 4,000 more miners than tin-plate workers. The number of labourers had also increased from around 1,100 to over 2,000 by 1921. By contrast the professional classes of the area remained fairly static at around 1,500, while the number of clerical workers actually fell very substantially.

It is against this socio-economic background that the political evolution of Labour in Llanelli must be considered. Three factors help to explain the replacement of Liberalism with Labour. In the first place, Liberalism itself was undergoing substantial change in the late nineteenth century and in Llanelli this was manifested by a greater willingness on the part of Liberals themselves to accommodate Labour. In time, this made it easier to elide the differences, especially when the Liberal Party in Britain became divided. Secondly, the organizational infrastructure of Labour developed rapidly from 1899 onwards, providing a firm base for future political campaigns. In particular, Labour profited by the radical constitutional and organizational changes made in 1917. Finally, the changes wrought both in the franchise and the electoral boundaries in 1918 worked to the advantage of Labour; the Labour divisional organization in the new Llanelli constituency after 1918 was an extension of trade union organization which

---

[14] E. H. Hunt, *Regional Wage Variations in Britain, 1850–1914* (Oxford, 1973), esp. pp. 21–7.
[15] *Report of the Medical Officer of Health for 1911* (Llanelli, 1912).

operated in that territory before the war, but it was better focused and its audience was more receptive.

The Carmarthen Districts, of which Llanelli was a component, changed hands between the political parties twice between 1886 and 1914; the Liberal Unionist candidate, who came within 200 votes of capturing the seat in 1892, succeeded in doing so with the slenderest of majorities in 1895, only to lose again in 1900. East Carmarthen, however, showed no such oscillation; Liberal majorities never fell below 2,000 and peaked in January 1910, taking over 62 per cent of the poll. Before 1900 there was no challenge to this hegemony from Labour. Trade unions kept strictly to the limited arena of wage politics. Given the occupational structure of the district, it is inevitable that the earliest trade unions in the area centred on tin-plate workers and miners, notably the Independent Association of Tin-plate Makers, the first distinctly Welsh trade union in the industry, which was formed in Swansea in 1871. The Amalgamated Association of Miners followed soon after. New Unionism affected Llanelli in the 1890s to the degree that branches of the Dockers' and Gasworkers' Unions were formed.[16] By 1900, there were some twenty major trade unions located in the town, including strong branches of the Engineers and Railway Servants. Yet these were often highly sectarian unions, incapable of committing themselves to joint strategies for political purposes. Some unions faced special difficulties in the recessions of the 1890s, notably the tin-plate industry which suffered grievously from the tariffs imposed by US President McKinley in 1890.

Early interest in socialism came, typically, from outside the trade unions. In 1892, the year when Keir Hardie won his first election as an Independent Labour candidate in South West Ham, London, a meeting was held at the Athenaeum, Llanelli, to provide a platform for H. W. Hobart, a touring propagandist from the London-based Marxist party, the Social Democratic Federation.[17] The significance of this meeting was the choice of chairman, David Randell, the Liberal MP for Gower. Randell has been almost entirely overlooked by historians, partly because he belongs to that crucial no man's land of Welsh politics, the Lib-Labs.[18] A lawyer of mid-Wales extraction, he had specialized in trade-union law and it was his work on behalf of the tin-plate workers, and later the steel smelters and anthracite miners, that enabled him to win the Liberal nomination for the Gower by-election in 1888, when he was thirty-four years old, an indication of the political influence of the tin-plate men at the time. Randell remained a member for twelve years and in that time carried through the House of Commons a bill giving wages a preferential claim on estates in liquidation cases.

---

[16] See, for example, M(odern) R(ecords) C(entre), *Annual Balance Sheet and Secretary's Report*, Llanelly Trades and Labour Council, 1900 ff.

[17] *Justice*, 3, 17 December 1892. Other meetings were held in Felinfoel, Ammanford, Pontarddulais (where it was claimed too many working men were voting Tory under the delusion that they were thus supporting socialism), Gorseinon, Kidwelly and Pen-clawdd. Few branches, however, were actually formed.

[18] The outlines of Randell's career are given in M. Stenton and F. Lees, *Who's Who of British MPs* (2 vols., Brighton, 1976), 2, p. 296. See also G. Thomas, 'Gower Politics', pp. 4–5. Additional information is found in Randell's obituaries, e.g. *SWDN*, 6 June 1912; *Llais Llafur*, 8 June 1912.

The real interest for historians lies in Randell's political evolution. In the 1880s he was a prominent member of Cymru Fydd, the advanced nationalist wing of the Liberal Party; indeed, he described himself in the 1888 election as a 'National Labourist'.[19] By 1892 he had begun to develop a more specific interest in socialism and in the politics of trade unions. He was present at a meeting of miners held to discuss federation in the same year as he chaired the inaugural meeting of the SDF in Llanelli.[20] At that meeting, he announced that he was 'tending more and more towards socialism'. He was not content, he told his audience, with the complex ritualistic theory of 'as it was in the beginning, is now and ever shall be'. The SDF, he declared, was 'in the very front rank of the new social movement'. Later, he even offered to help form a branch of the SDF. A branch was eventually formed, but it had a fragile existence. For a time there were regular meetings in People's Park, but when the SDF national campaigners returned in the autumn of 1893 they had to revive the Llanelli branch.[21] After that it seems to have petered out altogether, as did the initially more successful branches at Ammanford, Pontarddulais and Landore. There is no record of Randell having taken part in any of these activities, yet his public support of socialists continued. In 1894, during a bitter strike in the tin-plate industry when 1,500 men were locked out, Keir Hardie made his first visit to Llanelli and addressed an audience of several thousand, with David Randell again in the chair.[22] Six years later, in circumstances which have yet to be fully revealed, Randell resigned his seat and withdrew from politics. In 1903 he briefly reappeared, chairing a meeting of the ILP at the Royalty Theatre in Llanelli, when Keir Hardie made a return visit to the town, but soon afterwards he suffered a nervous breakdown which was given as a contributory cause of his death in 1912.[23] At that time, neither Liberals nor Labour claimed Randell as one of their own, an indication perhaps of the degree to which political polarization had occurred. Yet David Randell may be regarded as typical of a generation of Liberals who were disillusioned with their own party but reluctant to commit themselves totally to the uncertain destinies of the new Labour Party. It was their misfortune to be born a little too early; they were the casualties of the changing political climate.

If Randell was regarded as somewhat eccentric by more conventional Liberals, it is well to remind ourselves that there was, in fact, a close working relationship between many trade unionists and the Liberal Party. Although this relationship was never formalized in the way relations between unions and the Labour Party were to be, there is no doubt that money and effort were committed by many trade unions to the Liberal Party. Miners' leaders, in particular, were closely involved in Liberal politics, but other trade unions gave tacit support to Liberal candidates. Liberal MPs were well aware of this. Though somewhat less mercurial than David Randell, Major E. R. Jones, who sat for Carmarthen Districts

[19] *S[outh] W[ales] P[ress]*, 15, 22, 29 March 1888.
[20] *SWP*, 8 December 1892.
[21] *Justice*, 16 September 1893.
[22] *L[abour] L[eader]*, 23 June 1894.
[23] *LL*, 23 October 1908.

between 1892 and 1895, was said to be an 'advanced Liberal' and he proudly boasted his friendship with the radical, Joseph Cowen, whose biography he eventually wrote.[24] Alfred Davies, underwriter and financier, who won the Carmarthen Districts back from the Conservatives in 1900 at the height of the Boer War, was described as 'a Radical with a sound labour platform',[25] while Llewelyn Williams, his successor, sought and obtained the endorsement of the Llanelli Trades Council, and years later openly endorsed the candidature of J. H. Williams, the Labour candidate for Llanelli in 1918.[26]

Long before the formal emergence of the Labour Party in Llanelli, then, leading Liberals were demonstrating their awareness, even their sympathy, for its principles or, at the very least recognizing the voting power of those groups whose natural affinity was now with Labour. In 1910, countering an accusation that he had voted against the Feeding of Necessitous Children Bill, the Liberal MP for East Carmarthen, Abel Thomas, protested that he was no less a socialist than his accuser, the Labour candidate; the difference was a 'matter of degree and pace'.[27] Yet, however sympathetic or indulgent individual Liberals might be, they failed to satisfy the growing demands of trade unionists in Great Britain as a whole for greater political representation. This failure is in large measure the reason why so many trades councils were formed at the turn of the century, one of which was the Llanelli Trades and Labour Council, inaugurated on 4 January 1900, just before the founding conference of the Labour Party.[28] Immediately the Llanelli Trades Council was contesting local elections and won two seats on the Urban District Council within three months of its formation. The Dockers' Union had taken the initiative in forming the Trades Council, but eight other trade unions were involved in the inauguration. By 1910 fifteen trade unions representing 3,000 workers were affiliated to the Trades Council.

From the outset, moreover, the Trades Council had high political ambitions. After some early successes in local elections and despite several unsuccessful attempts to win county council seats, there was talk of Westminster. In 1903 the secretary wrote to the headquarters of the Labour Representation Committee to enquire who had been selected as Labour candidate, and was somewhat surprised to discover that the initiative lay with Llanelli itself. Discussions had already been held regarding the possibility of running the celebrated dockers' leader, Ben Tillett, and, although nothing came of it immediately, the prospect of a Labour candidate for Llanelli was firmly on the agenda.[29] Gradually the Trades Council became an influential body. When a new town hall was constructed in 1908, the Trades Council moved its headquarters to the former town hall and from there the officers ran a close-knit organization which kept a close watch on the activities of the local town council as well as trade unions themselves.

---

[24] Stenton and Lees, *Who's Who of British MPs*, 2, p. 195.

[25] Ibid.

[26] *LM*, 12 December 1918.

[27] *LM*, 8 December 1910.

[28] *Annual Balance Sheet and Secretary's Report*, Llanelly Trades and Labour Council, 1901.

[29] LPArch, Walworth Road, London, Labour Representation Committee Letter Files, 10/272, 15 July 1903; 10/273, 23 September 1903.

By contrast, despite an early start, socialism made little real headway in the town. The SDF never reappeared after the 1890s and it was not until 1906, during a period of general socialist revival in Wales, that a branch of the ILP was formed, thirteen years after the party had been formed in Bradford. The branch made up in energy what it lacked in numbers. In 1910, for example, the ILP held over twenty-five full-scale open-air meetings between May and September, with speakers from as far afield as Scotland and the USA as well as home-grown orators; and this was in addition to the regular weekly meetings in the YMCA.[30] Occasionally larger halls or theatres were booked for rallies addressed by some of the great names of the day—the mercurial Victor Grayson, the coldly brilliant and acid Philip Snowden, Bruce Glasier, Keir Hardie (on more than one occasion) and Ramsay MacDonald. More significantly, members of the Llanelli branch were actively proselytizing over a wide area of west Wales. In 1910 a special supper was held, attended by over 200 people.[31] Yet the national ILP statistics for 1910 to 1918 show that Llanelli remained a small branch, increasingly prone to extremist infiltration. In 1911, for example, it was nine months in arrears to the national party and in 1915 it was dissolved as 'a centre of impossibilism'. It was reformed a few months later, dissolved once again in 1916, and finally revived in 1918.[32]

Nevertheless, even in these difficult circumstances, the Llanelli ILP exercised a disproportionate political influence. Relationships between socialists and trade union organizations were often fraught and Llanelli was no exception. Where the ILP developed a clear strategic programme, the trade unions and the Trades Council operated on a pragmatic basis, concentrating on winning increased representation on local bodies without necessarily identifying priorities in policy. Besides, the trade unions themselves often acted independently. In 1906, at the very time when the ILP was being formed in Llanelli, the local Tin-plate District Committee had sought to establish its own branch of the LRC.[33] Six years later, the Trades Council itself changed its name to the Llanelli and District Labour Association and questions were raised as to whether the ILP was eligible to affiliate. In the event, the new Labour Association had difficulty affiliating to the Labour Party since Ramsay MacDonald was anxious to ensure that all trade unionists in the constituency, including Carmarthen, were party to this move; the Carmarthen trade unionists, however, were very reluctant to associate with the Labour Party.[34] In fact, such divisions between trade unions strengthened the hand of the ILP. In 1908 the National Administrative Council of the ILP had refused to endorse the ILP nomination for the parliamentary seat because the local party was too weak.[35] In 1910, however, the ILP was able

[30] Regular reports of the Llanelli ILP can be found in *LL* from 1906 onwards; e.g. 20 July 1906; 2 November 1906; 11 January 1907; 8 February 1907.

[31] *LM*, 27 January 1910.

[32] ILP membership statistics; BLPES, N[ational] A[dministrative] C[ouncil] Collection; for example, items 53–9.

[33] LPArch, Labour Party Letter Files, GC/3/177.

[34] Ibid., AFF/7/311–20; N(ational) E(xecutive) C(ommittee), 2 January 1913.

[35] NAC, 24 January 1908.

to fight the seat despite the claims of the miners that they alone should make the nomination. The miners' failure to agree amongst themselves ensured that in the second general election of 1910 and at the by-election of 1912 the unlikely figure of Dr J. H. Williams, President of the local ILP, became the Labour candidate. In both campaigns he was obliged to run with little trade union support and without even the official blessing of the national Labour Party.[36]

J. H. Williams was hardly the archetypal ILP candidate. In 1910 he was forty-one years of age, a medical practitioner with long experience in local government; for twenty-three years he served as county councillor and alderman, as chairman of Burry Port Urban District Council, and as a member of the Llanelli Board of Guardians. Yet he cannot be called a political heavyweight. His campaign speeches were often maudlin and emotional. He addressed himself to sentiment rather than substantial issues, drawing heavily on biblical quotations. Indeed, one observer in the election of 1910 wondered whether Dr Williams was, in fact, standing as a theologian.[37] In neither campaign was Dr Williams able to threaten the position of the defending Liberal Party. In 1910, the issue of the House of Lords had considerable appeal for the voters of East Carmarthen and, though the Conservatives had a credible candidate in Mervyn Peel, the Liberal Abel Thomas acquired 62 per cent of the poll and won with a majority (3,510) bigger than the combined votes of his two opponents (3,491). Dr Williams at his first attempt had got 1,176 votes, just 12.6 per cent of the poll. Doubtless the failure of the national Labour Party to endorse his candidature, on technical grounds, undermined his position somewhat and the campaign was also bedevilled by lack of funds. More indicative of Labour's weakness in these years, however, was its failure to take advantage of the by-election in East Carmarthen caused by the death of Abel Thomas in 1912. Although the Liberals were placed under a disadvantage by the loss of a sitting member, by the problems they encountered in selecting a successor, and by the relative ineffectiveness of the eventual nominee, the Revd Towyn Jones, Labour utterly failed to capitalize on these difficulties.[38] Their own search for a candidate exposed wide rifts in their ranks; having claimed the seat, the miners failed to produce a candidate, with some of them voting for John James, Cwm-gors, and even more voting solidly against the adoption of any Labour candidate.[39] Once again, Dr J. H. Williams, the ILP nominee, was left to contest the seat with little or no trade union support and with a shadow of the Llanelli riots of 1911 clouding the contest, a factor which probably worked to Labour's disadvantage.[40]

[36] NEC, 23 November 1910; NEC–Parliamentary Labour Party joint meeting, 15 October 1912. For details of Dr Williams's career, see obituaries; e.g. *Llanelly Star*, 8 February 1936; *LM*, 13 February 1936; *L(lanelly) G(uardian)*, 13 February 1936.

[37] *LG*, 15 December 1910. See his adoption speech, *LM*, 8 December 1910.

[38] For an account of the Liberal adoption meetings, see *LG*, 8 August 1910.

[39] A bitter controversy broke out after John James drew attention in the press to Williams's failure to get endorsement from the Labour Party. See *Llais Llafur*, 31 August, 7 September 1912; *LG*, 8 August 1912. It was felt in some quarters, however, that J. H. Williams was an acceptable candidate; ibid., 15 August 1912.

[40] See D. Hopkin, 'The Llanelli Riots, 1911', *WHR*, 11 (1982–3), 488–515.

Indeed, it would be fair to say that Labour had reached a plateau by 1912. Some members of the movement were beginning to be seen as unpleasant extremists, notably the two local activists, the dentist Neft and the New Dock schoolteacher, Dan Griffiths. The trade unions, notably the miners, were still uncertain of the new movement, so that it was difficult to present a united front. On the other hand, attempts to forge a more disciplined party led to accusations of authoritarian behaviour. The Trades Council, for example, was being accused of holding furtive and suspicious caucus meetings in their head-quarters in the old town hall.[41] Above all, perhaps, the composition of the electorate, especially the parliamentary electorate, made it difficult for Labour to achieve more than a small percentage of any poll.

At the outbreak of the First World War Labour was still the outsider in Llanelli, with few seats on the Borough Council, fewer still on the County Council, and no parliamentary prospects at all. Yet, four years later, the situation had changed dramatically both at the local and parliamentary level. Three factors can be held to explain this change: the psychological impact of war, improvements in the electoral organization of Labour and, perhaps most important of all, the franchise changes of 1918 and the accompanying redistribution of parliamentary seats.

First of all, while it is difficult to quantify the psychological and political impact of the First World War, there is no doubt that it was an important factor in changing the political climate. If the war challenged old assumptions and nostrums, it also introduced, directly or indirectly, a new political dimension, a sense of profound change, a new level of political optimism. In part this was due to the impact of the Russian Revolution, as the young secretary of Ammanford Trades Council, James Griffiths, proclaimed to his members in his report for 1917.[42] But the changing climate can also be felt in industrial relations and in the growing impact of anti-war dissent, both of which caused grave concern to the government. Pacifists and socialists appeared to engender as much fear and hatred as the German enemy, while the spectre of Bolshevism and other new political forces prompted newspaper proprietors like Lords Beaverbrook and Northcliffe to argue for the continuation of press censorship when the war was over.[43]

Secondly, the organization of the Labour movement was transformed in 1917–18. Before the war, the organization of the Labour Party was weak. In 1912, for example, nobody seriously gave Dr J. H. Williams the least chance. Largely as a result of the reluctance of trade unions to contribute either money or effort to his campaigns, the Labour campaigns were substantially disadvantaged

---

[41] *LM*, 7 April 1910.

[42] *First Annual Report of Ammanford Trades Council* (Ammanford, 1917).

[43] See D. Hopkin, 'Domestic Censorship in the First World War', *Journal of Contemporary History*, 5 (1970), 151–69.

compared with both Conservatives and Liberals (see Table 6). Indeed, in 1903 the Trades Council had supported the revived candidature of E. R. Jones, the former Liberal MP, because it was unable to afford its own candidate and chose instead 'the next best candidate in the interest of Labour who has promised to defray the whole of his election expenses'.[44] By 1918 a very different situation had arisen. The Labour Party in Britain was far better organized, with a properly developed headquarters staff and with all the benefits of constituency organization and individual membership beginning to make itself felt.[45]

This was reflected in far better organization in Llanelli than ever before. The boundary changes, the third factor, worked to Labour's advantage, integrating the industrial areas into one constituency and ensuring that the forces of the trade union movement were not divided, as they had been, between two constituencies. In the wake of these boundary changes, a Divisional Labour Party had been formed in 1918,[46] and this facilitated the introduction of new campaign techniques and new methods of propaganda, all of which were introduced, much to the surprise of the local press and Labour's adversaries, at the general election held in the same year; for example, the constituency was divided into districts, hundreds of young workers were used in a high profile campaign and, above all, a personal canvass of householders was undertaken.[47] None of this would have been possible, however, without the transformation in the attitude of trade unions towards Labour which took place during the war. Whereas the pre-war trade unions appear to have been suspicious of the ILP, a major shift in attitude took place during the war, partly fuelled by common opposition to government policies and partly by a growing recognition that the future of the Liberal Party was becoming insecure. This was underlined by the split between the Liberal leaders during 1917 which yawned wide during the general election campaign of 1918.

The change in the level and quality of Labour Party organization is reflected in both the structure of the political Labour movement in Llanelli and the range of its activities. By 1920, for example, the Divisional Labour Party contained representation not only from the trade unions and the Trades Council, but also the Socialist Society, the ILP, the Labour Group on both Borough and County Councils and a women's section. The Trades Council had broadened its range of activities considerably. In the first half of 1919, for example, it helped to organize the Labour group on Carmarthenshire County Council, and successfully campaigned for the reinstatement of the left-wing activist, Dan Griffiths, to the teaching job he had lost when he became a conscientious objector to military service. Less successful was an attempt to organize the local police into a trade union in 1919 but, undaunted, the Labour Party campaigned locally against British support for the White Armies in Russia, formed a Profiteering Committee

  [44] LP Arch, GC/11/291/30 October 1903.
  [45] For the most complete account of these changes, see R. I. McKibbin. *The Evolution of the Labour Party, 1910–24* (Oxford, 1973).
  [46] NEC, 24 June 1918.
  [47] See *LM*, 2 January 1919.

to monitor and report on food and commodity prices in the town, and began the process of acquiring a printing press and freehold premises.[48]

The range and vigour of Labour's activities attracted wide public attention, and there is a distinct impression that the political atmosphere had changed greatly from the pre-war years. Certainly contemporaries reported the activities of the Labour movement in a different spirit—either very critically, which suggests there was something to fear, or very enthusiastically, which again suggests there was something to play for.[49] This in turn may well have been due to the dramatic electoral impact of the franchise and boundary changes introduced by the Representation of the People Act of 1918, arguably the most important factor in the rise of Labour.

In recent years, historians have considered very closely the implications of high and low levels of enfranchisement in English constituencies on the rise of Labour and the decline of Liberalism. Colin Matthew and Ross McKibbin, for example, have suggested that substantial sections of the Edwardian working class, who might well have voted Labour, were denied the vote for procedural reasons and that their enfranchisement in 1918 was the crucial factor in improving Labour's electoral prospects.[50] This view has been challenged by a number of historians. Duncan Tanner has cast doubt on the notion that the bias was class-orientated, while Michael Hart has disputed the claim that pre-war Liberals did not form the majority of post-war Labour voters.[51] Using ingenious correlation techniques, moreover, John Turner suggests that, far from improving the electoral chances of Labour, the 1918 Act proved an impediment; he argues that Labour's electoral successes in 1918 and 1922 were inversely related to the proportion of new voters and that it was the male working-class voters enfranchised before 1918 who were most effectively mobilized, through a combination of unionization and economic circumstances, in support of the Labour Party.[52]

Hitherto no systematic work has been undertaken in the same field in Wales, largely because English historians have avoided what one historian has described as 'the peculiar cultural and political significance of religious allegiance and rurality' in the Celtic peripheries of Britain.[53] In the absence of psephological studies of all the Welsh constituencies, it is difficult, therefore, to offer anything more than tentative hypotheses and some provisional conclusions based on a

[48] DRO, D/POL/1/1, Minute Book of Llanelli Divisional Labour Party.

[49] By 1919 the *Llanelly Mercury*, a stalwart Liberal paper, was running a regular column by 'Socialist'; eventually the paper supported Labour.

[50] H. C. G. Matthew, R. I. McKibbin and J. A. Kay, 'The franchise factor in the rise of the Labour Party', *E[nglish] H[istorical] R[eview]*, 91 (1976), 723–54; also P. Clarke, 'The electoral position of the Liberal and Labour Parties, 1910–14', ibid., 90 (1975), 828–36. The municipal performance of Labour before 1914 is examined in M. G. Sheppard and J. Halstead, 'Labour's Municipal Election Performance in Provincial England and Wales, 1901–13', *Bulletin of the Society of the Study for Labour History*, 39 (1979), 39–62.

[51] D. Tanner, 'The Parliamentary Electoral System, the "Fourth Reform Act" and the Rise of Labour in England and Wales', *Bulletin of the Institute of Historical Research*, 56 (1983), 205–19; M. Hart, 'The Liberals, the War and the Franchise', *EHR*, 97 (1982), 820–32.

[52] J. Turner, 'The Labour Vote and the Franchise after 1913: an investigation of the English evidence', in P. Denley and D. Hopkin (eds.), *History and Computing* (Manchester, 1987), pp. 136–43.

[53] Ibid., p. 138.

limited exercise on the Llanelli electorate. There is the added difficulty that until 1918 Llanelli was divided into two constituencies. The borough itself was part of the Carmarthen District of Boroughs, while Llanelli rural district was joined with Llandeilo, Llangadog, Llandovery and Caeo as the Eastern Division of Carmarthenshire. In 1918 the boundaries were radically altered: the expanding industrial areas west of Llanelli around Burry Port and the eastern coalfield of the Aman and Gwendraeth valleys were combined with the borough itself to form a new Llanelli constituency, while the agricultural areas were detached to form the West Carmarthen constituency. This in itself is, of course, a factor of very considerable political importance. Quite apart from the change in what may be called the occupational balance of power, the new constituencies were very much larger than their predecessors. The total electorate of the three former constituencies in 1910 was around 28,500; the Llanelli constituency alone was almost 49,000 in 1922, and the new Western constituency was 36,000.

A comparison between the only extant pre-war electoral register for the urban district of Llanelli, that of 1913–14, and the post-war electoral registers for the same polling districts, is highly revealing.[54] It is generally agreed that the register which most accurately reflects the impact of the franchise changes of 1918 on individual polling districts is that of autumn 1922, when the post-war demobilization was complete and all valid registrations had been recorded. While the increase in Wales as a whole is substantial, as shown in Table 1, there is considerable variation from constituency to constituency and between different parts of each constituency. Table 2 reveals the magnitude of increase in the electorate in the eight polling districts which made up the three Llanelli urban wards.

Table 1: Electoral Change in Wales 1910–1922

	Jan 1910	Oct 1922	% change
Total Welsh electorate	415,786	1,018,627	+145
Carmarthenshire	28,473	85,008	+198
	(1913–14)		
Llanelli	5,061	18,080	+257

The changes, moreover, can be placed in context by examining the increase for Wales as a whole between January 1910 (the last pre-war election in which every Welsh seat was fought and for which electoral figures are therefore easily available) and 1922. The general increase for Wales was 145 per cent; for Carmarthenshire as a whole, including all three constituencies, the increase was 198 per cent. It is impossible to extract the relevant figures for the Llanelli wards for 1910, but the electorate in 1913, the date of the extant register, may well have been somewhat larger than in 1910, so that the increase of 257 per cent from the later date to 1922, shown in detail in Table 2, is an even more

---

[54] Llanelli Public Library, *Electoral Roll of the Burgesses of Llanelly, 1913–14* (Llanelly, 1914); DRO, Electoral register for October 1922.

Table 2: Llanelli Borough—Changes in Levels of Enfranchisement 1913–22

		1913	1922	% increase
Ward 1	Div 1	543	2,198	304.8
	Div 2	668	2,320	247.3
	Div 3	519	1,586	205.6
Ward 2	Div 4	884	3,046	244.6
	Div 5	557	1,807	224.4
	Div 6	706	2,771	292.5
Ward 3	Div 7	633	2,165	242
	Div 8	551	2,187	297
Total		5,061	18,080	
Average % increase				257.2
Median % increase				245.5
Standard deviation				34.135

emphatic indication of the degree to which the Llanelli electorate changed. The conclusion is that in the pre-war years, urban Llanelli was an area of low enfranchisement, especially in the poorer wards around the New Dock and Morfa. Even relatively prosperous areas such as College Hill and Glenalla Road, however, show an increase in the electorate well above the national average for Wales. This suggests, as Matthew and McKibbin have argued for Britain as a whole, that the Labour Party in Llanelli was suffering under particular disadvantages before 1914. But does it follow that Labour in Llanelli gained the majority of the new electors?

One way of assessing the character of the new electorate is to measure the turnover of electors between 1913 and 1922. This is achieved by conducting a Nominal Record Linkage of male electors between the two registers as well as measuring female enfranchisement. Tables 3 and 4 give the data and analysis of a random sample of streets in each polling district, from which it becomes apparent that the turnover of electors is far greater than the simple increase in the electorate. Only 12 per cent of the electorate in the sample of 1922 were old electors from 1913. Expressed in terms of male electors, since female enfranchisement was only achieved in 1918, it can be seen that 73 per cent of the male electors of 1922 were new to the register. The proportion of women on the register was relatively high, at 40 per cent, but this varied considerably from ward to ward, according to the random sample. In Coldstream Street, for example, women outnumbered men, while in Oxen Street there were almost twice as many men as women on the register. The reasons for this are difficult to establish. In Division 2 as a whole, the increase in the electorate was virtually identical with the median increase for Llanelli as a whole, which suggests that Coldstream Street was an exception, while the highest increase in the electorate was registered in Ward 1, where Oxen Street was located, but where the high density of population should not have produced such disproportion between men and women.

Table 3: Random Sample of Llanelli Polls 1913–1922

Ward and street	Total households	1913		1922				Men		Removals[c]	Widows
		Household registration[a]	Total individuals	Household registration[a]	Total individuals	Men	Women	Common[b]	New		
Ii Old Road	54	29	29	51	113	63	50	14	49	15	—
Oxen Street	37	18	18	24	48	31	17	5	26	12	1
Iii Coldstream Street	61	42	42	59	135	67	68	15	52	19	5
Iiii Lakefield Place	24	21	22	24	63	39	24	11	28	8	3
Glanmor Terrace	37	29	30	37	86	55	31	17	38	11	2
IIiv College Square	23	15	15	23	47	27	20	10	17	5	1
IIv Pottery Street	58	43	43	57	128	80	48	23	57	16	4
IIvi Bigyn Road	86	79	79	85	220	137	83	36	101	38	5
IIIviii Bryn Road	73	55	55	73	183	113	70	32	81	17	6
IIIviii Bidulph Street	28	26	26	28	71	41	30	10	31	16	—
Total	524	357	359	504	1,094	653	441	173	480	157	27

[a] The columns marked 'Household registration' record the number of households which appear in each register.

[b] 'Common' indicates how many individual electors appear on both registers.

[c] 'Removals' indicates how many individuals registered in 1913 had left the register by 1922.

Table 4: Analysis of Gender of Voters, 1922

		Household ratio Men:women electors	Electors per household		
			Men	Women	Total
Ii	Old Road	1.26:1	1.23	0.98	2.21
Ii	Oxen Street	1.82:1	1.29	0.70	1.99
Iii	Coldstream Street	0.98:1	1.13	1.15	2.28
Iiii	Lakefield Place	1.62:1	1.62	1.00	2.62
Iiii	Glanmor Terrace	1.77:1	1.48	0.83	2.31
Ward 1	*Total*	1.34:1	1.30	0.97	2.27
IIiv	College Square	1.35:1	1.17	0.86	2.03
IIv	Pottery Street	1.66:1	1.40	0.84	2.24
IIvi	Bigyn Road	1.65:1	1.61	0.97	2.58
Ward 2	*Total*	1.61:1	1.47	0.91	2.38
IIIvii	Bryn Road	1.61:1	1.55	0.95	2.50
IIIviii	Bidulph Street	1.36:1	1.46	1.07	2.53
Ward 3	*Total*	1.54:1	1.52	0.99	2.51
Totals:	*mean*	1.63:1	1.29	0.87	2.16
	median	1.61:1	1.43	0.96	2.39

What is clear is that a good deal more work needs to be done to trace the occupational and gender distribution of particular streets, as well as their rateable values, to establish whether there is a correlation between these variables and enfranchisement levels both pre- and post-war. However, it is evident from these simple calculations that not only was there an unusually large increase in the electorate in Llanelli borough but that the increase was not evenly distributed either between areas of the town or between social and gender groups. In Llanelli at least, it would appear that Labour was a beneficiary of these major changes in the electorate.

After 1918 it was difficult to ignore the Labour Party in Britain; by the same token, it was impossible to ignore the spectacular increase in the Labour vote in the new Llanelli constituency. In the general election of 1918, despite general hostility towards Labour and enthusiasm for Lloyd George, J. H. Williams increased his share of the poll from 10.3 per cent in 1912 to 46 per cent, increased his actual vote by over 1,300 per cent and, more important, came within 2,000 votes of actually taking the seat (Table 5). And there were some straws in the

Table 5: Increase in Votes and Share of Total Vote: East Carmarthenshire and Llanelli, 1910–1923

	1910 (Dec)	1912	1918	1922	1923	% change			
						1910–18	1912–18	1912–22	1912–23
Liberal	5,825	6,082	16,344	15,947	11,765	+280	+269	+262	+193
Conservative	2,315	3,354	—	—	5,442	—	—	—	+162
Labour	1,176	1,089	14,409	23,213	21,063	+1,225	+1,323	+2,131	+1,934

wind. The campaign was marked by a good deal of boisterous behaviour by supporters of Labour, with the Liberal meetings disrupted all over the constituency.[55] In the second place, the Liberal Party was obliged to create additional vice-presidential places in its local organization in order to try to attract 'Labour' representatives.[56]

In the months that followed, the tempo was maintained. Ramsay MacDonald addressed a huge rally in 1919, followed by the Revd Gordon Lang, Robert Williams, general secretary of the Transport Workers, and Morgan Jones, the pacifist who was soon to be MP for Caerphilly.[57] The local elections of 1919, moreover, underlined the progress of the party. In neighbouring Glamorgan, major changes were already occurring, with the County Council falling under Labour control. Elsewhere in south and north Wales, there was a tide of support for Labour. Wrexham saw its first Labour councillors; Colwyn Bay reeled under the impact of Labour victories in the borough elections; Labour men arrived at the Denbighshire County Council. Monmouthshire fell to Labour altogether, as did several boroughs. In Llanelli, all four Labour candidates did well, topping the poll in every ward and displacing two established councillors. Even if the turn-out was small and the general atmosphere apathetic, it is clear that Labour was advancing.[58]

The advance was not unchecked. The local elections of 1920 were something of a set-back for Labour as ratepayers showed their discontent at rising rates. Divisions within the Labour movement between the moderates and the new left wing, including the emerging Communist Party, brought some anxiety, and opponents of Labour quickly capitalized on this during the campaigns. Nor did the parliamentary candidate escape unscathed. The cross-currents in the Labour movement which had caused difficulties for his nominations in 1910 and 1912 had already surfaced in 1918 when attempts were made to run rival candidates. Among the nominees were Dan Griffiths, proposed by the local ILP, and the young S. O. Davies, the miners' choice, who left, however, to become

---

[55] For an indication of the vigour of the Labour campaign, see *LM*, 1, 19 December 1918.
[56] *LM*, 21 November 1918.
[57] See *LG*, 13 November 1919.
[58] *LM*, 6 November 1919.

the agent in Dowlais.[59] Several unions felt that Dr Williams was inappropriate or too old. There were rumours, well-founded in fact, about the state of his health, while the miners wanted to claim the new seat for their own. In the event, attempts to dislodge Williams failed, and he became, by default rather than by choice, the official Labour candidate. The increase in the Labour vote in 1918 had very little to do with the candidate himself. Despite the increased vote, Williams's difficulties continued. In 1921 the steelworkers and the railwaymen withdrew from the Llanelli Trades Council, claiming that it had been 'captured by a minority of extreme socialists, had ceased to be a purely trade union organization and had become instead a sort of wild political caucus'.[60]

Dr Williams survived as candidate largely because of the appointment by the constituency Labour Association of an able new organizer, James Griffiths, chosen out of a field of over 140 applicants from all over Britain.[61] He brought vigour and political flair to the organization but, above all, he helped to mollify some of the internal critics. In his days as secretary of Ammanford Trades Council, he was noted for his fiery left-wing views, and these gave him some cachet with the hard left. On the other hand, he was also emerging as a supreme pragmatist, highly acceptable to the trade unions in whose ranks he would shortly rise high. For the moment, his contribution to the progress of the Labour Party was to shore up support for J. H. Williams, thereby imposing some kind of order on the movement.

James Griffiths's appointment did not come a moment too soon. A crisis in the Coalition led to a swift general election. In Llanelli, the outlook for Labour was good. The Liberals were still hopelessly divided and to add to their difficulties, the sitting member, Towyn Jones, announced his retirement very late in the day. But the Conservatives decided not to fight the seat, presumably in order to try to prevent the Labour Party from benefiting from a three-way fight, and the Liberals put up a convincing candidate, Clark Williams. Lloyd George himself came down to speak for the candidate and there was strong support for the Liberals from the local press and the main local institutions. Even so, despite predictions of a Liberal victory and growing evidence that the Labour candidate was not really physically fit, Labour won by a handsome majority. In part this was due to British trends, but these in turn were influenced by the unpreparedness of the Liberal machine and the unpopularity of Lloyd George. In contrast to the vigour and youth of the Labour campaign machine, the Liberals seemed old and enervated. A League of Young Liberals was formed a fortnight after the election defeat.[62] In the constituency itself, the Liberals claimed that the resources available to Labour were vastly greater than theirs, but in fact the Liberals spent almost twice as much money on the campaign (£1,371 against £715). There is no doubt, however, that Labour was in a better position to raise £700 than it had been before the war, but even so the local

---

[59]   *LM*, 21 November 1918. See also R. Griffiths, *S. O. Davies, A Socialist Faith* (Llandysul, 1983), pp. 34, 44.

[60]   *The Cambrian*, 4 November 1921.

[61]   For a full list of applicants and other material, see NLW, James Griffiths Collection, A3/3.

[62]   *LM*, 23 November 1922.

James Griffiths as a young MP.

Dr J. H. Williams, Labour MP for Llanelli.

party ran into substantial debt and it took all the ingenuity of James Griffiths to pay it and raise enough money to fight another election twelve months later.[63] It is an index of the improving position of the Labour Party in the early twenties that it was able to afford two general election campaigns within twelve months (Table 6). More important, at the 1923 general election, James Griffiths, the

Table 6: Expenditure at Election Campaigns 1910–22

	1910 (Dec)		1922		1923	
	Total	Per voter	Total	Per voter	Total	Per voter
	£	*s. d.*	£	*s. d.*	£	*s. d.*
Liberal	494	1 8	1,371	1 8	1,158	1 11
Conservative	795	6 1	—	—	1,091	4 0
Labour	251	4 3	715	0 7	371	0 4

Source: *Parliamentary Papers*

Labour agent, spent only half as much money as in 1922 and yet managed to hold up the Labour vote; with the Conservatives belatedly putting up a candidate, Labour secured a majority of nearly 10,000 over the Liberals.

By 1924, the Labour Party had all but conquered Llanelli and was well on the way towards that domination which it has maintained over industrial Wales to the present day. In north Wales, too, there were important political changes working to the advantage of Labour. Symbolic of Labour's arrival in Wales was the fact that the first Labour Prime Minister, Ramsay MacDonald, represented a Welsh seat at Aberafan, and though the Labour Government was turned out at the end of 1924, the tide did not turn in Wales. Even in 1931, when the Labour Party was decimated elsewhere in Britain, Wales stood loyal to the Party, with a quarter of all Labour MPs occupying Welsh seats. And Llanelli remained rock-solid. In 1931 the constituency registered the largest Labour majority—over 16,000—in Britain. In 1935, moreover, Dr Williams was unopposed, even though it was well known that the local Labour Party was desperately trying to persuade him to retire. A year later he was dead. In a tribute to him, his former Liberal opponent R. T. Evans remarked:

> He has not made history in the House of Commons; his speeches do not stand out, no piece of legislation can be attributed to him. He will not be remembered for his great public services but for his great strength of character.[64]

He might well have added that Dr Williams was fortunate to have benefited from the changes in the political infrastructure of his home town for, despite his known limitations, the Labour Party progressed on all fronts in Llanelli. By now, there was no credible alternative to Labour.

Recent research has shown that the expansion of the Labour Party in the

---

[63] For an indication of the continuing financial difficulties of the Divisional Labour Party after 1918, see DLP minutes 26 July 1919, 15 November 1919; DRO, D/POL/1/1. The deficit from the 1922 election, for example, was £151; NLW, James Griffiths Collection, A3/4.

[64] *LM*, 13 February 1936.

1920s was not sustained everywhere.[65] Deceived by the early euphoria, many constituency parties committed themselves to increased expenditure in the form of full-time agents and office buildings, commitments which soon became an appalling burden as the membership and electoral support for the party waned. In Llanelli, too, membership was slack and many trade unions were reluctant to add to their own increasing financial burdens at a time of economic stagnation by putting money into the Labour Party. There is no doubt, too, that the 1926 defeat added to the party's difficulties. Yet, the infrastructure of support for Labour was well established by the mid-1920s, with the bulk of the electorate prepared to support the party through thick and thin.

There are, of course, many unresolved questions which a study of Llanelli alone cannot answer. Why did north-east and north-west Wales not experience the same enthusiasm for Labour which was so clearly shown in the south Wales coalfield? Why did Cardiff, which had grown so rapidly in the late nineteenth century, and which encapsulated all the problems of rapid growth, prove to be so resistant to Labour? Is it because the diversity of occupations and the dominance of the service sector produced a community which was more deferential in its politics?

It has been argued that the Labour Party did best in 1922 in those constituencies where the roots of Labourism were deep.[66] This can certainly be seen to apply to Llanelli, providing the traditions of 'Labourism' are interpreted broadly. We should not be beguiled by the electoral shortcomings of the Labour Party before 1914 into believing that, somehow, the Labour movement as a whole was ineffective. On the contrary, the trade unions were able to influence the Liberals to their own satisfaction. This was especially so in areas where there was little industrial conflict as, for example, in the tin-plate areas of Llanelli. Unlike the case of the miners, there were no minimum wage problems to galvanize political Labourism, nor was syndicalism part of the tin-plate vocabulary. But Liberalism was. When Abel Thomas expressed his regrets in December 1910 that the appearance of the Independent Labour candidate divided 'Liberalism', he was expressing a widely accepted political axiom.[67] Many of the conflicts which erupted in the 1920s and 1930s between the intellectual left and the more pragmatic leaders of the Labour Party had their roots in pre-war divisions. In the case of Llanelli, the separation between the ILP and the Labour Party remained throughout the inter-war years. The victory of Dr Williams in 1922 was the victory of a pragmatic Labourism, aided by the collapse of the Liberal organization and the inability of the Conservatives to improve their pre-war position. But above all, it was an indication that franchise changes had produced a new electorate, whose behaviour was altogether different from its pre-war counterpart, concentrated in new industrial constituencies which offered Labour a natural home. Llanelli was one of the very first of these electorates.

[65] See, for example, T. Lindley, 'The Barnsley Labour Party, 1918–45', *Bulletin of the Society for the Study of Labour History*, 39 (1979), 10.

[66] Turner, 'Labour Vote'.

[67] *LM*, 8 December 1910.

A Bibliography of the Writings of Ieuan Gwynedd Jones 1958–1987

Compiled by PHILIP HENRY JONES

1958

'Franchise reform and Glamorgan politics in the mid-nineteenth century', *Morgannwg*, 2 (1958), 47–64.

1960

'Wales and parliamentary reform', in A. J. Roderick (ed.), *Wales through the Ages* (Llandybïe, 1960), 2, pp. 132–9.

Review: M. Elsas (ed.), *Iron in the Making: Dowlais Iron Company Letters*. *Morgannwg*, 4 (1960), 81–2.

Review: E. Wyn Evans, *Mabon (William Abraham 1842–1922)*. *WHR*, 1 (1960–3), 240–2.

1961

'The election of 1868 in Merthyr Tydfil: a study in the politics of an industrial borough in the mid-nineteenth century', *Journal of Modern History*, 33 (1961), 270–86.

'The Liberation Society and Welsh politics, 1844 to 1868', *WHR*, 1 (1960–3), 193–224.

1963

Review: R. I. Parry, *Ymneilltuaeth*; Gwynfryn Richards, *Ein Hymraniadau Annedwydd 1662–1962*. *WHR*, 1 (1960–3), 444–7.

Review: R. Bryn Williams, *Y Wladfa*. *Taliesin*, 5 [1963], 69–72.

1964

'Cardiganshire politics in the mid-nineteenth century: a study of the elections of 1865 and 1868', *Ceredigion*, 5 (1964–7), 14–41.

'Dr Thomas Price and the election of 1868 in Merthyr Tydfil: a study in nonconformist politics', *WHR*, 2 (1964–5), 147–72, 251–70.

'The elections of 1865 and 1868 in Wales, with special reference to Cardiganshire and Merthyr Tydfil', *Trans. Cymmr.*, 1964 (Part 1), 41–68.

'Thomas Charles (1755–1814)', in C. Gittins (ed.), *Pioneers of Welsh Education* (Swansea, 1964), pp. 31–55.

Review: K. S. Inglis, *Churches and the working classes in Victorian England.* *History*, 49 (1964), 245–6.

Review: *South Wales and Monmouthshire Record Society Publications*, 5 (1963). *Morgannwg*, 8 (1964), 82.

1965

Review: J. F. Rees, *The Problem of Wales and other Essays.* *History*, 50 (1965), 404–5.

1966

'Dal ar y cyfeiriad', *Taliesin*, 13 (1966), 53–61. (Review-article discussing R. Tudur Jones, *Hanes Annibynwyr Cymru*).

'The Merthyr of Henry Richard', in G. Williams (ed.), *Merthyr Politics: the Making of a Working-Class Tradition* (Cardiff, 1966), pp. 28–57.

Review: E. T. Davies, *Religion in the Industrial Revolution in South Wales.* WHR, 3 (1966–7), 82–5.

Review: Chris Evans, *Industrial and Social History of Seven Sisters.* WHR, 3 (1966–7), 92–4.

Review: T. Evans, *The History of Miskin Higher or the Parishes of Aberdare and Llanwynno.* *Morgannwg*, 10 (1966), 83.

Review: K. Williams-Jones (ed.), *A Calendar of the Merioneth Quarter Sessions Rolls, Vol. I, 1733–65.* *Morgannwg*, 10 (1966), 75–6.

1967

'Merthyr Tydfil in 1850: impressions and contrasts', *Glamorgan Historian*, 4 (1967), 31–45.

1968

'Denominationalism in Swansea and district: a study of the Ecclesiastical Census of 1851', *Morgannwg*, 12 (1968), 67–96.

'Merioneth politics in mid-nineteenth century: the politics of a rural economy', *Journal of the Merioneth Historical and Record Society*, 5 (1965–8), 273–334.

Review: M. Stewart, *The Crawshays of Cyfarthfa Castle.* *Morgannwg*, 12 (1968), 113–14.

1969

Review: A. H. Dodd, *A History of Caernarvonshire, 1284–1900.* *Morgannwg*, 13 (1969), 114–15.

1970

'Denominationalism in Caernarvonshire in the mid-nineteenth century as shown in the Religious Census of 1851', *Transactions of the Caernarvonshire Historical Society*, 31 (1970), 78–114.

Review: James Griffiths, *Pages from Memory: an Autobiography.* *Anglo-Welsh Review*, 42 (1970), 266–8.

1971

The Dynamics of Politics in Mid-Nineteenth-Century Wales: an Inaugural Lecture delivered . . . 20 January 1971 (Cardiff, 1971), 32 pp.

'The South Wales collier in mid-nineteenth century', in *Victorian South Wales: Architecture, Industry and Society* (London, [1971]), pp. 34–51.

1972

Editor: *Gwilym Davies 1879–1955: a Tribute* (Llandysul, 1972), 100 pp.

'Rhai agweddau ar grefydd a chymdeithas yn hanner cyntaf y ganrif ddiwethaf', *Efrydiau Athronyddol*, 35 (1972), 50–63.

Review: P. M. H. Bell, *Disestablishment in Ireland and Wales*. *History*, 57 (1972), 299.

Review: L. Wynne Evans, *Education in Industrial Wales 1700–1900*. *Anglo-Welsh Review*, 46 (1972), 247–50.

1973

'The rebuilding of Llanrhystud church', *Ceredigion*, 7 (1972–5), 99–116.

'Religion and politics: the rebuilding of St Michael's church Aberystwyth and its political consequences', *Ceredigion*, 7 (1972–5), 117–30.

Review: D. J. V. Jones, *Before Rebecca*. *Carmarthen Antiquary*, 9 (1973), 191–3.

1974

'Glamorgan politics from 1660–1688', in G. Williams (ed.), *Early Modern Glamorgan . . . Glamorgan County History, Vol. IV* (Cardiff, 1974), pp. 375–94.

'Politics in Merthyr Tydfil', *Glamorgan Historian*, 10 (1974), 50–64.

'Radicaliaeth' in G. Bowen (ed.), *Atlas Meirionnydd* (Y Bala, [1974]), tt. 140–1.

'The religious condition of the counties of Brecon and Radnor as revealed in the Census of Religious Worship of 1851', in O. W. Jones and D. G. Walker (eds.), *Links with the Past: Swansea and Brecon Historial Essays* (Llandybïe, 1974), pp. 185–214.

Review: K. O. Morgan, *Lloyd George Family Letters 1885–1936*; John Grigg, *The Young Lloyd George*; E. Royston Pike, *Human Documents of the Lloyd George Era*. *Anglo-Welsh Review*, 52 (1974), 235–40.

1975

'Crefydd a'r gymuned yng Nghymru', *Y Traethodydd*, 130 (1975), 197–213.

'The Valleys: the making of community', in Paul H. Ballard and Erastus Jones (eds.), *The Valleys Call: a Self-Examination by People of the South Wales Valleys during the Year of the Valleys 1974* (Ferndale, 1975), pp. 55–67.

1976

'The building of St Elvan's church, Aberdare', *Glamorgan Historian*, 11 [1976], 71–81.

'Health and sanitary engineering in mid-nineteenth-century Merthyr Tydfil', *The Journal of the South East Wales Industrial Archaeology Society*, 2(2) (1976), 27–48.

'Merthyr Tydfil: the politics of survival', *Llafur*, 2 (1976–9), 18–31.

Joint editor (with David Williams): *The Religious Census of 1851: a calendar of the returns relating to Wales, Vol. I: South Wales* (Cardiff, 1976), pp. xxxvi, 698.

Foreword to R. I. Parry and Tom Whitney, *Old Aberdare and Merthyr Tydfil in photographs* (Barry, 1976).

1977

Editor: *Aberystwyth 1277–1977: Eight Lectures to celebrate the Seventh Centenary of the Foundation of the Borough* (Llandysul, 1977), pp. x, 141.

'Enwadaeth yn 1801 ac yn 1851', in T. M. Bassett and B. L. Davies, *Atlas Sir Gaernarfon* (Caernarfon, 1977), tt. 154–6. (Also published as 'Denominationalism in 1801 and 1851' in the English-language version of the *Atlas*).

'Government, religion and politics', in *Aberystwyth 1277–1977 . . .* pp. 96–113.

Additions to the final chapter of the second edition of David Williams, *A History of Modern Wales* (London, 1977).

Review: W. R. P. George, *The Making of Lloyd George. Y Traethodydd*, 132 (1977), 153–5.

1978

'The Anti-Corn Law letters of Walter Griffith', *BBCS*, 28 (1978–80), 95–128.

'Church reconstruction in North Cardiganshire in the nineteenth century', *NLWJ*, 20 (1977–8), 352–60.

Review: Donald Moore (ed.), *Wales in the Eighteenth Century*; Raphael Samuel (ed.), *Miners, Quarrymen and Saltworkers. Anglo-Welsh Review*, 61 (1978), 140–3.

1979

Health, Wealth and Politics in Victorian Wales (Swansea, 1979), 39 pp.

'Language and community in nineteenth century Wales', in Paul H. Ballard and D. Huw Jones (eds.), *This Land and People . . . a Symposium on Christian and Welsh National Identity* (Cardiff, 1979), pp. 22–39.

Review: D. W. Howell, *Land and People in Nineteenth-Century Wales. American Historical Review*, 84 (1979), 160–1.

Review: D. T. W. Price, *A History of Saint David's College Lampeter, Vol. I. WHR*, 9 (1978–9), 374–7.

1980

'Church building in Flintshire in the mid-nineteenth century', *Flintshire Historical Society Journal*, 29 (1979–80), 89–112.

'Language and community in nineteenth-century Wales', in D. Smith (ed.), *A People and a Proletariat: Essays in the History of Wales 1780–1980* (London, 1980), pp. 47–71.

'Patterns of religious worship in Montgomeryshire in the mid-nineteenth century', *Montgomeryshire Collections*, 68 (1980), 93–118.

1981

With E. D. Lewis: 'Capel y Cymer: llanw a thrai', *Morgannwg*, 25 (1981), 137–63.

'Church reconstruction in Breconshire in the nineteenth century', *Brycheiniog*, 19 (1980–1), 7–26.

Explorations and Explanations: Essays in the Social History of Victorian Wales (Llandysul, 1981), 338 pp.

Editor: *The Religious Census of 1851: a Calendar of the Returns relating to Wales. Volume II: North Wales* (Cardiff, 1981), pp. viii, 430.

'The Religious frontier in nineteenth-century Wales', *Cylchgrawn Cymdeithas Hanes y Methodistiaid Calfinaidd*, new series, 5 (1981), 3–24.

The Valleys in the Mid-Nineteenth Century (Torfaen Museum Trust, 1981), 30 pp.

1983

Review: Harold Carter and Sandra Wheatley, *Merthyr Tydfil in 1851*. *Morgannwg*, 27 (1983), 91–5.

1984

'The County and its history, 1909–1984', *Ceredigion*, 10 (1984–7), 1–17.

'Ecclesiastical economy: aspects of church building in Victorian Wales', in R. R. Davies *et al.* (eds.), *Welsh Society and Nationhood: Historical Essays presented to Glanmor Williams* (Cardiff, 1984), pp. 216–31.

'Glanmor Williams', in R. R. Davies *et al.* (eds.), *Welsh Society and Nationhood: Historical Essays presented to Glanmor Williams* (Cardiff, 1984), pp. 1–4.

'The people's health in mid-Victorian Wales', *Trans. Cymmr.*, 1984, 115–47.

'The Swansea Valley: life and labour in the nineteenth century', *Llafur*, 4(1) (1984), 57–71.

Joint editor (with R. R. Davies, Ralph A. Griffiths and Kenneth O. Morgan): *Welsh Society and Nationhood: Historical Essays presented to Glanmor Williams* (Cardiff, 1984).

Review: J. E. Wynne Davies (ed.), *Gwanwyn Duw, Diwygwyr a Diwygiadau*. *WHR*, 12 (1984–5), 122–3.

1985

Communities: the Observers and the Observed (Cardiff, 1985), 20 pp.

Review: G. E. Jones, *Controls and Conflicts in Welsh Secondary Education*. *History*, 70 (1985), 330–1.

1986

Contributions to *The Oxford Companion to the Literature of Wales/Cydymaith i Lenyddiaeth Cymru*.

Review: John Williams, *Digest of Welsh Historical Statistics*. *Llais Llyfrau/Book News from Wales* (Summer 1986), 9–10.

1987

Communities: Essays in the Social History of Victorian Wales (Llandysul, 1987), pp. xvi, 370.

Review: David W. Howell, *Patriarchs and Parasites.* *Llais Llyfrau/Book News from Wales* (Spring 1987), 11–12.

Index

List of Subscribers

The following have associated themselves with the publication of this volume through subscription.

Mary Bevan, Barnet
Eleonore Breuning, University College of Swansea
Dafydd J. Burns, Pontypridd
T. Duncan Cameron, Aberaeron
A. D. Carr, University College of North Wales, Bangor
J. E. R. Carson, Aberystwyth
Harold Carter, University College of Wales, Aberystwyth
Muriel E. Chamberlain, University College of Swansea
Stuart Clark, University College of Swansea
John Cochlin, Tenby
F. G. Cowley, Swansea
Sir Goronwy Daniel, Letterston
Wayne David, Bridgend
Mr and Mrs Alun Eirug Davies, Aberystwyth
Mr and Mrs Aneurin Davies, Swansea
David H. Davies, Blandford Forum
Derek and Jayne Davies, Newtown
Hywel Davies OBE, Narberth
R. R. Davies, Coleg Prifysgol Cymru, Aberystwyth
Hugh Dunthorne, University College of Swansea
D. W. Dykes, National Museum of Wales
Martin Eckley, Harlech
Dr and Mrs Richard Edwards, Aberystwyth
C. C. Eldridge, St David's University College, Lampeter
Joe England, Coleg Harlech
Elizabeth Evans, Felinfach
D. Gareth Evans, Trinity College, Carmarthen
J. F. Fuggles, The National Trust, Oxford
Hywel Francis, University College of Swansea
W. R. P. George, Cricieth
E. L. Gibson, Penmynydd
William P. Griffith, Llanfair Pwllgwyngyll
Ralph A. Griffiths, University College of Swansea
John R. Guy, Yeovil

H. J. Hanham, University of Lancaster
C. C. Harris, University College of Swansea
Marged Haycock, Coleg Prifysgol Cymru, Aberystwyth
Harry Hearder, University of Wales College of Cardiff
C. S. Hewitt, Aberteifi
Bert Hogenkamp, Amsterdam, The Netherlands
David Howell, University College of Swansea
A. D. Howells, Guildford
Brian Howells, Lampeter
V. G. Hubbard, Welsh Joint Education Committee
Aneurin Rhys Hughes, EC Delegation, Oslo, Norway
Ieuan and Mac Hughes, Cardiff
John H. Hughes, Aberystwyth
John Vivian Hughes, Port Talbot
Margaret Hughes, Newtown
Graham Humphrys, University College of Swansea
E. L. ac M. A. James, Penrhyn-coch, Aberystwyth
David Jenkins, Penrhyn-coch, Aberystwyth
David Jenkins, Ffynnon Taf
Dafydd Jenkins, Coleg Prifysgol Cymru, Aberystwyth
Gwyn Jenkins, Tal-y-bont
Angela V. John, Thames Polytechnic
Anthony M. Johnson, University of Wales College of Cardiff
Alun Gwynedd Jones, University College of North Wales, Bangor
Anthony Jones, The Art Institute of Chicago, USA
Benjamin G. Jones, London
Beti a Tegwyn Jones, Bow Street, Aberystwyth
Dafydd Morris Jones, Aberarth
David Jones, University College of Swansea
Gareth Elwyn Jones, University College of Swansea
Glanville R. J. Jones, University of Leeds
Goronwy Owen Jones, Aberafon
J. Gwynfor Jones, University of Wales College of Cardiff
Huw Bevan Jones, Llandysul
Malcolm Morgan Jones, Caerfyrddin
Marian Henry Jones, Aberystwyth
M. J. Jones, Yr Wyddgrug
R. M. Jones, Colege Prifysgol Cymru, Aberystwyth
R. Merfyn Jones, University of Liverpool
Rosemary A. N. Jones, Aberystwyth
Simeon Jones, Porthcawl
The Rt. Hon. Neil Kinnock MP
Clive H. Knowles, University of Wales College of Cardiff
W. R. Lambert, Welsh Joint Education Committee
Ceri W. Lewis, Treorci
John H. Lewis, Llandysul

Nêst Llywelyn Lewis, Aberystwyth
Lewis W. Lloyd, Harlech
Ceridwen Lloyd-Morgan, Llanafan
Dafydd Llŷr, Welsh Industrial and Maritime Museum, Cardiff
David Loades, University College of North Wales, Bangor
Lionel Madden, Aberystwyth
Kenneth and Jane Morgan, The Queen's College, Oxford
Prys Morgan, Coleg Prifysgol Abertawe
W. John Morgan, University of Nottingham
Ichiro Nagai, Tokyo, Japan
The Most Revd George Noakes, Archbishop of Wales
D. Huw Owen, Llyfrgell Genedlaethol Cymru, Aberystwyth
Gareth Owen, University College of Wales, Aberystwyth
Morfudd E. Owen, Canolfan Uwchefrydiau Cymreig a Cheltaidd, Aberystwyth
Robert John Owen, Conwy
Jon Parry, London
Teifion Phillips, Barry
Nia M. W. Powell, Coleg Prifysgol Gogledd Cymru, Bangor
David Pretty, Tonteg, Pontypridd
D. T. W. Price, St David's University College, Lampeter
Eunice Price, Hong Kong
Roger Price, University of East Anglia
Canon Thomas J. Pritchard, Pwllheli
Iorwerth Prothero, University of Manchester
Bryan Rayner, Burry Port
Gwynfor and Margaret Rees, Llanilar
Nan a Graham Rees, Aberystwyth
John Rhys, Gwasg Prifysgol Cymru, Caerdydd
Philip Richards, Aberdare
Keith Robbins, University of Glasgow
Brynley F. Roberts, National Library of Wales
Dafydd Roberts, Amgueddfa Lechi Cymru, Llanberis
David Roberts, University College of North Wales, Bangor
R. O. Roberts, Abertawe
J. S. Rowett, Brasenose College, Oxford
John David Ruston, Harlech
Wynne I. Samuel, Caerdydd
R. T. Shannon, University College of Swansea
J. G. T. Sheringham, Machynlleth
David B. Smith, University of Wales College of Cardiff
Robert a Huw Beverley Smith, Aberystwyth
P. Smith, Royal Commission on Ancient and Historical Monuments in Wales
Christopher Smout, University of Edinburgh
Meic Stephens, Welsh Arts Council, Cardiff

Nora Temple, University of Wales College of Cardiff
Brynmor Thomas, Aberystwyth
Daniel Cynan Thomas, Ystalyfera
D. O. Thomas, Aberystwyth
Gareth J. Thomas, Aberdare
J. E. Thomas, University of Nottingham
Roy Thomas, University of Wales College of Cardiff
Mr and Mrs T. W. Thomas, Neath
Dorothy Thompson, University of Birmingham
Katherine J. Turner, Kent
David and Margaret Walker, Swansea
Ryland Wallace, Crickhowell
Huw Walters, Llyfrgell Genedlaethol Cymru
T. Mervyn Ll. Walters, Loughborough
Sandra Wheatley, University College of Wales, Aberystwyth
The Baroness White of Rhymney, House of Lords
Emyr W. Williams, Aberhosan, Machynlleth
Enid and Moelwyn Williams, Aberystwyth
Ernest Charles Williams, Caerdydd
Gareth Williams, Coleg Prifysgol Cymru, Aberystwyth
Huw Williams, Dowlais
Ieuan M. Williams, Swansea
J. Dewi Williams, Brentwood
J. Gwynn Williams, Bangor
C. J. Wrigley, University of Nottingham

Amgueddfa Werin Cymru, Sain Ffagan
Brotherton Library, University of Leeds
Centre de Recherche Bretonne et Celtique, Brest, Brittany
Clwyd Library and Museum Service
Clwyd Record Office
Coleg Harlech, Harlech
Dictionary of Labour Biography
Gwasanaeth Llyfrgell Gwynedd
Harvard College Library, Cambridge, Massachusetts, USA
Institute of Historical Research, University of London
The Library, University College of North Wales, Bangor
The Library, University College of Swansea
The Library, University of Wales College of Cardiff
Y Llyfrgell, Athrofa Addysg Uwch De Morgannwg
Y Llyfrgell, Coleg y Drindod, Caerfyrddin
Y Llyfrgell, Coleg Prifysgol Dewi Sant, Llanbedr Pont Steffan
Llyfrgell Gyhoeddus, Aberystwyth
Llyfrgell Hugh Owen, Coleg Prifysgol Cymru, Aberystwyth
The London Library

Merthyr Tydfil Heritage Trust
Mid Glamorgan County Library
National Museum of Wales
South Glamorgan County Council
Swansea Museum
West Glamorgan County Library